DATE DUE			

GAYLORD M-2   PRINTED IN U.S.A.

THE *American Society*

THE AMERICAN IMAGE SERIES
Ernest R. May, General Editor

THE AMERICAN SOCIETY
Edited by Kenneth S. Lynn

THE AMERICAN FOREIGN POLICY
Edited by Ernest R. May

THE AMERICAN POLITICAL PROCESS
Edited by Leonard W. Levy and John P. Roche

THE AMERICAN ECONOMY
Edited by Jesse W. Markham

THE
American
Society

EDITED BY *Kenneth S. Lynn*

George Braziller   NEW YORK   1963

PREFACE

*I*N THE AUTUMN of 1961 Harvard University was asked to organize an orientation program for seventy-five Brazilian student leaders being sent to the United States by the Cultural Union of São Paulo and the Department of State. The Office of Latin American Studies at Harvard arranged for four of us, specialists in American studies, to work with these students during the ten days they were to be in Cambridge.

When we began to prepare the program, we discovered that there were no suitable texts either in Portuguese or English. Such books of readings as existed were designed for college courses or, at the very least, assumed some specialized knowledge on the part of the reader. While we could expect the Brazilian students to be intelligent and well-informed about Brazil, we had to assume that they would know almost nothing about how the United States had grown, what its culture was, or how its democracy or economic system worked. To meet their needs, we felt we should put together four entirely new volumes containing basic readings.

When the Brazilian students arrived, these volumes were not yet ready. The four of us circulated some of the readings among them. We also talked with them at length and tried to answer their questions and find out what about the United States interested and puzzled them.

We are not sure yet what effect our teaching may have had. Among those hostile to the United States, we did not look for conversion. What we hoped was merely that all of them would go home knowing more about America, unable any longer to voice oversimplifications, and to this extent we think we did succeed. In any event, we hope that these four volumes, with their introductions, will enable others to undertake similar ventures.

Unlike comparable works, these volumes are designed for readers who have no specialized background in these fields, and, because they were constructed with a foreign audience in mind, they introduce perspectives that may be interesting even to specialists. While foreign readers should find in them the profile of America, readers nearer home may get, as well, a sense of the American image.

Of none is this more true than of Kenneth Lynn's *American Society*. Professor of American Literature at Harvard and author of works on American humor and the American dream of success, he has put together writings from all three centuries of the nation's history. Someone looking merely at the table of contents might think them merely shards of a long past; reading them through, he would realize that they fit together seamlessly in an excitingly, perhaps shockingly, faithful mirror, not only for America as it has been, but as it is. From this volume a reader comes away understanding how Americans can take inordinate pride in what they have done and at the same time feel inordinate shame at what they have failed to do. In the imaginative literature of the nation, here truly is its image and reflection.

ERNEST R. MAY

CONTENTS

IV. New Beginnings

V. Faith and Doubt

VI. Varieties of Present Experience

INTRODUCTION

Kenneth S. Lynn

THE PROBLEM of who we are and what we are has always been of acute concern to the American people, so any new attempt at defining the national character should properly begin with the observation that the attempt has been made a thousand times before. From the very beginning of our cultural existence, we have been the most self-conscious people on earth.

The Pilgrims of Plymouth and the Puritans of Massachusetts Bay subjected their lives to continuous self-examination, for fear they might overlook evidence of divine displeasure with their efforts to found a New Salem in the wilderness of North America. Anxious citizens like Samuel Sewall kept diaries in which they probed for the hidden meanings of daily events with a skill no less deft and a resolution no less unswerving than that of a psychoanalyst pursuing the origins of his patient's neurosis. (That the United States in the twentieth century has accepted the principles of Freudian theory with unexampled enthusiasm should occasion no surprise; our fascination with symbolical interpretations of human behavior has an ancient history.) More self-assured Puritans like Thomas Shepard and Cotton Mather published autobiographies and histories of New England not only in order to enhance their own self-awareness, but to provide maps to guide the steps of later generations of pilgrims en route to the Celestial City—a didactic motive which in various secular forms has continued ever since to inspire American leaders to write their memoirs.

Benjamin Franklin, for example, who firmly believed that contributions to the self-consciousness of one's children were a desideratum, conceived of his *Autobiography* as an extended piece of advice to his "Dear Son" as to how to get ahead in the world, and innumerable self-made men have subsequently followed Franklin's literary lead, to the point where the "success story" has become an established genre of American writing. Sagas of spiritual travail were thus transmogrified into chronicles of how poor boys rose from rags to riches, and in this evolution from religious idealism to the crassest materialism we catch sight of a recurrent American pattern. Our highest aspirations are forever dissolving into cynical self-seeking; our belief in God, or in the special destiny of America, or in the justice of some grand national effort ceases to uplift us, and we forthwith fall on our knees before the altar of what William James memorably termed the "bitch-goddess, SUCCESS." Yet the very fact that James was capable of such a brilliantly corrosive phrase attests in itself to the unconquerable vitality of an American tradition which scorns the materialistic ethic as a debasement of the national spirit.

In spite of all the "success stories" that have been published, the most distinguished American autobiography we have is *The Education of Henry Adams,* a book which deliberately mocks the success-story form by presenting Adams's career as a sequence of failures, and which is as concerned as Cotton Mather ever was with the spiritual salvation of the country. Just as the Puritan autobiographies, with their emphasis on the conscientious performance of duties, reveal an other-worldliness that contained within itself the seeds of its own dissolution (hard work performed in the name of serving God was a perfect formula, after all, for serving Mammon), so the thoroughly worldly works of Henry Adams—and of Mark Twain, Sinclair Lewis, Thorstein Veblen, and many other American writers—betray a truly Puritanical outrage at the commercialization of American life.

While Adams's *Education* is unrivaled as a literary document, the most rewarding autobiography for the student of the American character is undoubtedly Benjamin Franklin's. Probably the most illuminating book about America ever written, it can be seen to best advantage by contrasting Franklin's advice to his son with the famous set of instructions given by Lord Chesterfield, Franklin's English contemporary, to *his* son. The dissimilarities of their advice may serve to illustrate certain key differences between two English-speaking civilizations.

Like Franklin, Chesterfield was concerned that his son should get on in the world, and there was no question in his mind as to what was the best policy for doing so. To Chesterfield, manners, *i.e.*, the social demeanor sanctioned by custom and authority, were clearly the best policy. For Chesterfield was an aristocrat; he lived and moved in a formal, hierarchical world, based on elaborate traditions:

to get ahead in this world, one had to conform to the rules. Thus Chesterfield's advice to his son consisted largely of maxims which were designed to acquaint him with immutable patterns of gentlemanly behavior. Be reserved, Chesterfield told his son; be moderate; and above all, always be the same: never break the Roman principles, as Chesterfield called them, of a traditional and orderly society.

Compared to Chesterfield's London, America in the eighteenth century was a chaos. People were constantly in motion, whether they were immigrants debarking from ships, adventurers bound for the trans-Allegheny frontier, or merchants with commercial interests up and down the seaboard, and this geographical movement was accompanied by a social mobility of unprecedented fluidity. That famous picture Franklin gives of himself in the *Autobiography* as a boy of seventeen newly arrived in Philadelphia, walking up Market Street with a baker's roll under each arm and eating a third, epitomizes the eighteenth-century American experience. Contemporary Europe was also full of young men on the move and on the rise—one thinks of Samuel Johnson walking to London, or Jean Jacques Rousseau on his way to Paris—but the American experience was nonetheless qualitatively different. Not only were there greater economic opportunities in this country, but there were far fewer social barriers to brake the fluidity, to slow it down and assimilate the young men who were riding the crest of the tide. Chesterfield's England had its roots in feudalism; families had a history; people knew who you were. In America, no one knew who you were. An indentured servant could arrive on a ship, serve out his five-year term, and a few years later be worth more money than the man to whom he had been indentured. Not only that, but he might have changed his residence a dozen times, taught himself to read, and married a minister's daughter.

In many of the colonies, sumptuary laws were passed which attempted to put a stop to this sort of social-climbing. These laws sought to regulate the kind of clothes one wore, to define what kind of house was appropriate to one's social station, to estimate what one was entitled to be addressed as—"Sir," "Goodman," or whatever. Significantly enough, there were no comparable laws in England, for the simple reason that they were unnecessary. The social stabilization that the American colonies vainly sought to achieve by law was accomplished in England by other means. For a time, the Puritan concept of the calling—that a man should labor all his days in the vineyard that the Lord had originally placed him in—exercised a restraining influence on the mobility of New England society. But by the end of the seventeenth century, the pressures making for mobility could no longer be contained, not even in the Boston of the Mathers. The concept of the calling could not stop Benjamin Franklin, the son of a candlemaker, from passing on to other occupations and other roles.

In a society in which nobody knew who you were or where you came from, in which the escape from one's original identity could be effected with ridiculous ease, a man could often change his luck by inventing a new character for himself. The possibilities for self-assertion were enormous. American writers, reflecting on these possibilities, have been obsessed throughout our history with the idea of masquerade. Floating down the Mississippi on a raft, Huck Finn encounters those two four-flushers, the King and the Duke, who in addition to their basic disguise as the lost Dauphin of France and the Duke of Bridgewater, admit to having taken "a turn" at mesmerism, phrenology, schoolteaching, doctoring, and preaching. To cite two other examples from literature dealing with the Mississippi, Herman Melville's novel about the river is called *The Confidence Man: His Masquerade*, the very title of which is sufficient to suggest its theme, while *The White Rose of Memphis*, by a novelist who is remembered today primarily because he was William Faulkner's great-grandfather, establishes a similar theme in its opening scene—in which the crowd at a masked ball on board a steamboat decides to wear its masks for the rest of the voyage.

Faulkner himself, in *Absalom, Absalom!*, the story of a poor boy named Thomas Sutpen from the mountains of Virginia who spends his whole life trying to live up to his Platonic conception of himself as a wealthy cotton planter with a Greek Revival house, an army of slaves, and a distinguished line of descendants, is as fascinated by masquerades as his great-grandfather was. Indeed, wherever one turns in American history and literature, one encounters men and women who are acting out their dreams, like Dreiser's Sister Carrie or Scott Fitzgerald's Gatsby, and who are haunted, as Melville's

Captain Ahab was, by the discrepancies between appearance and reality, both as they feel those discrepancies within themselves and in the universe around them. The social and geographical mobility of American life, which has given unlimited freedom to the Self, which has permitted the human personality to develop any way it dared, has furnished the American imagination with its most persistent preoccupation. Even if our minds had never been stained by the Puritan habit of searching for the secret (as opposed to the Biblically revealed) Will of God, the elusive quality of our social experience would have been sufficient to ensure our everlasting concern with the differences between the Word and the flesh.

In such a wide-open world, it is not surprising to find that Benjamin Franklin does not attempt, as Lord Chesterfield constantly did, to justify his advice to his son by appeals to external authority; since there are no social precedents which apply to the American situation, Franklin appeals only to his own experience to back up what he says, never to the classical authors of whom Chesterfield was so fond. His strategy for self-advancement is also entirely different. Instead of Chesterfield's consistent response to consistent situations, Franklin responds to the novel situations of a fast-changing society by adjusting his behavior *ad hoc*. We all know that Franklin was a jack-of-all-trades, a scientist, a philosopher, a diplomat, a printer, that he was the man who invented bifocal glasses, contributed to the theory of electricity, and interested himself in a variety of reforms from phonetic spelling to improved methods of paving city streets, but it is equally important to an understanding of Franklin to realize that he was also a master of the histrionic art—that, in fact, his being a jack-of-all-trades depended not only on his intellectual breadth, but on the amazing plasticity of his personality. As good an illustration as any of his acting talent is the familiar story of his career in Paris, where he arrived in December, 1776, as the agent of the Revolutionary cause in America charged with enlisting French support for the American side. Among the nobility, the intellectuals, and the people of Paris he enjoyed a vogue such as no American diplomat of his time or any other time has ever experienced. His face was reproduced everywhere—on medallions, in scores of paintings, on rings, on books. Louis XVI was reputed to have become so jealous of Franklin that he commissioned a chamber pot with Franklin's face on the inside bottom, and that he kept the pot in the royal chambers.

Now this extraordinary vogue was partly deserved and partly not. On the one hand, there was Franklin's great record of public service, his international reputation as a scientist, his winningly sincere patriotism. But on the other hand there is no doubt that Franklin's popularity was considerably enhanced by his deliberate deceptiveness. For when Franklin arrived in Paris he found that the French *philosophes* were enchanted with the myth of an ideal American society made up of pious, tolerant, philosophical farmers living in Quakerly harmony on the edge of Penn's woods. Although Franklin had lived among men of fashion in London for most of the previous twenty years, where one of his jobs had been to fight the Quaker heirs of William Penn, he recognized that the role of religious pacifist was the perfect disguise for the agent of a revolution and immediately assumed the part. Here is the Paris police report on Franklin three weeks after he arrived in France:

This Quaker wears the full costume of his sect. He has an agreeable physiognomy. Spectacles always on his eyes; but little hair—a fur cap is always on his head.

That fur cap of Franklin's is an authentic emblem of our civilization. It expresses, for one thing, our genius for salesmanship, our gift for packaging, our belief that it's not what you're selling that counts with the customers so much as how you sell it. The advertising executives of Madison Avenue, those gray-flanneled masters of the hidden persuasion whom our sociologists and sociological novelists are forever describing as if they were an entirely new race of men, have a lineage that goes straight back to Benjamin Franklin—and beyond Franklin to the fabled Yankee peddler of our earliest frontier days, the first American master of the hard sell. Constance Rourke in *American Humor* has caught this creature of legend marvelously well as he descends, some time toward the end of the eighteenth century, upon a frontier community in the South:

A close view of his figure brought consternation to the men and women lounging at the tavern or near the sheds that clustered around the planter's gate. "I'll be shot if it ain't a Yankee!" cried one. The yard was suddenly

vacant. Doors banged and windows were shut. The peddler moved relentlessly nearer, reached a doorway, and laid his pack on the half hatch. The
inhabitants had barred their doors and double-locked their money-tills in
vain. With scarcely a halt the peddler made his way into their houses and
silver leapt into his pockets. When his pack was unrolled, calicoes, glitter-
ing knives, razors, scissors, clocks, cotton caps, shoes, and notions made a
holiday at a fair. His razors were bright as the morning star, cut quick as
thought, and had been made by the light of a diamond in Andalusia. He
showed hickory cups and bowls and plates, and mentioned the haste with
which people in a neighboring village had broken their crockery and
thrown it into the street since crockery was known to spread the plague.
He told stories of the plague. In the end he invaded every house. Every one
bought. The Negroes came up from their cabins to watch his driving
pantomime and hear his slow, high talk. Staying the night at a tavern, he
traded the landlord out of bed and breakfast and left with most of the
money in the settlement.

As Miss Rourke amply recognized, such salesmanship constituted
an essential part of a national humor, and in this respect, too, Franklin's fur cap is emblematic. For the essence of American humor is
exaggeration. Thus our mode of combating criticism by foreigners—
to which we have always been extraordinarily sensitive—has been to
acknowledge the criticisms, exaggerate them to the very limits of belief, and laugh them out of existence (or so we have hoped). When
Franklin wrote a description of America for a British newspaper in
which he talked straight-facedly about how the tails of American
sheep are so laden with wool they have to be supported by little four-
wheel carts, and about how the grand leap of the whale up the falls
of the Niagara was a spectacle not to be missed, he was imitating the
immemorial routine of the American frontiersman whose response to
European sneers that he was nothing but a savage was to flap his
arms, leap into the air, and crow like a rooster. If such behavior did
not rid the frontiersman of his inferiority complex, at least there was
contemptuous satisfaction for him in the knowledge that the sophisti-
cates of Europe were stupid enough to believe in his ignorant performance—a satisfaction that Mark Twain would also partake in
while going through the elaborate act, in *The Innocents Abroad,* of
not knowing what the Renaissance was.

Yet for all the fury with which our humorists have flung back the accusation that we are innocents into the teeth of our accusers, we have also cherished the notion of American innocence, with lamentable consequences. When Franklin donned his fur cap, or indicated to his son—as he did in a notorious passage in the *Autobiography*—that he might ingratiate himself with important individuals by "imitating" Jesus and Socrates, he was setting a dangerous example. For the policy of deceiving others could easily end, unless one were as realistically aware of the differences between appearance and reality as Franklin was, in self-deception—and this ultimate fraudulency has in fact been the last laugh in many an American life. Confusing aspiration with accomplishment, the nineteenth-century historian George Bancroft took the ambition of the Puritans to found a "city on a hill," the utopian visions of Thomas Jefferson, and the political oratory of his own day—which magniloquently proclaimed the "Manifest Destiny" of America—as solid evidence that Jacksonian America represented the moral culmination of human history. The same sentiment is voiced today from many a pulpit and political platform.

These wistful Americans yearn to believe that their country is in some fundamental sense still the virgin wilderness that the first explorers saw—an unfallen Eden, a land of innocence. They resent political commentators who speak of the moral ambiguities of American foreign policy, because they know in their hearts that the United States is the one nation in the world that has never fought an unjust war. They lend encouragement to local authorities who would ban the books of Henry Miller and D. H. Lawrence, because they know that in so doing they are protecting the innocence of our youth—and that those who suggest that American boys and girls are no longer innocent are terribly wrong. Confronted by our crime rate, our divorce rate, our suicide rate, they suspect deleterious foreign influences—for how otherwise could such evils flourish in a nation where the churches are filled to overflowing every Sunday? The nostalgic wish to return to a lost innocence can also be detected among more sophisticated citizens. Our college students, for example, and our younger faculty members take justifiable pride in the fact that the western world's intellectual center of gravity has shifted from the universities of the Old World to those of the New, yet the contemporary novel that means the most to them is *The Catcher in the Rye*, an escapist fantasy involving a youth who flees the halls of learning in pursuit of an innocent childhood world which he fears he may never be able to find again.

No wonder, then, that our greatest writers have concentrated their imaginative energies on attacking our self-delusions. Jonathan Edwards's account of the "Great Awakening" of the 1740's is not only a narrative history of that fantastic outburst of religious conversions, but a brilliant, probing examination of the ways in which Americans of his time deceived themselves into believing that a momentary and hysterical fervor was evidence that God's grace was working within them. Although Melville's *Moby Dick* displays a profound indebtedness to Emerson's celebration of self-reliant, democratic man, its greatness consists in its exposure of the evils of self-intoxication. Henry James's *Portrait of a Lady* and Mark Twain's *Huckleberry Finn* dramatize the folly of romanticizing one's experience into a series of fairy-tale adventures wherein one's innocence is a shield against all dangers and everyone lives happily ever after. Dreiser's *An American Tragedy*, the sociological sermons of David Riesman, the slashing invective of H. L. Mencken's essays, and the nightmare-novels of Nathaniel West are all dedicated to revealing the emptiness that lies behind the beguiling false-fronts of middle-class American culture.

Yet beneath the rage, the despair, the cynicism, beneath all the disillusionments, disenchantments, and denunciations with which our national literature is replete, behind all the American attacks on American innocence, one finds, paradoxically, another innocence. It consists, this other, deeper innocence, in a persistent vision of the possibilities of American life. Huck Finn incarnates our desire to create a newer, better world, and so do the eager, morally spontaneous young girls who are the heroines of Henry James's novels, and so does Sinclair Lewis's Arrowsmith. Now the fact that our severest critics are themselves incorrigible idealists is very significant. It explains, first of all, why these critics so often seem to be excessively angry with their fellow countrymen—why Mark Twain and John Dos Passos at times seem to despise America, and why Melville seems so bitter. These writers are not merely deriding our tendency to pomposity and moral complacency for the sake of derision, nor do they attack those who believe that America is perfect simply because such a belief is manifestly wrong; they attack them because the belief is *not yet true*, because a complacency with our present lot—or a wistful yearning that the past might be recaptured—impedes the future realization of the American Dream.

As to the exact nature of that Dream, it is difficult to speak with precision, for in the course of three hundred years the Dream has had many prophets. Dr. Paul Tillich, a recent interpreter who brings to the problem of the American character the perspective of Europe as well as an immense scholarship, has written that the historic, cultural vocation of the United States has been to realize the Kingdom of Heaven on earth, and certainly the religious motive for the settling of Massachusetts Bay, the saga of the Mormons, and many other sectarian experiments lend credence to his contention. However, while Tillich's interpretation has many merits, it hardly encompasses the breadth of our national experience. Religious belief was not the only reason for the "Atlantic migration," nor was it the motivation that prompted most pioneers to cross the Alleghenies, the Mississippi, and the Rockies. The "Kingdom" which Thomas Jefferson envisaged, or that Walt Whitman sang of, or that the political radicals of the 1930's agitated for, was not the heavenly society the Puritans had in mind. There is, however, one element of the Puritanical ambition that recurs repeatedly in later definitions of the American character. And that is the idea of *e pluribus unum*. Americans, it is true, have always honored the concept of individual freedom; the openness of our society sufficiently testifies to that. There is even an anarchic strain in our national make-up which dates back to the time when a man who did not like the restraints of society could always move deeper into the wilderness to some remote place where he himself was the only law, and which is manifested today in the startling violence of American life. Then, too, there is an individualistic logic at work in the social dynamics of democracy that tends to drive men apart from one another, rather than to bring them together. As de Tocqueville observed,

Thus not only does democracy make every man forget his ancestors, but it hides his descendants and separates his contemporaries from him; it throws him back forever upon himself alone and threatens in the end to confine him entirely within the solitude of his own heart.

The overwhelming sense of loneliness that emerges from Hawthorne's stories, and from the work of so many American writers of our own time, certainly tends to confirm the truth of de Tocqueville's brilliant observation. We are perhaps the most modern of peoples in that our individual sense of alienation from society is very keen.

Nevertheless the idea that liberty is indivisible, that the American purpose is a communal one, persists, as it has from the beginning: the dream of a "more perfect union" which is the American Dream. The Puritans' "errand into the wilderness" was an effort to found a community of saints, not a pursuit of individual salvation. As Jonathan Edwards's theology makes clear, the love of God and the sense of man's sinfulness both operated to bind believers together in an existential democracy. Significantly, the followers of Edwards became enthusiastic supporters of Thomas Jefferson's radical egalitarianism, because while Jefferson's deistic religion was light years removed from Edwards's Calvinism, Jefferson's belief in a free society constituted a vision of American communality that was no less exalted, no less mystical—for all of Jefferson's rationalism—than Edwards's. In Jefferson's public writings, and especially in the private correspondence that sprang up between him and John Adams in the old age of these ancient foes, one can feel the throb of a faith in democratic comradeship that draws on the religious energies of two centuries of American history and that would swell into a mighty vibration, in the century ahead, in the oratory of Andrew Jackson and Abraham Lincoln, the poetry of Walt Whitman, Mark Twain's reminiscences of steamboat days, and Oliver Wendell Holmes, Jr.'s speeches on the Civil War.

One finds a concern with communality even in the writings of professedly antidemocratic Americans of the nineteenth century. When, for example, the antebellum Southern sociologist George Fitzhugh endeavored to defend the existence of Negro slavery in the South, he did so on the ground that the master-slave relationship, with its mutual obligations, was a more tightly wound communal fabric than the exploitative, factory owner-wage earner relationship that obtained in the North. (Conversely, when Harriet Beecher Stowe attacked the "peculiar institution," she struck out against its power to destroy communities both small and large—Negro families, because slave owners in the United States had the right to sell slave children away from their parents, and parents away from each other; white families, because of the existence, on every plantation, of an utterly available black harem for every Southern gentleman who wanted one; and the United States itself. "Every nation," Mrs. Stowe warned, "that carries in its bosom great and unredressed injustice has in it the elements of . . . convulsion.") Our writers of the twentieth century have been more doubtful about our ability to reach the Promised Land of our dreams, yet they have never given up on it. As Robert Frost says in "The Gift Outright,"

> Such as we were we gave ourselves outright
> (The deed of gift was many deeds of war)
> To the land vaguely realizing westward,
> But still unstoried, artless, unenhanced,
> Such as she was, such as she would become.

The grand American design that a younger nation clearly apprehended has become terribly blurred. Nevertheless, in the midst of the chaos of our times, we continue to be stirred by the sense of a "vaguely realizing" national purpose in which we all participate.

I.   A City on the Hill

WILLIAM BRADFORD (1590–1657)

*William Bradford, governor and leader of the Plymouth Colony
for more than thirty years, was born in Yorkshire, England, the son
of a yeoman farmer. From his early boyhood he was intensely religious, and at the age of sixteen, despite his family's disapproval, he
joined a group of Separatists who wished to worship God in accord-
ance with what they thought were the purer principles of the early
Christian Church.*

*Because of religious persecution, Bradford's group was forced to
flee from England. From 1609 until their removal to America, the
group lived in Holland. In November, 1620,* The Mayflower, *with
more than a hundred men, women, and children aboard, reached the
New World, and a settlement was built at what is now Plymouth,
Massachusetts.*

*If the climate was harsh, the soil rocky, and the forests inhabited
by Indians and wild animals, Bradford and his fellow settlers were
equal to the challenge. Inspired by a deep religious faith, they saw
themselves as soldiers battling for God against the dark forces of
Satan—and no obstacle was allowed to stand in the way of God's
glory.*

*Of all the accounts of seventeenth-century New England, none
gives a clearer picture of the religious conviction and great courage of
the Pilgrims than Bradford's history,* Of Plymouth Plantation. *Book
I deals with the origin of their church in England and recounts their
stay in Holland and arrival in America. Book II consists of annals
from 1620-1646 and tells of the hardships and trials, Indian con-
spiracies, impostors, debts, pestilence, and death which the colony
endured in the first years of its life.*

Arrival in America

OF THEIR VOYAGE, AND HOW THEY PASSED THE SEA; AND OF
THEIR SAFE ARRIVAL AT CAPE COD

September 6. These troubles being blown over, and now all being compact together in one ship, they put to sea again with a prosperous wind, which continued divers days together, which was some encouragement unto them; yet, according to the usual manner, many were afflicted with seasickness. And I may not omit here a special work of God's providence. There was a proud and very profane young man, one of the seamen, of a lusty, able body, which made him the more haughty; he would always be contemning the poor people in their sickness and cursing them daily with grievous execrations; and did not let to tell them that he hoped to help to cast half of them overboard before they came to their journey's end, and to make merry with what they had; and if he were by any gently reproved, he would curse and swear most bitterly. But it pleased God before they came half seas over, to smite this young man with a grievous disease, of which he died in a desperate manner, and so was himself the first that was thrown overboard. Thus his curses light on his own head, and it was an astonishment to all his fellows for they noted it to be the just hand of God upon him.

After they had enjoyed fair winds and weather for a season, they were encountered many times with cross winds and met with many fierce storms with which the ship was shroudly shaken, and her upper works made very leaky; and one of the main beams in the midships was bowed and cracked, which put them in some fear that the ship could not be able to perform the voyage. So some of the chief of the company, perceiving the mariners to fear the sufficiency of the ship as appeared by their mutterings, they entered into serious consultation with the master and other officers of the ship, to consider in time of the danger, and rather to return than to cast themselves into a desperate and inevitable peril. And truly there was great distraction and

From William Bradford, *Of Plymouth Plantation*. Edited by Samuel Eliot Morison (New York, Alfred A. Knopf, 1952), pp. 58-63.

difference of opinion amongst the mariners themselves; fain would they do what could be done for their wages' sake (being now near half the seas over) and on the other hand they were loath to hazard their lives too desperately. But in examining of all opinions, the master and others affirmed they knew the ship to be strong and firm under water; and for the buckling of the main beam, there was a great iron screw the passengers brought out of Holland, which would raise the beam into his place; the which being done, the carpenter and master affirmed that with a post put under it, set firm in the lower deck and otherways bound, he would make it sufficient. And as for the decks and upper works, they would caulk them as well as they could, and though with the working of the ship they would not long keep staunch, yet there would otherwise be no great danger, if they did not overpress her with sails. So they committed themselves to the will of God and resolved to proceed.

In sundry of these storms the winds were so fierce and the seas so high, as they could not bear a knot of sail, but were forced to hull for divers days together. And in one of them, as they thus lay at hull in a mighty storm, a lusty young man called John Howland, coming upon some occasion above the gratings was, with a seele of the ship, thrown into sea; but it pleased God that he caught hold of the topsail halyards which hung overboard and ran out at length. Yet he held his hold (though he was sundry fathoms under water) till he was hauled up by the same rope to the brim of the water, and then with a boat hook and other means got into the ship again and his life saved. And though he was something ill with it, yet he lived many years after and became a profitable member both in church and commonwealth. In all this voyage there died but one of the passengers, which was William Butten, a youth, servant to Samuel Fuller, when they drew near the coast.

But to omit other things (that I may be brief) after long beating at sea they fell with that land which is called Cape Cod; the which being made and certainly known to be it, they were not a little joyful. After some deliberation had amongst themselves and with the master of the ship, they tacked about and resolved to stand for the southward (the wind and weather being fair) to find some place about Hudson's River for their habitation. But after they had sailed that course about half the day, they fell amongst dangerous shoals and roaring breakers, and they were so far entangled therewith as they conceived themselves in great danger; and the wind shrinking upon them withal, they resolved to bear up again for the Cape and thought themselves happy to get out of those dangers before night overtook them, as by God's good providence they did. And the next day they got into the Cape Harbor where they rid in safety. . . .

. . . Being thus arrived in a good harbor, and brought safe to land, they fell upon their knees and blessed the God of Heaven who had brought them over the vast and furious ocean, and delivered them from all the perils and miseries thereof, again to set their feet on the firm and stable earth, their proper element. And no marvel if they were thus joyful, seeing wise Seneca was so affected with sailing a few miles on the coast of his own Italy, as he affirmed, that he had rather remain twenty years on his way by land than pass by sea to any place in a short time, so tedious and dreadful was the same unto him.

But here I cannot but stay and make a pause, and stand half amazed at this poor people's present condition; and so I think will the reader, too, when he well considers the same. Being thus passed the vast ocean, and a sea of troubles before in their preparation (as may be remembered by that which went before), they had now no friends to welcome them nor inns to entertain or refresh their weatherbeaten bodies; no houses or much less towns to repair to, to seek for succour. It is recorded in Scripture as a mercy to the Apostle and his shipwrecked company, that the barbarians showed them no small kindness in refreshing them, but these savage barbarians, when they met with them (as after will appear) were readier to fill their sides full of arrows than otherwise. And for the season it was winter, and they that know the winters of that country know them to be sharp and violent, and subject to cruel and fierce storms, dangerous to travel to known places, much more to search an unknown coast. Besides, what could they see but a hideous and desolate wilderness, full of wild beasts and wild men—and what multitudes there might be of them they knew not. Neither could they, as it were, go up to the top of Pisgah to view from this wilderness a more goodly country to feed their hopes; for which way soever they turned their eyes (save upward to the heavens) they could have little solace or content in respect of any outward objects. For summer being done, all things stand upon them with a weatherbeaten face, and the whole country, full of woods and thickets, represented a wild and savage hue. If they looked behind them, there was the mighty ocean which they had passed and was now as a main bar and gulf to separate them from all the civil parts of the world. If it be said they had a ship to succour them, it is true; but what heard they daily from the master and company? But that with speed they should look out a place (with their shallop) where they would be, at some near distance; for the season was such as he would not stir from thence till a safe harbor was discovered by them, where they would be, and he might go without danger; and that victuals consumed apace but he must and would keep sufficient for themselves and their return. Yea, it was muttered by some that if they got not a place in time, they would turn them and their goods ashore and leave them. Let it also be considered what weak hopes of supply and succour they left behind them, that might bear up their minds in this sad condition and trials they were under; and they could not but be very small. It is true, indeed, the affections and love of their brethren at Leyden was cordial and entire towards them, but they had little power to help them or themselves; and how the case stood between them and the merchants at their coming away hath already been declared.

What could now sustain them but the Spirit of God and His grace? May not and ought not the children of these fathers rightly say: "Our fathers were Englishmen which came over this great ocean, and were ready to perish in this wilderness; but they cried unto the Lord, and He heard their voice and looked on their adversity," etc. "Let them therefore praise the Lord, because He is good: and His mercies endure forever." "Yea, let them which have been redeemed of the Lord, shew how He hath delivered them from the hand of the oppressor. When they wandered in the desert wilderness out of the way, and found no city to dwell in, both hungry and thirsty, their soul was overwhelmed in them. Let them confess before the Lord His lovingkindness and His wonderful works before the sons of men."

BENJAMIN FRANKLIN (1706–90)

Franklin's Autobiography, *from which the following selection is taken, is only a partial record of Franklin's full and rewarding life. The major part of the book was written in 1771 and covered the years from 1706 to 1730. The remainder was composed in bits and pieces in 1784, 1788, and 1790. Franklin's many interests and projects did not leave him enough time to do justice to the latter half of his career. Yet as it stands the* Autobiography *is an American classic.*

A Bold and Arduous Project

I HAD BEEN religiously educated as a Presbyterian; and tho' some of the dogmas of that persuasion, such as *the eternal decrees of God, election, reprobation, etc.*, appeared to me unintelligible, others doubtful, and I early absented myself from the public assemblies of the sect, Sunday being my studying day, I never was without some religious principles. I never doubted, for instance, the existence of the Deity; that he made the world, and govern'd it by his Providence; that the most acceptable service of God was the doing good to man; that our souls are immortal; and that all crime will be punished, and virtue rewarded, either here or hereafter. These I esteem'd the essentials of every religion; and, being to be found in all the religions we had in our country, I respected them all, tho' with different degrees of respect, as I found them more or less mix'd with other articles, which, without any tendency to inspire, promote, or confirm morality, serv'd principally to divide us, and make us unfriendly to one another. This

From Benjamin Franklin, *Autobiography of Benjamin Franklin*, John Bigelow, ed., Philadelphia, 1868.

respect to all, with an opinion that the worst had some good effects, induc'd me to avoid all discourse that might tend to lessen the good opinion another might have of his own religion; and as our province increas'd in people, and new places of worship were continually wanted, and generally erected by voluntary contribution, my mite for such purpose, whatever might be the sect, was never refused.

Tho' I seldom attended any public worship, I had still an opinion of its propriety, and of its utility when rightly conducted, and I regularly paid my annual subscription for the support of the only Presbyterian minister or meeting we had in Philadelphia. He us'd to visit me sometimes as a friend, and admonish me to attend his administrations, and I was now and then prevail'd on to do so, once for five Sundays successively. Had he been in my opinion a good preacher, perhaps I might have continued, notwithstanding the occasion I had for the Sunday's leisure in my course of study; but his discourses were chiefly either polemic arguments, or explications of the peculiar doctrines of our sect, and were all to me very dry, uninteresting, and unedifying, since not a single moral principle was inculcated or enforc'd, their aim seeming to be rather to make us Presbyterians than good citizens.

At length he took for his text that verse of the fourth chapter of Philippians, *"Finally, brethren, whatsoever things are true, honest, just, pure, lovely, or of good report, if there be any virtue, or any praise, think on these things."* And I imagin'd, in a sermon on such a text, we could not miss of having some morality. But he confin'd himself to five points only, as meant by the apostle, viz.: 1. Keeping holy the Sabbath day. 2. Being diligent in reading the holy Scriptures. 3. Attending duly the publick worship. 4. Partaking of the Sacrament. 5. Paying a due respect to God's ministers. These might be all good things; but, as they were not the kind of good things that I expected from that text, I despaired of ever meeting with them from any other, was disgusted, and attended his preaching no more. I had some years before compos'd a little Liturgy, or form of prayer, for my own private use (viz., in 1728), entitled, *Articles of Belief and Acts of Religion.* I return'd to the use of this, and went no more to the public assemblies. My conduct might be blameable, but I leave it, without attempting further to excuse it; my present purpose being to relate facts, and not to make apologies for them.

It was about this time I conceiv'd the bold and arduous project of arriving at moral perfection. I wish'd to live without committing any fault at any time; I would conquer all that either natural inclination, custom, or company might lead me into. As I knew, or thought I knew, what was right and wrong, I did not see why I might not always do the one and avoid the other. But I soon found I had undertaken a task of more difficulty than I had imagined. While my care was employ'd in guarding against one fault, I was often surprised by another; habit took the advantage of inattention; inclination was sometimes too strong for reason. I concluded, at length, that the mere speculative conviction that it was our interest to be completely virtuous, was not sufficient to prevent our slipping; and that the contrary habits must be broken, and good ones acquired and established, before we can have any dependence on a steady, uniform rectitude of conduct. For this purpose I therefore contrived the following method.

In the various enumerations of the moral virtues I had met with in my reading, I found catalogue more or less numerous, as different writers included more or fewer ideas under the same name. Temperance, for example, was by some confined to eating and drinking, while by others it was extended to mean the moderating every other pleasure, appetite, inclination, or passion, bodily or mental, even to our avarice and ambition. I propos'd to myself, for the sake of clearness, to use rather more names, with fewer ideas annex'd to each, than a few names with more ideas; and I included under thirteen names of virtues all that at that time occur'd to me as necessary or desirable, and annexed to each a short precept, which fully express'd the extent I gave to its meaning.

These names of virtues, with their precepts were:

1. TEMPERANCE. Eat not to dullness; drink not to elevation.

2. SILENCE. Speak not but what may benefit others or yourself; avoid trifling conversation.

3. ORDER. Let all your things have their places; let each part of your business have its time.

4. RESOLUTION. Resolve to perform what you ought; perform without fail what you resolve.

5. FRUGALITY. Make no expense but to do good to others or yourself; i.e., waste nothing.

6. INDUSTRY. Lose no time; be always employ'd in something useful; cut off all unnecessary actions.

7. SINCERITY. Use no hurtful deceit; think innocently and justly; and, if you speak, speak accordingly.

8. JUSTICE. Wrong none by doing injuries, or omitting the benefits that are your duty.

9. MODERATION. Avoid extreams; forbear resenting injuries so much as you think they deserve.

10. CLEANLINESS. Tolerate no uncleanliness in body, cloaths, or habitation.

11. TRANQUILLITY. Be not disturbed at trifles, or at accidents common or unavoidable.

12. CHASTITY. Rarely use venery but for health or offspring, never to dullness, weakness, or the injury of your own or another's peace or reputation.

13. HUMILITY. Imitate Jesus and Socrates.

My intention being to acquire the *habitude* of all these virtues, I judg'd it would be well not to distract my attention by attempting the whole at once, but to fix it on one of them at a time; and, when I should be master of that, then to proceed to another, and so on, till I should have gone thro' the thirteen; and, as the previous acquisition of some might facilitate the acquisition of certain others, I arrang'd them with that view, as they stand above. Temperance first, as it tends to procure that coolness and clearness of head, which is so necessary where constant vigilance was to be kept up, and guard maintained against the unremitting attraction of ancient habits, and the force of perpetual temptations. This being acquir'd and establish'd, Silence would be more easy; and my desire being to gain knowledge at the same time that I improv'd in virtue, and considering that in conversation it was obtain'd rather by the use of ears than of the tongue, and therefore wishing to break a habit I was getting into of prattling, punning, and joking, which only made me acceptable to a trifling company, I gave *Silence* the second place. This and the next, *Order*, I expected would allow me more time for attending to my project and my studies. *Resolution*, once become habitual, would keep me firm in my endeavours to obtain all the subsequent virtues; *Frugality* and Industry freeing me from my remaining debt, and producing affluence and independence, would make more easy the practice of Sincerity and Justice, etc., etc. Conceiving then, that, agreeably to the advice of Pythagoras in his Golden Verses, daily examination would be necessary, I contrived the following method for conducting that examination.

I made a little book, in which I allotted a page for each of the virtues. I rul'd each page with red ink, so as to have seven columns, one for each day of the week, marking each column with a letter for the day. I cross'd these columns with thirteen red lines, marking the beginning of each line with the first letter of one of the virtues, on which line, and in its proper column, I might mark, by a little black spot, every fault I found upon examination to have been committed respecting that virtue upon that day.

FORM OF THE PAGES.

TEMPERANCE.						
EAT NOT TO DULLNESS; DRINK NOT TO ELEVATION.						
	S.	M.	T.	W.	T.	F.	S.
T.							
S.	*	*		*		*	
O.	**	*	*		*	*	*
R.			*			*	
F.		*			*		
I.			*				
S.							
J.							
M.							
C.							
T.							
C.							
H.							

I determined to give a week's strict attention to each of the virtues successively. Thus, in the first week, my great guard was to avoid even the least offence against *Temperance,* leaving the other virtues to their ordinary chance, only marking every evening the faults of the day. Thus, if in the first week I could keep my first line, marked T, clear of spots, I suppos'd the habit of that virtue so much strengthen'd, and its opposite weaken'd, that I might venture extending my attention to include the next, and for the following week keep both lines clear of spots. Proceeding thus to the last, I could go thro' a course compleat in thirteen weeks, and four courses in a year. And like him who, having a garden to weed, does not attempt to eradicate all the bad herbs at once, which would exceed his reach and his strength, but works on one of the beds at a time, and, having accomplish'd the first, proceeds to a second, so I should have, I hoped, the encouraging pleasure of seeing on my pages the progress I made in virtue, by clearing successively my lines of their spots, till in the end, by a number of courses, I should be happy in viewing a clean book, after a thirteen weeks' daily examination.

This my little book had for its motto these lines from Addison's *Cato:*

> "Here will I hold. If there's a power above us
> (And that there is, all nature cries aloud
> Thro' all her works), He must delight in virtue;
> And that which he delights in must be happy."

Another from Cicero,

"O vitae Philosophia dux! O virtutum indagatrix expultrixque vitiorum! Unus dies, bene et ex praeceptis tuis actus, peccanti immortalitati est anteponendus."

Another from the Proverbs of Solomon, speaking of wisdom or virtue:

"Length of days is in her right hand, and in her left hand riches and honour. Her ways are ways of pleasantness, and all her paths are peace." i. 1-6, 17.

And conceiving God to be the fountain of wisdom, I thought it right and necessary to solicit his assistance for obtaining it; to this end

I formed the following little prayer, which was prefix'd to my tables of examination, for daily use.

"O powerful Goodness! bountiful Father! merciful Guide! Increase in me that wisdom which discovers my truest interest. Strengthen my resolutions to perform what that wisdom dictates. Accept my kind offices to thy other children as the only return in my power for thy continual favours to me."

I used also sometimes a little prayer which I took from Thomson's Poems, viz.:

> "Father of light and life, thou Good Supreme!
> O teach me what is good; teach me Thyself!
> Save me from folly, vanity, and vice,
> From every low pursuit; and fill my soul
> With knowledge, conscious peace, and virtue pure;
> Sacred, substantial, never-fading bliss!"

The precept of *Order* requiring that *every part of my business should have its allotted time*, one page of my little book contain'd the following scheme of employment for the twenty-four hours of a natural day.

THE MORNING. *Question.* What good shall I do this day?	5 6 7	Rise, wash, and address *Powerful Goodness!* Contrive day's business, and take the resolution of the day; prosecute the present study, and breakfast.
	8 9 10 11	Work.
NOON.	12 1	Read, or overlook my accounts, and dine
	2 3 4 5	Work.

EVENING.
  Question. What good have
I done today?

$\left. \begin{array}{c} 6 \\ 7 \\ 8 \\ 9 \end{array} \right\}$ Put things in their places. Supper. Music or diversion, or conversation. Examination of the day.

NIGHT.

$\left. \begin{array}{c} 10 \\ 11 \\ 12 \\ 1 \\ 2 \\ 3 \\ 4 \end{array} \right\}$ Sleep.

I enter'd upon the execution of this plan for self-examination, and continu'd it with occasional intermissions for some time. I was surpris'd to find myself so much fuller of faults than I had imagined; but I had the satisfaction of seeing them diminish. To avoid the trouble of renewing now and then my little book, which, by scraping out the marks on the paper of old faults to make room for new ones in a new course, became full of holes, I transferr'd my tables and precepts to the ivory leaves of a memorandum book, on which the lines were drawn with red ink, that made a durable stain, and on those lines I mark'd my faults with a black-lead pencil, which marks I could easily wipe out with a wet sponge. After a while I went thro' one course only in a year, and afterward only one in several years, till at length I omitted them entirely, being employ'd in voyages and business abroad, with a multiplicity of affairs that interfered; but I always carried my little book with me.

My scheme of ORDER gave me the most trouble; and I found that, tho' it might be practicable where a man's business was such as to leave him the disposition of his time, that of a journeyman printer, for instance, it was not possible to be exactly observed by a master, who must mix with the world, and often receive people of business at their own hours. *Order,* too, with regard to places for things, papers, etc., I found extreamly difficult to acquire. I had not been early accustomed to it, and, having an exceeding good memory, I was not so sensible of the inconvenience attending want of method. This article, therefore, cost me so much painful attention, and my faults in it vexed me so much, and I made so little progress in amendment, and had such frequent relapses, that I was almost ready to give up the attempt, and content myself with a faulty character in that respect, like the man who, in buying an ax of a smith, my neighbor, desired to have the whole of its surface as bright as the edge. The smith consented to grind it bright for him if he would turn the wheel; he turn'd, while the smith press'd the broad face of the ax hard and heavily on the stone, which made the turning of it very fatiguing. The man came every now and then from the wheel to see how the work went on, and at length would take his ax as it was, without farther grinding. "No," said the smith, "turn on, turn on; we shall have it bright by-and-by; as yet it is only speckled." "Yes," says the man, *"but I think I like a speckled ax best."* And I believe this may have been the case with many, who, having, for want of some such means as I employ'd, found the difficulty of obtaining good and breaking bad habits in other points of vice and virtue, have given up the struggle, and concluded that *"a speckled ax was best;"* for something, that pretended to reason, was every now and then suggesting to me that such extream nicety as I exacted of myself might be a kind of foppery in morals, which, if it were known, would make me ridiculous; that a perfect character might be attended with the inconvenience of being envied and hated; and that a benevolent man should allow a few faults in himself, to keep his friends in countenance.

In truth, I found myself incorrigible with respect to Order; and now I am grown old, and my memory bad, I feel very sensibly the want of it. But, on the whole, tho' I never arrived at the perfection I had been so ambitious of obtaining, but fell far short of it, yet I was, by the endeavour, a better and a happier man than I otherwise should have been if I had not attempted it; as those who aim at perfect writing by imitating the engraved copies, tho' they never reach the wish'd-for excellence of those copies, their hand is mended by the endeavour, and is tolerable while it continues fair and legible.

It may be well my posterity should be informed that to this little artifice, with the blessing of God, their ancestor ow'd the constant felicity of his life, down to his 79th year, in which this is written. What reverses may attend the remainder is in the hand of Providence; but, if they arrive, the reflection on past happiness enjoy'd ought to help his bearing them with more resignation. To Temperance he ascribes his long-continued health, and what is still left to him of a good constitution; to Industry and Frugality, the early easiness of his circumstances and acquisition of his fortune, with all that knowledge that enabled him to be a useful citizen, and obtained for him some degree of reputation among the learned; to Sincerity and Justice, the confidence of his country, and the honourable employs it conferred upon him; and to the joint influence of the whole mass of the virtues, even in the imperfect state he was able to acquire them, all that evenness of temper, and that cheerfulness in conversation, which makes his company still sought for, and agreeable even to his younger acquaintance. I hope, therefore, that some of my descendants may follow the example and reap the benefit.

It will be remark'd that, tho' my scheme was not wholly without religion, there was in it no mark of any of the distinguishing tenets of any particular sect. I had purposely avoided them; for, being fully persuaded of the utility and excellency of my method, and that it might be serviceable to people in all religions, and intending some time or other to publish it, I would not have any thing in it that should prejudice any one of any sect, against it. I purposed writing a little comment on each virtue, in which I would have shown the advantages of possessing it, and the mischiefs attending its opposite vice; and I should have called my book THE ART OF VIRTUE, because it would have shown the means and manner of obtaining virtue, which would have distinguished it from the mere exhortation to be good, that does not instruct and indicate the means, but is like the apostle's man of verbal charity, who only without showing to the naked and hungry how or where they might get clothes or victuals, exhorted them to be fed and clothed.—James ii. 15, 16.

But it so happened that my intention of writing and publishing this comment was never fulfilled. I did, indeed, from time to time, put down short hints of the sentiments, reasonings, etc., to be made use of in it, some of which I have still by me; but the necessary close attention to private business in the earlier part of my life, and public business since, have occasioned my postponing it; for, it being connected in my mind with *a great and extensive project*, that required the whole man to execute, and which an unforeseen succession of employs prevented my attending to, it has hitherto remain'd unfinish'd.

In this piece it was my design to explain and enforce this doctrine, that vicious actions are not hurtful because they are forbidden, but forbidden because they are hurtful, the nature of man alone considered; that it was, therefore, every one's interest to be virtuous who wish'd to be happy even in this world; and I should, from this circumstance (there being always in the world a number of rich merchants, nobility, states, and princes, who have need of honest instruments for the management of their affairs, and such being so rare), have endeavoured to convince young persons that no qualities were so likely to make a poor man's fortune as those of probity and integrity.

My list of virtues contain'd at first but twelve; but a Quaker friend having kindly informed me that I was generally thought proud; that my pride show'd itself frequently in conversation; that I was not content with being in the right when discussing any point, but was overbearing, and rather insolent, of which he convinc'd me by mentioning several instances; I determined endeavouring to cure myself, if I could, of this vice or folly among the rest, and I added *Humility* to my list, giving an extensive meaning to the word.

I cannot boast of much success in acquiring the *reality* of this virtue, but I had a good deal with regard to the *appearance* of it. I made it a rule to forbear all direct contradiction to the sentiments of others, and all positive assertion of my own. I even forbid myself, agreeably to the laws of our Junto, the use of every word or expression in the language that imported a fix'd opinion, such as *certainly, undoubtedly*, etc., and I adopted, instead of them, *I conceive, I apprehend*, or *I imagine* a thing to be so or so; or it *so appears to me at present*. When another asserted something that I thought an error, I deny'd myself the pleasure of contradicting him abruptly, and of showing immediately some absurdity in his proposition; and in answering I began by observing that in certain cases or circumstances his opinion would be right, but in the present case there *appear'd* or *seem'd* to me some differences, etc. I soon found the advantage of this change in my manner; the conversations I engag'd in went on more pleasantly. The modest way in which I propos'd my opinions procur'd them a readier reception and less contradiction; I had less mortification when I was found to be in the wrong, and I more easily prevail'd with others to give up their mistakes and join with me when I happened to be in the right.

And this mode, which I at first put on with some violence to natural inclination, became at length so easy, and so habitual to me, that perhaps for these fifty years past no one has ever heard a dogmatical expression escape me. And to this habit (after my character of integrity) I think it principally owing that I had early so much weight with my fellow citizens when I proposed new institutions, or alterations in the old, and so much influence in public councils when I became a member; for I was but a bad speaker, never eloquent, subject to much hesitation in my choice of words, hardly correct in language, and yet I generally carried my points.

In reality, there is, perhaps, no one of our natural passions so hard to subdue as *pride*. Disguise it, struggle with it, beat it down, stifle it, mortify it as much as one pleases, it is still alive, and will every now and then peep out and show itself; you will see it, perhaps, often in this history; for, even if I could conceive that I had compleatly overcome it, I should probably be proud of my humility.

JONATHAN EDWARDS (1703–58)

For Benjamin Franklin, God was the rational and urbane ruler of the universe, and man a creature of reason. For Jonathan Edwards, the outstanding theologian and philosopher of colonial America, God was inscrutable, hidden in omnipotence and glory, and man was inherently evil, capable of being saved only by the grace of God. This overpowering sense of God's majesty pervades all of Edwards's thoughts and writings, and it is very evident in the Personal Narrative.

A native of Connecticut, Edwards went to Yale, where he studied Locke's psychology and the physical discoveries of Newton. He was graduated in 1720 and spent the next six years studying and teaching theology. In 1726 he was called to Northampton, Massachusetts, as the colleague of his grandfather, Solomon Stoddard, whom he succeeded in 1729.

The Puritans' strict requirements for church membership had been gradually relaxed in the late seventeenth and early eighteenth centuries. However, Edwards insisted that man's salvation did not depend on his own reason and will, but rather on God's infinite and mysterious mercy, and that only those who could profess their spiritual regeneration by divine grace could be admitted to full communion as church members.

This emphasis on man's evil nature and on grace as an emotional experience in the Lockean sense helped to spur the Great Awakening of 1734, the first in a series of religious revivals which swept from New England to the Carolinas and Georgia. But Edwards's exclusion of many people from church membership aroused the ire of the Northampton congregation, and in 1750 Edwards and his large family were forced to moved to Stockbridge, Mass., where he served as missionary to the Indians. In 1757 he became president of the College of New Jersey, but died shortly afterward.

Edwards has had a great influence on American literature and philosophy. His idea that grace is an emotional experience links him with William James. His acceptance of the natural world as an emblem of the spiritual universe points forward to Melville, Hawthorne, Emerson, and Whitman.

Personal Narrative

I HAD A VARIETY of concerns and exercises about my soul from my childhood; but had two more remarkable seasons of awakening, before I met with that change by which I was brought to those new dispositions, and that new sense of things, that I have since had. The first time was when I was a boy, some years before I went to college, at a time of remarkable awakening in my father's congregation, I was then very much affected for many months, and concerned about the things of religion, and my soul's salvation; and was abundant in duties. I used to pray five times a day in secret, and to spend much time in religious talk with other boys; and used to meet with them to pray together. I experienced I know not what kind of delight in religion. My mind was much engaged in it, and had much selfrighteous pleasure; and it was my delight to abound in religious duties. I with some of my schoolmates joined together, and built a booth in a swamp, in a very retired spot, for a place of prayer. And besides, I had particular secret places of my own in the woods, where I used to retire by myself; and was from time to time much affected. My affections seemed to be lively and easily moved, and I seemed to be in my element when engaged in religious duties. And I am ready to think, many are deceived with such affections, and such a kind of delight as I then had in religion, and mistake it for grace.

But in process of time, my convictions and affections wore off; and I entirely lost all those affections and delights and left off secret prayer, at least as to any constant performance of it; and returned like a dog to his vomit, and went on in the ways of sin. Indeed I was at times very uneasy, especially towards the latter part of my time at

From Jonathan Edwards, *Personal Narrative, Works,* Samuel Austin, ed., 1808-09.

college; when it pleased God, to seize me with a pleurisy; in which
he brought me nigh to the grave, and shook me over the pit of hell.
And yet, it was not long after my recovery, before I fell again into
my old ways of sin. But God would not suffer me to go on with any
quietness; I had great and violent inward struggles, till, after many
conflicts with wicked inclinations, repeated resolutions, and bonds that
I laid myself under by a kind of vows to God, I was brought wholly
to break off all former wicked ways, and all ways of known outward
sin; and to apply myself to seek salvation, and practise many religious duties; but without that kind of affection and delight which I
had formerly experienced. My concern now wrought more by inward struggles and conflicts, and selfreflections. I made seeking my
salvation the main business of my life. But yet, it seems to me, I
sought after a miserable manner; which has made me sometimes
since to question, whether ever it issued in that which was saving;
being ready to doubt, whether such miserable seeking ever succeeded.
I was indeed brought to seek salvation in a manner that I never was
before; I felt a spirit to part with all things in the world, for an
interest in Christ. My concern continued and prevailed, with many
exercising thoughts and inward struggles; but yet it never seemed to
be proper to express that concern by the name of terror.

From my childhood up, my mind had been full of objections
against the doctrine of God's sovereignty, in choosing whom he
would to eternal life, and rejecting whom he pleased; leaving them
eternally to perish, and be everlastingly tormented in hell. It used to
appear like a horrible doctrine to me. But I remember the time very
well, when I seemed to be convinced, and fully satisfied, as to this
sovereignty of God, and his justice in thus eternally disposing of men,
according to his sovereign pleasure. But never could give an account,
how, or by what means, I was thus convinced, not in the least imagining at the time, nor a long time after, that there was any extraordinary influence of God's Spirit in it; but only that now I saw further,
and my reason apprehended the justice and reasonableness of it.
However, my mind rested in it; and it put an end to all those cavils
and objections. And there has been a wonderful alteration in my
mind, in respect to the doctrine of God's sovereignty, from that day
to this; so that I scarce ever have found so much as the rising of an

objection against it, in the most absolute sense, in God's shewing mercy to whom he will shew mercy, and hardening whom he will. God's absolute sovereignty and justice, with respect to salvation and damnation, is what my mind seems to rest assured of, as much as of any thing that I see with my eyes; at least it is so at times. But I have often, since that first conviction, had quite another kind of sense of God's sovereignty than I had then. I have often since had not only a conviction, but a delightful conviction. The doctrine has very often appeared exceeding pleasant, bright, and sweet. Absolute sovereignty is what I love to ascribe to God. But my first conviction was not so.

The first instance that I remember of that sort of inward, sweet delight in God and divine things that I have lived much in since, was on reading those words, I Tim. i. 17. *Now unto the King eternal, immortal, invisible, the only wise God, be honor and glory for ever and ever, Amen.* As I read the words, there came into my soul, and was as it were diffused through it, a sense of the glory of the Divine Being; a new sense, quite different from any thing I ever experienced before. Never any words of scripture seemed to me as these words did. I thought with myself, how excellent a Being that was, and how happy I should be, if I might enjoy that God, and be rapt up to him in heaven, and be as it were swallowed up in him for ever! I kept saying, and as it were singing over these words of scripture to myself; and went to pray to God that I might enjoy him, and prayed in a manner quite different from what I used to do; with a new sort of affection. But it never came into my thought, that there was any thing spiritual, or of a saving nature in this.

From about that time, I began to have a new kind of apprehensions and ideas of Christ, and the work of redemption, and the glorious way of salvation by him. An inward, sweet sense of these things, at times, came into my heart; and my soul was led away in pleasant views and contemplations of them. And my mind was greatly engaged to spend my time in reading and meditating on Christ, on the beauty and excellency of his person, and the lovely way of salvation by free grace in him. I found no books so delightful to me, as those that treated of these subjects. Those words Cant. ii. 1, used to be abundantly with me, *I am the Rose of Sharon, and the Lilly of the valleys.* The words seemed to me, sweetly to represent the loveliness and beauty of Jesus Christ. The whole book of Canticles used to be pleasant to me, and I used to be much in reading it, about that time; and found, from time to time, an inward sweetness, that would carry me away, in my contemplations. This I know not how to express otherwise, than by a calm, sweet abstraction of soul from all the concerns of this world; and sometimes a kind of vision, or fixed ideas and imaginations, of being alone in the mountains, or some solitary wilderness, far from all mankind, sweetly conversing with Christ, and wrapt and swallowed up in God. The sense I had of divine things, would often of a sudden kindle up, as it were, a sweet burning in my heart; an ardor of soul, that I know not how to express.

Not long after I first began to experience these things, I gave an account to my father of some things that had passed in my mind. I was pretty much affected by the discourse we had together; and when the discourse was ended, I walked abroad alone, in a solitary place in my father's pasture, for contemplation. And as I was walking there, and looking up on the sky and clouds, there came into my mind so sweet a sense of the glorious *majesty* and *grace* of God, that I know not how to express. I seemed to see them both in a sweet conjunction; majesty and meekness joined together; it was a sweet, and gentle, and holy majesty; and also a majestic meekness, an awful sweetness; a high, and great, and holy gentleness.

After this my sense of divine things gradually increased, and became more and more lively, and had more of that inward sweetness. The appearance of every thing was altered; there seemed to be, as it were, a calm, sweet cast, or appearance of divine glory, in almost every thing. God's excellency, his wisdom, his purity and love, seemed to appear in every thing; in the sun, moon, and stars; in the clouds, and blue sky; in the grass, flowers, trees; in the water, and all nature; which used greatly to fix my mind. I often used to sit and view the moon for continuance; and in the day, spent much time in viewing the clouds and sky, to behold the sweet glory of God in these things; in the mean time, singing forth, with a low voice my contemplations of the Creator and Redeemer. And scarce any thing, among all the works of nature, was so sweet to me as thunder and lightning; formerly, nothing had been so terrible to me. Before, I used to be uncommonly terrified with thunder, and to be struck with terror when I saw a thunder storm rising; but now, on the contrary, it rejoiced me. I felt God, so to speak, at the first appearance of a thunder storm; and used to take the opportunity, at such times, to fix myself in order to view the clouds, and see the lightnings play, and hear the majestic and awful voice of God's thunder, which often-times was exceedingly entertaining, leading me to sweet contempla-tions of my great and glorious God. While thus engaged, it always seemed natural to me to sing, or chant for my meditations; or, to speak my thoughts in soliloquies with a singing voice.

I felt then great satisfaction, as to my good state; but that did not content me. I had vehement longings of soul after God and Christ, and after more holiness, wherewith my heart seemed to be full, and ready to break; which often brought to my mind the words of the Psalmist, Psal. cxix. 28. *My soul breaketh for the longing it hath.* I often felt a mourning and lamenting in my heart, that I had not turned to God sooner, that I might have had more time to grow in grace. My mind was greatly fixed on divine things; almost per-petually in the contemplation of them. I spent most of my time in thinking of divine things, year after year; often walking alone in the woods, and solitary places, for meditation, soliloquy, and prayer, and converse with God; and it was always my manner, at such times, to sing forth my contemplations. I was almost constantly in ejaculatory prayer, wherever I was. Prayer seemed to be natural to me, as the breath by which the inward burnings of my heart had vent. The de-lights which I now felt in the things of religion, were of an exceeding different kind from those before mentioned, that I had when a boy; and what I then had no more notion of, than one born blind has of pleasant and beautiful colors. They were of a more inward, pure, soul animating and refreshing nature. Those former delights never reached the heart; and did not arise from any sight of the divine excellency of the things of God; or any taste of the soul satisfying and life-giving good there is in them.

My sense of divine things seemed gradually to increase, until I went to preach at Newyork, which was about a year and a half after they began; and while I was there, I felt them, very sensibly, in a much higher degree than I had done before. My longings after God and holiness, were much increased. Pure and humble, holy and heav-

enly Christianity, appeared exceeding amiable to me. I felt a burning
desire to be in every thing a complete Christian; and conformed to
the blessed image of Christ; and that I might live, in all things, according to the pure, sweet and blessed rules of the gospel. I had an
eager thirsting after progress in these things; which put me upon
pursuing and pressing after them. It was my continual strife day and
night, and constant inquiry, how I should *be* more holy, and *live*
more holily, and more becoming a child of God, and a disciple of
Christ. I now sought an increase of grace and holiness, and a holy
life, with much more earnestness, than ever I sought grace before I
had it. I used to be continually examining myself, and studying and
contriving for likely ways and means, how I should live holily, with
far greater diligence and earnestness, than ever I pursued any thing
in my life; but yet with too great a dependence on my own strength;
which afterwards proved a great damage to me. My experience had
not then taught me, as it has done since, my extreme feebleness and
impotence, every manner of way; and the bottomless depths of secret
corruption and deceit there was in my heart. However, I went on
with my eager pursuit after more holiness, and conformity to Christ.

The heaven I desired was a heaven of holiness; to be with God,
and to spend my eternity in divine love, and holy communion with
Christ. My mind was very much taken up with contemplations on
heaven, and the enjoyments there; and living there in perfect holiness, humility and love: And it used at that time to appear a great
part of the happiness of heaven, that there the saints could express
their love to Christ. It appeared to me a great clog and burden, that
what I felt within, I could not express as I desired. The inward ardor
of my soul, seemed to be hindered and pent up, and could not freely
flame out as it would. I used often to think, how in heaven this principle should freely and fully vent and express itself. Heaven appeared exceedingly delightful, as a world of love; and that all happiness consisted in living in pure, humble, heavenly, divine love.

I remember the thoughts I used then to have of holiness; and said
sometimes to myself, "I do certainly know that I love holiness, such
as the gospel prescribes." It appeared to me, that there was nothing
in it but what was ravishingly lovely; the highest beauty and amia-
bleness . . . a *divine* beauty; far purer than any thing here upon

earth; and that every thing else was like mire and defilement, in comparison of it.

Holiness, as I then wrote down some of my contemplations on it, appeared to me to be of a sweet, pleasant, charming, serene, calm, nature; which brought an inexpressible purity, brightness, peacefulness and ravishment to the soul. In other words, that it made the soul like a field or garden of God, with all manner of pleasant flowers; all pleasant, delightful, and undisturbed; enjoying a sweet calm, and the gently vivifying beams of the sun. The soul of a true Christian, as I then wrote my meditations, appeared like such a little white flower as we see in the spring of the year; low and humble on the ground, opening its bosom to receive the pleasant beams of the sun's glory; rejoicing as it were in a calm rapture; diffusing around a sweet fragrancy; standing peacefully and lovingly, in the midst of other flowers round about; all in like manner opening their bosoms, to drink in the light of the sun. There was no part of creature holiness, that I had so great a sense of its loveliness, as humility, brokenness of heart and poverty of spirit; and there was nothing that I so earnestly longed for. My heart panted after this, to lie low before God, as in the dust; that I might be nothing, and that God might be ALL, that I might become as a little child.

MICHEL-GUILLAUME JEAN DE CRÈVECOUER (1735–1813)

Crèvecoeur came to Canada from his native France in 1754 and served under Montcalm in the Seven Years' War. Later, Crèvecoeur explored the Great Lakes region and the Ohio River, and after further travels in Pennsylvania and New York, married an American girl and settled down on a farm in Orange County, New York. The next ten years were spent farming and writing essays, some of which were collected under the title, Letters from an American Farmer *(1782). The remaining essays,* Sketches of Eighteenth Century America, *were not published until the twentieth century.*

A Tory, Crèvecoeur left the country when the Revolution broke out and did not return until the war was over. On his arrival, he found that his wife had been killed, his three children had disappeared (two of them eventually turned up in Boston), and his farm had been burned. With the help of American friends, he became French consul in New York, but in 1790 he returned to Normandy where he spent the rest of his life.

The Letters from an American Farmer *contains essays which are a curious mixture of Rousseauistic evocations of a farmer's intimate communion with nature, and acute, realistic observations of American life. The following passage is perhaps the most famous in all of Crèvecoeur's writings. It presents the familiar image of America as the great melting pot.*

The American
"... WHAT A CHANGE ...!"

HE IS AN AMERICAN, who, leaving behind him all his ancient prejudices and manners, receives new ones from the new mode of

From Michel-Guillaume Jean de Crèvecouer, *Letters from an American Farmer*, 1782.

life he has embraced, the new government he obeys, and the new rank he holds. He becomes an American by being received in the broad lap of our great *Alma Mater*.

Here individuals of all nations are melted into a new race of men, whose labors and posterity will one day cause great changes in the world. Americans are the western pilgrims, who are carrying along with them that great mass of arts, sciences, vigour, and industry, which began long since in the east; they will finish the great circle. The Americans were once scattered all over Europe; here they are incorporated into one of the finest systems of population which has ever appeared, and which will hereafter become distinct by the power of the different climates they inhabit. The American ought, therefore, to love this country much better than that wherein either he or his forefathers were born. Here the rewards of his industry follow with equal steps the progress of his labour, his labour is founded on the basis of nature, *self-interest*; can it want a stronger allurement? Wives and children, who before in vain demanded of him a morsel of bread, now, fat and frolicsome, gladly help their father to clear those fields whence exuberant crops are to arise to feed and to clothe them all; without any part being claimed, either by a despotic prince, a rich abbot, or a mighty lord. Here religion demands but little of him; a small voluntary salary to the minister, and gratitude to God; can he refuse these? The American is a new man, who acts upon new principles; he must therefore entertain new ideas, and form new opinions. From involuntary idleness, servile dependence, penury, and useless labor, he has passed to toils of a very different nature, rewarded by ample subsistence.—This is an American. . . .

An European, when he first arrives, seems limited in his intentions, as well as in his views; but he very suddenly alters his scale; two hundred miles formerly appeared a very great distance; it is now but a trifle; he no sooner breathes out air than he forms schemes, and embarks in designs he never would have thought of in his own country. There the plenitude of society confines many useful ideas, and often extinguishes the most laudable schemes which here ripen into maturity. Thus Europeans become Americans.

But how is this accomplished in that crowd of low, indigent people, who flock here every year from all parts of Europe? I will tell you;

they no sooner arrive than they immediately feel the good effects of
that plenty of provisions we possess: they fare on our best food, and
they are kindly entertained; their talents, character, and peculiar
industry are immediately enquired into; they find countrymen everywhere disseminated, let them come from whatever part of Europe.

Let me select one as an epitome of the rest; he is hired, he goes to
work, and works moderately; instead of being employed by a
haughty person, he finds himself with his equal, placed at the substantial table of the farmer, or else at an inferior one as good; his wages
are high, his bed is not like that bed of sorrow on which he used to
lie: if he behaves with propriety, and is faithful, he is caressed, and
becomes, as it were, a member of the family. He begins to feel the
effects of a sort of resurrection; hitherto he had not lived, but simply
vegetated; he now feels himself a man, because he is treated as such;
the laws of his own country had overlooked him in his insignificancy;
the laws of this cover him with their mantle. Judge what an alteration there must arise in the mind and thoughts of this man; he begins
to forget his former servitude and dependence; his heart involuntarily swells and glows; this first swell inspires him with those new
thoughts which constitute an American. What love can he entertain
for a country where his existence was a burden to him! if he is a generous good man, the love of this new adoptive parent, will sink deep
into his heart. He looks around, and sees many a prosperous person,
who but a few years before was as poor as himself. This encourages
him much; he begins to form some little scheme, the first, alas, he
ever formed in his life. If he is wise, he thus spends two or three
years, in which time he acquires knowledge, the use of tools, the
modes of working the lands, felling trees, etc. This prepares the
foundation of a good name, the most useful acquisition he can make.
He is encouraged; he has gained friends; he is advised and directed;
he feels bold; he purchases some land; he gives all the money he
has brought over, as well as what he has earned, and trusts to the
God of harvests for the discharge of the rest. His good name pro-
cures him credit; he is now possessed of the deed, conveying to him
and his posterity the fee simple, and absolute property of two hundred acres of land, situated on such a river. What an epoch in this
man's life! He is become a freeholder, from perhaps a German boor

—he is now an American, a Pennsylvanian. He is naturalized; his name is enrolled with those of the other citizens of the province. Instead of being a vagrant, he has a place of residence; he is called the inhabitant of such a county, or of such a district, and for the first time in his life counts for something; for hitherto he had been a cypher. I only repeat what I have heard many say, and no wonder their hearts should glow, and be agitated with a multitude of feelings, not easy to describe. From nothing to start into being; from a servant to the rank of a master; from being the slave of some despotic prince, to become a free man, invested with lands, to which every municipal blessing is annexed! What a change indeed! It is in consequence of that change, that he becomes an American.

THOMAS JEFFERSON (1743–1804)

On Jefferson's gravestone are inscribed the following words, composed by Jefferson himself: "Here was buried Thomas Jefferson, Author of the Declaration of American Independence, of the Statute of Virginia for Religious Freedom, and Father of the University of Virginia."

At first glance, the inscription may seem slightly strange for a man who was also governor of Virginia, member of Congress, minister to France, Secretary of State, Vice-President of the United States, and President.

Yet, in a deeper sense, the inscription is immensely fitting and significant, for it reveals Jefferson's overwhelming faith in the three touchstones of democracy: political, religious, and intellectual freedom.

Jefferson, who was by birth and marriage connected with some of the wealthiest and most powerful families in Virginia, envisioned a nation of independent farmers living on their own land in close relation to nature and God. From their ranks the leaders of society, the natural aristocracy, would emerge. Jefferson's dream of an agrarian republic was not to be realized, however. The rapid growth of cities, the industrial revolution, and the development of better means of communication were soon to create the foundation for an industrial, rather than an agrarian, America.

Yet the ideas which Jefferson formulated and practiced have had the greatest influence on the development of the American mind. To join men together in a free society remains the American ideal.

On Christianity

LETTER TO DR. BENJAMIN RUSH

WASHINGTON, April 21, 1803.

DEAR SIR,—

In some of the delightful conversations with you, in the evenings of 1798-99, and which serve as an anodyne to the afflictions of the crisis through which our country was then laboring, the Christian religion was sometimes our topic; and I then promised you, that one day or other, I would give you my views of it. They are the result of a life of inquiry and reflection, and very different from that anti-Christian system imputed to me by those who know nothing of my opinions. To the corruptions of Christianity I am, indeed, opposed; but not to the genuine precepts of Jesus himself. I am a Christian, in the only sense he wished any one to be; sincerely attached to his doctrines, in preference to all others; ascribing to himself every *human* excellence; and believing he never claimed any other. At the short interval since these conversations, when I could justifiably abstract my mind from public affairs, the subject has been under my contemplation. But the more I considered it, the more it expanded beyond the measure of either my time or information. In the moment of my late departure from Monticello, I received from Dr. Priestley, his little treatise of "Socrates and Jesus Compared." This being a section of the general view I had taken of the field, it became a subject of reflection while on the road, and unoccupied otherwise. The result was, to arrange in my mind a syllabus, or outline of such an estimate of the comparative merits of Christianity, as I wished to see executed by some one of more leisure and information for the task, than myself. This I now send you, as the only discharge of my promise I can probably ever execute. And in confiding it to you, I know it will not be exposed to the malignant perversions of those who make every word from me a text for new misrepresentations and calumnies. I am moreover averse to the communication of my religious tenets to the public; because it would countenance the presumption of those who

From Thomas Jefferson, *Thomas Jefferson Correspondence*, W. C. Ford, ed., Boston, 1916.

have endeavored to draw them before that tribunal, and to seduce public opinion to erect itself into that inquisition over the rights of conscience, which the laws have so justly proscribed. It behooves every man who values liberty of conscience for himself, to resist invasions of it in the case of others; or their case may, by change of circumstances, become his own. It behooves him, too, in his own case, to give no example of concession, betraying the common right of independent opinion, by answering questions of faith, which the laws have left between God and himself. Accept my affectionate salutations.

SYLLABUS OF AN ESTIMATE OF THE MERIT OF THE DOCTRINES OF JESUS, COMPARED WITH THOSE OF OTHERS.

In a comparative view of the Ethics of the enlightened nations of antiquity, of the Jews and of Jesus, no notice should be taken of the corruptions of reason among the ancients, to wit, the idolatry and superstition of the vulgar, nor of the corruptions of Christianity by the learned among its professors.

Let a just view be taken of the moral principles inculcated by the most esteemed of the sects of ancient philosophy, or of their individuals; particularly Pythagoras, Socrates, Epicurus, Cicero, Epictetus, Seneca, Antoninus.

I. Philosophers. 1. Their precepts related chiefly to ourselves, and the government of those passions which, unrestrained, would disturb our tranquility of mind. In this branch of philosophy they were really great.

2. In developing our duties to others, they were short and defective. They embraced, indeed, the circles of kindred and friends, and inculcated patriotism, or the love of our country in the aggregate, as a primary obligation; toward our neighbors and countrymen they taught justice, but scarcely viewed them as within the circle of benevolence. Still less have they inculcated peace, charity, and love to our fellow men, or embraced with benevolence the whole family of mankind.

II. Jews. 1. Their system was Deism; that is, the belief of one only God. But their ideas of him and of his attributes were degrading and injurious.

2. Their Ethics were not only imperfect, but often irreconcilable with the sound dictates of reason and morality, as they respect intercourse with those around us; and repulsive and anti-social, as respecting other nations. They needed reformation, therefore, in an eminent degree.

III. Jesus. In this state of things among the Jews, Jesus appeared. His parentage was obscure; his condition poor; his education null; his natural endowments great; his life correct and innocent; he was meek, benevolent, patient, firm, disinterested, and of the sublimest eloquence.

The disadvantages under which his doctrines appear are remarkable.

1. Like Socrates and Epictetus, he wrote nothing himself.

2. But he had not, like them, a Xenophon or an Arrian to write for him. I name not Plato, who only used the name of Socrates to cover the whimsies of his own brain. On the contrary, all the learned of his country, entrenched in its power and riches, were opposed to him, lest his labors should undermine their advantages; and the committing to writing his life and doctrines fell on unlettered and ignorant men; who wrote, too, from memory, and not till long after the transactions had passed.

3. According to the ordinary fate of those who attempt to enlighten and reform mankind, he fell an early victim to the jealousy and combination of the altar and the throne, at about thirty-three years of age, his reason having not yet attained the *maximum* of its energy, nor the course of his preaching, which was but of three years at most, presented occasions for developing a complete system of morals.

4. Hence the doctrines which he really delivered were defective as a whole, and fragments only of what he did deliver have come to us mutilated, misstated, and often unintelligible.

5. They have been still more disfigured by the corruptions of schismatizing followers, who have found an interest in sophisticating and perverting the simple doctrines he taught, by engrafting on them the mysticisms of a Grecian sophist, frittering them into subtleties, and obscuring them with jargon, until they have caused good men

to reject the whole in disgust, and to view Jesus himself as an impostor.

Notwithstanding these disadvantages, a system of morals is presented to us, which, if filled up in the true style and spirit of the rich fragments he left us, would be the most perfect and sublime that has ever been taught by man.

The question of his being a member of the Godhead, or in direct communication with it, claimed for him by some of his followers, and denied by others, is foreign to the present view, which is merely an estimate of the intrinsic merit of his doctrines.

1. He corrected the Deism of the Jews, confirming them in their belief of one only God, and giving them juster notions of his attributes and government.

2. His moral doctrines, relating to kindred and friends, were more pure and perfect than those of the most correct of the philosophers, and greatly more so than those of the Jews; and they went far beyond both in inculcating universal philanthropy, not only to kindred and friends, to neighbors and countrymen, but to all mankind, gathering all into one family, under the bonds of love, charity, peace, common wants and common aids. A development of this head will evince the peculiar superiority of the system of Jesus over all others.

3. The precepts of philosophy, and of the Hebrew code, laid hold of actions only. He pushed his scrutinies into the heart of man; erected his tribunal in the region of his thoughts, and purified the waters at the fountain head.

4. He taught, emphatically, the doctrines of a future state, which was either doubted, or disbelieved by the Jews; and wielded it with efficacy, as an important incentive, supplementary to the other motives to moral conduct.

On the True Aristocracy

LETTER TO JOHN ADAMS

MONTICELLO, October 28, 1813.
* * * I agree with you that there is a natural aristocracy among men. The grounds of this are virtue and talents. Formerly, bodily

powers gave place among the aristoi. But since the invention of gunpowder has armed the weak as well as the strong with missile death, bodily strength, like beauty, good humor, politeness and other accomplishments, has become but an auxiliary ground for distinction. There is also an artificial aristocracy, founded on wealth and birth, without either virtue or talents; for with these it would belong to the first class. The natural aristocracy I consider as the most precious gift of nature, for the instruction, the trusts, and government of society. And indeed, it would have been inconsistent in creation to have formed man for the social state, and not to have provided virtue and wisdom enough to manage the concerns of the society. May we not even say, that that form of government is the best, which provides the most effectually for a pure selection of these natural aristoi into the offices of government? The artificial aristocracy is a mischievous ingredient in government, and provision should be made to prevent its ascendency. On the question, what is the best provision, you and I differ; but we differ as rational friends, using the free exercise of our own reason, and mutually indulging its errors. You think it best to put the pseudo-aristoi into a separate chamber of legislation, where they may be hindered from doing mischief by their co-ordinate branches, and where, also, they may be a protection to wealth against the Agrarian and plundering enterprises of the majority of the people. I think that to give them power in order to prevent them from doing mischief, is arming them for it, and increasing instead of remedying the evil. For if the co-ordinate branches can arrest their action, so may they that of the co-ordinates. Mischief may be done negatively as well as positively. Of this, a cabal in the Senate of the United States has furnished many proofs. Nor do I believe them necessary to protect the wealthy; because enough of these will find their way into every branch of the legislation, to protect themselves. From fifteen to twenty legislatures of our own, in action for thirty years past, have proved that no fears of an equalization of property are to be apprehended from them. I think the best remedy is exactly that provided by all our constitutions, to leave to the citizens the free election and separation of the aristoi from the pseudo-aristoi, of the wheat from the chaff. In general they will elect the really good and wise. In some instances, wealth may corrupt, and birth blind them; but not in sufficient degree to endanger the society.

It is probable that our difference of opinion may, in some measure, be produced by a difference of character in those among whom we lived. From what I have seen of Massachusetts and Connecticut myself, and still more from what I have heard, and the character given of the former by yourself (volume I, page 111), who know them so much better, there seems to be in those two States a traditionary reverence for certain families, which has rendered the offices of the government nearly hereditary in those families. I presume that from an early period of your history, members of those families happening to possess virtue and talents, have honestly exercised them for the good of the people, and by their services have endeared their names to them. In coupling Connecticut with you, I mean it politically only, not morally. For having made the Bible the common law of their land, they seemed to have modeled their morality on the story of Jacob and Laban. But although this hereditary succession to office with you, may, in some degree, be founded in real family merit, yet in a much higher degree, it has proceeded from your strict alliance of Church and State. These families are canonised in the eyes of the people on common principles, "you tickle me, and I will tickle you." In Virginia we have nothing of this. Our clergy, before the revolution, having been secured against rivalship by fixed salaries, did not give themselves the trouble of acquiring influence over the people. Of wealth, there were great accumulations in particular families, handed down from generation to generation, under the English law of entails. But the only object of ambition for the wealthy was a seat in the King's Council. All their court then was paid to the crown and its creatures; and they Philipised in all collisions between the King and the people. Hence they were unpopular; and that unpopularity continues attached to their names. A Randolph, a Carter, or a Burwell must have great personal superiority over a common competitor to be elected by the people even at this day. At the first session of our legislature after the Declaration of Independence, we passed a law abolishing entails. And this was followed by one abolishing the privilege of primogeniture, and dividing the lands of intestates equally among all their children, or other representatives. These laws, drawn by myself, laid the ax to the foot of pseudo-aristocracy. And had another which I prepared been adopted by the legislature, our work would have been complete. It was a bill for the more general diffusion of learning. This proposed to divide every county into wards of five or six miles square, like your townships; to establish in each ward a free school for reading, writing and common arithmetic; to provide for the annual selection of the best subjects from these schools, who might receive, at the public expense, a higher degree of education at a district school; and from these district schools to select a certain number of the most promising subjects, to be completed at an University, where all the useful sciences should be taught. Worth and genius would thus have been sought out from every condition of life, and completely prepared by education for defeating the competition of wealth and birth for public trusts. My proposition had, for a further object, to impart to these wards those portions of self-government for which they are best qualified, by confiding to them the care of their poor, their roads, police, elections, the nomination of jurors, administration of justice in small cases, elementary exercises of militia; in short, to have made them little republics, with a warden at the head of each, for all those concerns which, being under their eye, they would better manage than the larger republics of the county or State. A general call of ward meetings by their wardens on the same day through the State, would at any time produce the genuine sense of the people on any required point, and would enable the State to act in mass, as your people have so often done, and with so much effect by their town meetings. The law for religious freedom, which made a part of this system, having put down the aristocracy of the clergy, and restored to the citizen the freedom of the mind, and those of entails and descents nurturing an equality of condition among them, this on education would have raised the mass of the people to the high ground of moral respectability necessary to their own safety, and to orderly government; and would have completed the great object of qualifying them to select the veritable aristoi, for the trusts of government, to the exclusion of the pseudalists; and the same Theognis who has furnished the epigraphs of your two letters, assures us that Οὐδεμίαν πω Κύρὶ, ἀγαθοί πόλιν ὤλεσαν ἄνδρες.

Although this law has not yet been acted on but in a small and inefficient degree, it is still considered as before the legislature, with other bills of the revised code, not yet taken up, and I have great hope that some patriotic spirit will, at a favorable moment, call it up, and make it the keystone of the arch of our government.

With respect to aristocracy, we should further consider, that before the establishment of the American States, nothing was known to history but the man of the old world, crowded within limits either small or overcharged, and steeped in the vices which that situation generates. A government adapted to such men would be one thing; but a very different one, that for the man of these States. Here every one may have land to labor for himself, if he chooses; or, preferring the exercise of any other industry, may exact for it such compensation as not only to afford a comfortable subsistence, but wherewith to provide for a cessation from labor in old age. Every one, by his property, or by his satisfactory situation, is interested in the support of law and order. And such men may safely and advantageously reserve to themselves a wholesome control over their public affairs, and a degree of freedom, which, in the hands of the *canaille* of the cities of Europe, would be instantly perverted to the demolition and destruction of everything public and private. The history of the last twenty-five years of France, and of the last forty years in America, nay of its last two hundred years, proves the truth of both parts of this observation.

But even in Europe a change has sensibly taken place in the mind of man. Science had liberated the ideas of those who read and reflect, and the American example had kindled feelings of right in the people. An insurrection has consequently begun, of science, talents, and courage, against rank and birth, which have fallen into contempt. It has failed in its first effort, because the mobs of the cities, the instrument used for its accomplishment, debased by ignorance, poverty and vice, could not be restrained to rational action. But the world will recover from the panic of this first catastrophe. Science is progressive, and talents and enterprise on the alert. Resort may be had to the people of the country, a more governable power from their principles and subordination; and rank, and birth, and tinsel-aristocracy will finally shrink into insignificance, even there. This, however, we have no right to meddle with. It suffices for us, if the moral and physical condition of our own citizens qualifies them to select the able and good for the direction of their government, with a recurrence of elections at such short periods as will enable them to displace an unfaithful servant, before the mischief he meditates may be irremediable.

I have thus stated my opinion on a point on which we differ, not with a view to controversy, for we are both too old to change opinions which are the result of a long life of inquiry and reflection; but on the suggestions of a former letter of yours, that we ought not to die before we have explained ourselves to each other. We acted in perfect harmony, through a long and perilous contest for our liberty and independence. A constitution has been acquired, which, though neither of us thinks perfect, yet both consider as competent to render our fellow citizens the happiest and the securest on whom the sun has ever shone. If we do not think exactly alike as to its imperfections, it matters little to our country, which, after devoting to its long lives of disinterested labor, we have delivered over to our successors in life, who will be able to take care of it and of themselves.

Of the pamphlet on aristocracy which has been sent to you, or who may be its author, I have heard nothing but through your letter. If the person you suspect, it may be known from the quaint, mystical, and hyperbolical ideas, involved in affected, new-fangled and pedantic terms which stamp his writings. Whatever it be, I hope your quiet is not to be affected at this day by the rudeness or intemperance of scribblers; but that you may continue in tranquillity to live and to rejoice in the prosperity of our country, until it shall be your own wish to take your seat among the aristoi who have gone before you. Ever and affectionately yours.

II.   The Course of Empire

CONSTANCE ROURKE (1885-1941)

Born in Cleveland, Ohio, Constance Rourke was educated at Vassar (A. B., 1907) and at the Sorbonne. From 1910 to 1915, she taught at Vassar, but resigned in order to devote all her time to studying and writing.

The wide scope of Constance Rourke's published work, which ranges from Trumpets of Jubilee *(1927)—a book about the Beecher family and P. T. Barnum—to* American Humor *(1931);* Davy Crockett *(1934);* Troupers of the Gold Coast *(1928)—dealing with actresses on the California frontier—and* Audubon *(1936), manifests her belief that the study of American culture cannot be confined to rigidly limited disciplines, but must be concerned with the subtle, often hidden interactions between society and the imagination.*

In American Humor, *her finest achievement, Miss Rourke attempted to carry out Van Wyck Brooks's idea that American artists must be provided with a sense of the national past, if their work is to be truly American. Her description of the effect of the wilderness on the frontiersman's imagination establishes a comic tradition in terms of which we can better understand later American humorists.*

The Gamecock of the West

*I*N 1822, at a theater in New Orleans whose pit and parquet were crowded with flatboatmen, an actor stepped out in buckskin shirt and leggings, moccasins and fur cap, with a rifle on his shoulder. He

From Constance Rourke, *American Humor* (New York; Harcourt, Brace; 1931), pp. 34-38.

might have come from the audience. To a familiar air he sang a new
song by the author of "The Old Oaken Bucket"—

> But Jackson he was wide awake, and wasn't scar'd at trifles,
> For well he knew what aim we take with our Kentucky rifles;
> So he led us down to Cypress Swamp, the ground was low and mucky;
> There stood John Bull in martial pomp: *but here was old Kentucky!*

With this he threw his cap on the ground and took aim. The response
was a deafening Indian yell, and cataclysms of applause greeted each
of the eight stanzas with their refrain—

> Oh, Kentucky! the hunters of Kentucky,
> Oh, Kentucky! the hunters of Kentucky!

Thereafter the song was sung at theater after theater in the South
and West, sometimes half a dozen times in an evening. Sweeping
eastward, it reached fame in New York with "symphonies" and ac-
companiments and elaborations—

> We raised a bank to hide our breasts, not that we thought of dying,
> But that we always liked to rest unless the game is flying;
> Behind it stood our little force; none wished it to be greater,
> For every man was half a horse and half an alligator.

Like the Yankee in the Revolution the backwoodsman had leapt
up out of war as a noticeable figure—the War of 1812; in the scattered western country his portrait had taken shape slowly. Once on
the national horizon, however, he made up in noise what he had lost
in time. He grew rhapsodic—about himself—and like the Reverend
Samuel Peters betrayed a strong leaning toward natural history.
He was not only half horse, half alligator, he was also the sea-horse
of the mountain, a flying whale, a bear with a sore head. He had
sprung from the Potomac of the world. He was a steamboat, or an
earthquake that shook an enemy to pieces, and he could wade the
Mississippi. "I'm a regular tornado, tough as hickory and long-
winded as a nor'wester. I can strike a blow like a falling tree, and
every lick makes a gap in the crowd that lets in an acre of sunshine."
He was the most cunning of the creatures of the backwoods, a raccoon
"a ring-tailed roarer." Oddly enough, he was also a flower. "I'm the
yaller blossom of the forest!" Heels cracking, he leapt into the air

to proclaim his attributes against all comers like an Indian preparing for warfare. As a preliminary to a fight he neighed like a stallion or crowed like a cock. He was "the gamecock of the wilderness" and the "Salt River Roarer." "Down thar you go, war you a buffalo," he chanted in wrestling matches, with hands placed on the shoulder and hip of his opponent.

Strength was his obsession—size, scale, power: he seemed obliged to shout their symbols as if after all he were not wholly secure in their possession. He shouted as though he were intoxicated by shouting. He shouted in ritual, as though the emotions by which he was moved were bending him to some primitive celebration. Leaping, crowing, flapping his wings, he indulged in dances resembling beast-dances among savages; his heel-crackings and competitive matches were like savage efforts to create strength for the tribe by exhibiting strength. They even appeared, in the fertile new country, like those primitive ceremonies to produce growth by which the sower leaps high to make the hemp grow high.

He not only created a bestiary; with the single digression to the floral he insisted that he was a beast—a new beast, and the records prove that in this contention he was often right. Gouging was his favorite method of attack in affairs not settled with a gun or knife. Men of the backwoods joined in mortal combat stark naked, strapped within a few inches of each other to a bench, armed only with bowie-knives. A steamboat captain, once a flatboatman, finding that one of his men had been badly treated in a house on the river near New Orleans, fastened a cable round the pier on which the house rested, and starting the steamer, pulled it into the river, drowning the inmates.

Horror, terror, death, were written large in the life of the rivers and forests. Yet the backwoodsman kept a comic oblivious tone; he seemed to possess "a certain jollity of mind, pickled in a scorn of fortune." A traveler floundering through the mire of a cypress swamp in Ohio saw a beaver hat lying crown upward in the mud. It moved, and he lifted it with his whip. Underneath was a man's head—a laughing head that cried, "Hello, stranger!" The traveler offered his assistance, but the head declined, saying that he had a good horse under him.

RALPH WALDO EMERSON (1803–82)

The descendant of a long line of New England ministers, Emerson was born in Boston in 1803. His father died in 1811, and a few years later the family moved to Concord, Massachusetts, where Emerson was to spend most of his life.

A graduate of the Boston Latin School and Harvard College (A.B., 1821), Emerson entered the Harvard Divinity School in 1825 and was licensed the following year. In 1829, he was installed as minister of the Second Church of Boston. However, the death of his wife, his brother's insanity, his own ill health, and his increasing doubts about the validity of orthodox Christianity caused him to resign his pulpit in 1831. Searching for a meaning to life, Emerson went to Europe. In England he met Coleridge, Wordsworth, and Carlyle, who introduced him to German idealism and romanticism.

Two years later he returned to Concord, married Lydia Jackson, and took up his vocation as lecturer and essayist. He published Nature *in 1836, a little book, but the seminal document of American Transcendentalism. His address to Harvard's Phi Beta Kappa society on "The American Scholar" (1837) and his address to the Divinity School in Cambridge (1838) spread his fame and influence among the younger generation, but the latter brought down upon him the wrath of official Harvard, which ignored him until 1866—when Emerson was given an honorary degree.*

The dynamic optimism of Emerson's philosophy, first published to the world in Nature, *but then elaborated in* Essays, First Series *(1841),* Essays, Second Series *(1844),* The Conduct of Life *(1860), and other books, made Emerson the representative American of his time. His belief that the divine principle of the universe is manifested in nature and communicated to man through his intuition re-*

captured for nineteenth-century America the religious ecstasy of Edwardsean revivalism.

Self-Reliance

. . . . A foolish consistency is the hobgoblin of little minds, adored by little statesmen and philosophers and divines. With consistency a great soul has simply nothing to do. He may as well concern himself with his shadow on the wall. Speak what you think now in hard words and to-morrow speak what to-morrow thinks in hard words again, though it contradict every thing you said to-day.—"Ah, so you shall be sure to be misunderstood."—Is it so bad then to be misunderstood? Pythagoras was misunderstood, and Socrates, and Jesus, and Luther, and Copernicus, and Galileo, and Newton, and every pure and wise spirit that ever took flesh. To be great is to be misunderstood.

I suppose no man can violate his nature. All the sallies of his will are rounded in by the law of his being, as the inequalities of Andes and Himmaleh are insignificant in the curve of the sphere. Nor does it matter how you gauge and try him. A character is like an acrostic or Alexandrian stanza;—read it forward, backward, or across, it still spells the same thing. In this pleasing contrite wood-life which God allows me, let me record day by day my honest thought without prospect or retrospect, and, I cannot doubt, it will be found symmetrical, though I mean it not and see it not. My book should smell of pines and resound with the hum of insects. The swallow over my window should interweave that thread or straw he carries in his bill into my web also. We pass for what we are. Character teaches above our wills. Men imagine that they communicate their virtue or vice only by overt actions, and do not see that virtue or vice emit a breath every moment.

There will be an agreement in whatever variety of actions, so they be each honest and natural in their hour. For of one will, the actions will be harmonious, however unlike they seem. These varieties are

From Ralph Waldo Emerson, *Essays, First Series,* 1841.

lost sight of at a little distance, at a little height of thought. One tendency unites them all. The voyage of the best ship is a zigzag line of a hundred tacks. See the line from a sufficient distance, and it strengthens itself to the average tendency. Your genuine action will explain itself and will explain your other genuine actions. Your conformity explains nothing. Act singly, and what you have already done singly will justify you now. Greatness appeals to the future. If I can be firm enough to-day to do right and scorn eyes, I must have done so much right before as to defend me now. Be it how it will, do right now. Always scorn appearances and you always may. The force of character is cumulative. All the foregone days of virtue work their health into this. What makes the majesty of the heroes of the senate and the field, which so fills the imagination? The consciousness of a train of great days and victories behind. They shed a united light on the advancing actor. He is attended as by a visible escort of angels. That is it which throws thunder into Chatham's voice, and dignity into Washington's port, and America into Adams's eye. Honor is venerable to us because it is no ephemera. It is always ancient virtue. We worship it to-day because it is not of to-day. We love it and pay it homage because it is not a trap for our love and homage, but is self-dependent, self-derived, and therefore of an old immaculate pedigree, even if shown in a young person.

I hope in these days we have heard the last of conformity and consistency. Let the words be gazetted and ridiculous henceforward. Instead of the gong for dinner, let us hear a whistle from the Spartan fife. Let us never bow and apologize more. A great man is coming to eat at my house. I do not wish to please him; I wish that he should wish to please me. I will stand here for humanity, and though I would make it kind, I would make it true. Let us affront and reprimand the smooth mediocrity and squalid contentment of the times, and hurl in the face of custom and trade and office, the fact which is the upshot of all history, that there is a great responsible Thinker and Actor working wherever a man works; that a true man belongs to no other time or place, but is the centre of things. Where he is, there is nature. He measures you and all men and all events. Ordinarily, every body in society reminds us of somewhat else, or of some other person. Character, reality, reminds you of nothing else; it takes place of the whole creation. The man must be so much that he must make all circumstances indifferent. Every true man is a cause, a country, and an age; requires infinite spaces and numbers and time fully to accomplish his design;—and posterity seem to follow his steps as a train of clients. A man Caesar is born, and for ages after we have a Roman Empire. Christ is born, and millions of minds so grow and cleave to his genius that he is confounded with virtue and the possible of man. An institution is the lengthened shadow of one man; as, Monachism, of the Hermit Antony; the Reformation, of Luther; Quakerism, of Fox; Methodism, of Wesley; Abolition, of Clarkson. Scipio, Milton called "the height of Rome;" and all history resolves itself very easily into the biography of a few stout and earnest persons.

Let a man then know his worth, and keep things under his feet. Let him not peep or steal, or skulk up and down with the air of a charity-boy, a bastard, or an interloper in the world which exists for him. But the man in the street, finding no worth in himself which corresponds to the force which built a tower or sculptured a marble god, feels poor when he looks on these. To him a palace, a statue, or a costly book have an alien and forbidding air, much like a gay equipage, and seem to say like that, "Who are you, Sir?" Yet they all are his, suitors for his notice, petitioners to his faculties that they will come out and take possession. The picture waits for my verdict; it is not to command me, but I am to settle its claims to praise. That popular fable of the sot who was picked up dead-drunk in the street, carried to the duke's house, washed and dressed and laid in the duke's bed, and, on his waking, treated with all obsequious ceremony like the duke, and assured that he had been insane, owes its popularity to the fact that it symbolizes so well the state of man, who is in the world a sort of sot, but now and then wakes up, exercises his reason and finds himself a true prince.

Our reading is mendicant and sycophantic. In history our imagination plays us false. Kingdom and lordship, power and estate, are a gaudier vocabulary than private John and Edward in a small house and common day's work; but the things of life are the same to both; the sum total of both is the same. Why all this deference to Alfred and Scanderbeg and Gustavus? Suppose they were virtuous; did they wear out virtue? As great a stake depends on your private act to-day as followed their public and renowned steps. When private men shall act with original views, the lustre will be transferred from the actions of kings to those of gentlemen.

The world has been instructed by its kings, who have so magnetized the eyes of nations. It has been taught by this colossal symbol the mutual reverence that is due from man to man. The joyful loyalty with which men have everywhere suffered the king, the noble, or the great proprietor to walk among them by a law of his own, make his own scale of men and things and reverse theirs, pay for benefits not with money but with honor, and represent the law in his person, was the hieroglyphic by which they obscurely signified their consciousness of their own right and comeliness, the right of every man.

The magnetism which all original action exerts is explained when we inquire the reason of self-trust. Who is the Trustee? What is the aboriginal Self, on which a universal reliance may be grounded? What is the nature and power of that science-baffling star, without parallax, without calculable elements, which shoots a ray of beauty even into trivial and impure actions, if the least mark of independence appear? The inquiry leads us to that source, at once the essence of genius, of virtue, and of life, which we call Spontaneity or Instinct. We denote this primary wisdom as Intuition, whilst all later teachings are tuitions. In that deep force, the last fact behind which analysis cannot go, all things find their common origin. For the sense of being which in calm hours arises, we know not how, in the soul, is not diverse from things, from space, from light, from time, from man, but one with them and proceeds obviously from the same source whence their life and being also proceed. We first share the life by which things exist and afterwards see them as appearances in nature and forget that we have shared their cause. Here is the fountain of action and of thought. Here are the lungs of that inspiration which giveth man wisdom and which cannot be denied without impiety and atheism. We lie in the lap of immense intelligence, which makes us receivers of its truth and organs of its activity. When we discern justice, when we discern truth, we do nothing of ourselves, but allow a passage to its beams. If we ask whence this comes, if we seek to pry into the soul that causes, all philosophy is at fault. Its presence or its absence is all we can affirm. Every man discriminates between the voluntary acts of his mind and his involuntary perceptions, and knows that to his involuntary perceptions a perfect faith is due. He may err in the expression of them, but he knows that these things are so, like day and night, not to be disputed. My wilful actions and acquisitions are but roving;—the idlest reverie, the faintest native emotion, command my curiosity and respect. Thoughtless people contradict as readily the statement of perception as of opinions, or rather much more readily; for they do not distinguish between perception and notion. They fancy that I choose to see this or that thing. But perception is not whimsical, but fatal. If I see a trait, my children will see it after me, and in course of time all mankind,—although it may chance that no one has seen it before me. For my perception of it is as much a fact as the sun.

The relations of the soul to the divine spirit are so pure that it is profane to seek to interpose helps. It must be that when God speaketh he should communicate, not one thing, but all things; should fill the world with his voice; should scatter forth light, nature, time, souls, from the centre of the present thought; and new date and new create the whole. Whenever a mind is simple and receives a divine wisdom, old things pass away,—means, teachers, texts, temples fall; it lives now, and absorbs past and future into the present hour. All things are made sacred by relation to it,—one as much as another. All things are dissolved to their centre by their cause, and in the universal miracle petty and particular miracles disappear. If therefore a man claims to know and speak of God and carries you backward to the phraseology of some old mouldered nation in another country, in another world, believe him not. Is the acorn better than the oak which is its fulness and completion? Is the parent better than the child into whom he has cast his ripened being? Whence then this worship of the past? The centuries are conspirators against the sanity and authority of the soul. Time and space are but physiological colors which the eye makes, but the soul is light: where it is, is day; where it was, is night; and history is an impertinence and an injury if it be any thing more than a cheerful apologue or parable of my being and becoming.

Man is timid and apologetic; he is no longer upright; he dares not say "I think," "I am," but quotes some saint or sage. He is ashamed before the blade of grass or the blowing rose. These roses under my window make no reference to former roses or to better ones; they are for what they are; they exist with God to-day. There is no time to them. There is simply the rose; it is perfect in every moment of its existence. Before a leaf-bud has burst, its whole life acts; in the full-blown flower there is no more; in the leafless root there is no less. Its nature is satisfied and it satisfies nature in all moments alike. But man postpones or remembers; he does not live in the present, but with reverted eye laments the past, or, heedless of the riches that surround him, stands on tiptoe to foresee the future. He cannot be happy and strong until he too lives with nature in the present, above time. . . .

JAMES FENIMORE COOPER

The son of William Cooper, a wealthy land owner and judge, James Fenimore Cooper grew up in the knowledge that he was an aristocrat. His father's aristocratic domain, however, was on the edge of the frontier in Cooperstown, New York.

Expelled from Yale in 1805 for refusing to obey regulations, Cooper became a sailor in the merchant marine. From 1808 to 1811, he was a midshipman in the United States Navy. But after his marriage to Susan DeLancey, the daughter of an influential New York family, Cooper settled into the life of well-to-do country squire.

Cooper's first important book, The Spy, *was published in 1821. In 1823, he began the famous Leatherstocking series by writing* The Pioneers. The Last of the Mohicans *appeared in 1826,* The Prairie *in 1827,* The Pathfinder *in 1840 and* The Deerslayer *in 1841.*

Appointed American consul in Lyons, France, in 1826, Cooper spent the next seven years in Europe. Among the most important books in this period are The Bravo *(1831),* The Heidenmauer *(1832), and* The Headsman *(1833), a trilogy aimed at dispelling the false glamor with which Sir Walter Scott had portrayed the Middle Ages.*

During his stay in Europe, Cooper had defended American democracy against its European critics, but upon his return home he was repelled by the changes which had taken place in his absence. Cooper was a Federalist by upbringing and marriage who had become a Jeffersonian out of conviction, but the threat of popular demagoguery in the age of Jackson, and the concomitant rise to power of a new commercial class, incited Cooper to a full-scale attack on American society in The American Democrat *(1838),* Homeward Bound *(1838), and* Home As Found *(1838). These onslaughts made him extremely unpopular, and he was enthusiastically abused in the news-*

papers. Cooper's response was to sue his critics for libel. These legal battles consumed an enormous amount of Cooper's time, but did little to halt the defamations of his character.

The Advantages and Disadvantages of Democracy

ADVANTAGES OF A DEMOCRACY

*T*HE PRINCIPAL advantage of a democracy, is a general elevation in the character of the people. If few are raised to a very great height, few are depressed very low. As a consequence, the average of society is much more respectable than under any other form of government. The vulgar charge that the tendency of democracies is to levelling, meaning to drag all down to the level of the lowest, is singularly untrue, its real tendency being to elevate the depressed to a condition not unworthy of their manhood. In the absence of privileged orders, entails and distinctions, devised permanently to separate men into social castes, it is true none are great but those who become so by their acts, but, confining the remark to the upper classes of society, it would be much more true to say that democracy refuses to lend itself to unnatural and arbitrary distinctions, than to accuse it of a tendency to level those who have a just claim to be elevated. A denial of a favor, is not an invasion of a right.

Democracies are exempt from the military charges, both pecuniary and personal, that become necessary in governments in which the majority are subjects, since no force is required to repress those who, under other systems, are dangerous to the state, by their greater physical power.

As the success of democracies is mainly dependant on the intelligence of the people, the means of preserving the government are precisely those which most conduce to the happiness and social progress of man. Hence we find the state endeavoring to raise its citizens in the scale of being, the certain means of laying the broadest foundation of national prosperity. If the arts are advanced in aristocracies,

From James Fenimore Cooper, *The American Democrat*, 1838.

through the taste of patrons, in democracies, though of slower growth, they will prosper as a consequence of general information; or as a superstructure reared on a wider and more solid foundation.

Democracies being, as nearly as possible, founded in natural justice, little violence is done to the sense of right by the institutions, and men have less occasion than usual, to resort to fallacies and false principles in cultivating the faculties. As a consequence, common sense is more encouraged, and the community is apt to entertain juster notions of all moral truths, than under systems that are necessarily sophisticated. Society is thus a gainer in the greatest element of happiness, or in the right perception of the different relations between men and things.

Democracies being established for the common interests, and the publick agents being held in constant check by the people, their general tendency is to serve the whole community, and not small portions of it, as is the case in narrow governments. It is as rational to suppose that a hungry man will first help his neighbor to bread, when master of his own acts, as to suppose that any but those who feel themselves to be truly public sevants, will first bethink themselves of the publick, when in situations of publick trust. In a government of one, that one and his parasites will be the first and best served; in a government of a few, the few; and in a government of many, the many. Thus the general tendency of democratical institutions is to equalize advantages, and to spread its blessings over the entire surface of society.

Democracies, other things being equal, are the cheapest form of government, since little money is lavished in representation, and they who have to pay the taxes, have also, directly or indirectly, a voice in imposing them.

Democracies are less liable to popular tumults than any other polities, because the people, having legal means in their power to redress wrongs, have little inducement to employ any other. The man who can right himself by a vote, will seldom resort to a musket. Grievances, moreover, are less frequent, the most corrupt representatives of a democratick constituency generally standing in awe of its censure.

As men in bodies usually defer to the right, unless acting under erroneous impressions, or excited by sudden resentments, democracies pay more respect to abstract justice, in the management of their foreign concerns, than either aristocracies or monarchies, an appeal always lying against abuses, or violations of principle, to a popular sentiment, that, in the end, seldom fails to decide in favor of truth.

In democracies, with a due allowance for the workings of personal selfishness, it is usually a motive with those in places of trust, to consult the interests of the mass, there being little doubt, that in this system, the entire community has more regard paid to its wants and wishes, than in either of the two others.

DISADVANTAGES OF A DEMOCRACY

Democracies are liable to popular impulses, which, necessarily arising from imperfect information, often work injustice from good motives. Tumults of the people are less apt to occur in democracies than under any other form of government, for, possessing the legal means of redressing themselves, there is less necessity to resort to force, but, public opinion constituting, virtually, the power of the state, measures are more apt to be influenced by sudden mutations of sentiment, than under systems where the rulers have better opportunities and more leisure for examination. There is more feeling and less design in the movements of masses than in those of small bodies, except as design emanates from demagogues and political managers.

The efforts of the masses that are struggling to obtain their rights, in monarchies and aristocracies, however, are not to be imputed to democracy; in such cases, the people use their natural weapon, force, merely because they are denied any participation in the legal authority.

When democracies are small, these impulses frequently do great injury to the public service, but in large states they are seldom of sufficient extent to produce results before there is time to feel the influence of reason. It is, therefore, one of the errors of politicians to imagine democracies more practicable in small than in large communities, an error that has probably arisen from the fact that, the ignorance of masses having hitherto put men at the mercy of the combinations of the affluent and intelligent, democracies have been permitted to exist only in countries insignificant by their wealth and numbers.

Large democracies, on the other hand, while less exposed to the principal evil of this form of government, than smaller, are unable to scrutinize and understand character with the severity and intelligence that are of so much importance in all representative governments, and consequently the people are peculiarly exposed to become the dupes of demagogues and political schemers, most of the crimes of democracies arising from the faults and designs of men of this character, rather than from the propensities of the people, who, having little temptation to do wrong, are seldom guilty of crimes except through ignorance.

Democracies are necessarily controlled by publick opinion, and failing of the means of obtaining power more honestly, the fraudulent and ambitious find a motive to mislead, and even to corrupt the common sentiment, to attain their ends. This is the greatest and most pervading danger of all large democracies, since it is sapping the foundations of society, by undermining its virtue. We see the effects of this baneful influence, in the openness and audacity with which men avow improper motives and improper acts, trusting to find support in a popular feeling, for while vicious influences are perhaps more admitted in other countries, than in America, in none are they so openly avowed.

It may also be urged against democracies, that, nothing being more corrupting than the management of human affairs, which are constantly demanding sacrifices of permanent principles to interests that are as constantly fluctuating, their people are exposed to assaults on their morals from this quarter, that the masses of other nations escape. It is probable, however, that this evil, while it ought properly to be enumerated as one of the disadvantages of the system, is more than counterbalanced by the main results, even on the score of morals.

The constant appeals to public opinion in a democracy, though excellent as a corrective of public vices, induce private hypocrisy, causing men to conceal their own convictions when opposed to those of the mass, the latter being seldom wholly right, or wholly wrong. A want of national manliness is a vice to be guarded against, for the man who would dare to resist a monarch, shrinks from opposing an entire community. That the latter is quite often wrong, however, is abundantly proved by the fact, that its own judgments fluctuate, as it reasons and thinks differently this year, or this month even, from what it reasoned and thought the last.

The tendency of democracies is, in all things, to mediocrity, since the tastes, knowledge and principles of the majority form the tribunal of appeal. This circumstance, while it certainly serves to elevate the average qualities of a nation, renders the introduction of a high standard difficult. Thus do we find in literature, the arts, architecture and in all acquired knowledge, a tendency in America to gravitate towards the common center in this, as in other things; lending a value and estimation to mediocrity that are not elsewhere given. It is fair to expect, however, that a foundation so broad, may in time sustain a superstructure of commensurate proportions, and that the influence of masses will in this, as in the other interests, have a generally beneficial effect. Still it should not be forgotten that, with the exception of those works, of which, as they appeal to human sympathies or the practices of men, an intelligent public is the best judge, the mass of no community is qualified to decide the most correctly on any thing, which, in its nature, is above its reach.

It is a besetting vice of democracies to substitute public opinion for law. This is the usual form in which masses of men exhibit their tyranny. When the majority of the entire community commits this fault it is a sore grievance, but when local bodies, influenced by local interests, pretend to style themselves the publick, they are assuming powers that properly belong to the whole body of the people, and to them only under constitutional limitations. No tyranny of one, nor any tyranny of the few, is worse than this. All attempts in the publick, therefore, to do that which the publick has no right to do, should be frowned upon as the precise form in which tyranny is the most apt to be displayed in a democracy.

Democracies, depending so much on popular opinion are more liable to be influenced to their injury, through the management of foreign and hostile nations, than other governments. It is generally known that, in Europe, secret means are resorted to, to influence sentiment in this way, and we have witnessed in this country open appeals to the people, against the acts of their servants, in matters of foreign relations, made by foreign, not to say, hostile agents. Perhaps no stronger case can be cited of this weakness on the part of democracies, than is shown in this fact, for here we find men sufficiently audacious to build the hope of so far abusing opinion, as to persuade a people to act directly against their own dignity and interests.

The misleading of publick opinion in one way or another, is the parent of the principal disadvantages of a democracy, for in most instances it is first corrupting a community in order that it may be otherwise injured. Were it not for the counteracting influence of reason, which, in the end, seldom, perhaps never fails to assert its power, this defect would of itself, be sufficient to induce all discreet men to decide against this form of government. The greater the danger, the greater the necessity that all well-intentioned and right-minded citizens should be on their guard against its influence.

It would be hazardous, however, to impute all the peculiar faults of American character, to the institutions, the country existing under so many unusual influences. If the latter were overlooked, one might be induced to think frankness and sincerity of character were less encouraged by popular institutions than was formerly supposed, close observers affirming that these qualities are less frequent here, than in most other countries. When the general ease of society is remembered, there is unquestionably more deception of opinion practised than one would naturally expect, but this failing is properly to be imputed to causes that have no necessary connection with democratical institutions, though men defer to publick opinion, right or wrong, quite as submissively as they defer to princes. Although truths are not smothered altogether in democracies, they are often temporarily abandoned under this malign influence, unless there is a powerful motive to sustain them at the moment. While we see in our own democracy this manifest disposition to defer to the wrong, in matters that are not properly subject to the common sentiment, in deference to the popular will of the hour, there is a singular boldness in the use of personalities, as if men avenged themselves for the restraints of the one case by a licentiousness that is without hazard.

The base feelings of detraction and envy have more room for exhibition, and perhaps a stronger incentive in a democracy, than in other forms of government, in which the people get accustomed to personal deference by the artificial distinctions of the institutions. This is the reason that men become impatient of all superiority in a democracy, and manifest a wish to prefer those who affect a deference to the publick, rather than those who are worthy.

ALEXIS DE TOCQUEVILLE (1800–58)

The most famous foreign commentator on the American democracy, de Tocqueville came to the United States in May, 1831. Before he returned to France in February, 1832, he had visited most of the states in the Union and had traveled more than 7,000 miles.

Ostensibly, de Tocqueville and his companion, Beaumont, were studying the penitentiary system of the United States, but both men were far more interested in the problems which American democracy posed for the Old World. De Tocqueville was convinced that democracy was the wave of the future, and that Europe could benefit by studying the system in its American setting. "I confess," de Tocqueville wrote, "that in America I saw more than America; I sought the image of democracy itself, with its inclinations, its character, its prejudices, and its passions, in order to learn what we have to fear or hope from its progress."

Democracy in America

WHY THE AMERICANS ARE SO RESTLESS IN THE MIDST OF THEIR PROSPERITY.

IN CERTAIN remote corners of the Old World, you may still sometimes stumble upon a small district which seems to have been forgotten amidst the general tumult, and to have remained stationary whilst everything around it was in motion. The inhabitants are, for the most part, extremely ignorant and poor; they take no part in the business of the country, and are frequently oppressed by the govern-

From Alexis de Tocqueville, *Democracy in America*, Henry Reeve, ed., 1862.

ment; yet their countenances are generally placid, and their spirits light.

In America, I saw the freest and most enlightened men placed in the happiest circumstances which the world affords: it seemed to me as if a cloud habitually hung upon their brow, and I thought them serious, and almost sad, even in their pleasures.

The chief reason of this contrast is, that the former do not think of the ills they endure, while the latter are forever brooding over advantages they do not possess. It is strange to see with what feverish ardor the Americans pursue their own welfare; and to watch the vague dread that constantly torments them, lest they should not have chosen the shortest path which may lead to it.

A native of the United States clings to this world's goods as if he were certain never to die; and he is so hasty in grasping at all within his reach, that one would suppose he was constantly afraid of not living long enough to enjoy them. He clutches everything, he holds nothing fast, but soon loosens his grasp to pursue fresh gratifications.

In the United States, a man builds a house in which to spend his old age, and he sells it before the roof is on; he plants a garden, and lets it just as the trees are coming into bearing; he brings a field into tillage, and leaves other men to gather the crops; he embraces a profession, and gives it up; he settles in a place, which he soon afterwards leaves, to carry his changeable longings elsewhere. If his private affairs leave him any leisure, he instantly plunges into the vortex of politics; and if, at the end of a year of unremitting labor, he finds he has a few days' vacation, his eager curiosity whirls him over the vast extent of the United States, and he will travel fifteen hundred miles in a few days, to shake off his happiness. Death at length overtakes him, but it is before he is weary of his bootless chase of that complete felicity which forever escapes him.

At first sight, there is something surprising in this strange unrest of so many happy men, restless in the midst of abundance. The spectacle itself is, however, as old as the world; the novelty is, to see a whole people furnish an exemplification of it.

Their taste for physical gratifications must be regarded as the original source of that secret inquietude which the actions of the Americans betray, and of that inconstancy of which they daily afford fresh examples. He who has set his heart exclusively upon the pursuit of worldly welfare is always in a hurry, for he has but a limited time at his disposal to reach, to grasp, and to enjoy it. The recollection of the shortness of life is a constant spur to him. Besides the good things which he possesses, he every instant fancies a thousand others, which death will prevent him from trying if he does not try them soon. This thought fills him with anxiety, fear, and regret, and keeps his mind in ceaseless trepidation, which leads him perpetually to change his plans and his abode.

If, in addition to the taste for physical well-being, a social condition be superadded, in which neither laws nor customs retain any person in his place, there is a great additional stimulant to this restlessness of temper. Men will then be seen continually to change their track, for fear of missing the shortest cut to happiness.

It may readily be conceived, that, if men, passionately bent upon physical gratifications, desire eagerly, they are also easily discouraged: as their ultimate object is to enjoy, the means to reach that object must be prompt and easy, or the trouble of acquiring the gratification would be greater than the gratification itself. Their prevailing frame of mind, then, is at once ardent and relaxed, violent and enervated. Death is often less dreaded by them than perseverance in continuous efforts to one end.

The equality of conditions leads by a still straighter road to several of the effects which I have here described. When all the privileges of birth and fortune are abolished, when all professions are accessible to all, and a man's own energies may place him at the top of any one of them, an easy and unbounded career seems open to his ambition, and he will readily persuade himself that he is born to no vulgar destinies. But this is an erroneous notion, which is corrected by daily experience. The same equality which allows every citizen to conceive these lofty hopes, renders all the citizens less able to realize them: it circumscribes their powers on every side, whilst it gives freer scope to their desires. Not only are they themselves powerless, but they are met at every step by immense obstacles, which they did not at first perceive. They have swept away the privileges of some of their fellow-creatures which stood in their way, but they have opened the door to universal competition; the barrier has changed its shape rather than its position. When men are nearly alike, and all follow the same track, it is very difficult for any one individual to walk quick and cleave a way through the dense throng which surrounds and presses him. This constant strife between the inclinations springing from the equality of condition and the means it supplies to satisfy them, harasses and wearies the mind.

It is possible to conceive men arrived at a degree of freedom which should completely content them; they would then enjoy their independence without anxiety and without impatience. But men will never establish any equality with which they can be contented. Whatever efforts a people may make, they will never succeed in reducing all the conditions of society to a perfect level; and even if they unhappily attained that absolute and complete equality of position, the inequality of minds would still remain, which, coming directly from the hand of God, will forever escape the laws of man. However democratic, then, the social state and the political constitution of a people may be, it is certain that every member of the community will always find out several points about him which overlook his own position; and we may foresee that his looks will be doggedly fixed in that direction. When inequality of conditions is the common law of society, the most marked inequalities do not strike the eye: when everything is nearly on the same level, the slightest are marked enough to hurt it. Hence, the desire of equality always becomes more insatiable in proportion as equality is more complete.

Amongst democratic nations, men easily attain a certain equality of condition; but they can never attain as much as they desire. It perpetually retires from before them, yet without hiding itself from their sight, and in retiring draws them on. At every moment they think they are about to grasp it; it escapes at every moment from their hold. They are near enough to see its charms, but too far off to enjoy them; and before they have fully tasted its delights, they die.

To these causes must be attributed that strange melancholy which oftentimes haunts the inhabitants of democratic countries in the midst of their abundance, and that disgust at life which sometimes seizes upon them in the midst of calm and easy circumstances. Complaints are made in France that the number of suicides increases; in America suicide is rare, but insanity is said to be more common there than anywhere else. These are all different symptoms of the same disease. The Americans do not put an end to their lives, however disquieted they may be, because their religion forbids it; and amongst them materialism may be said hardly to exist, notwithstanding the general passion for physical gratification. The will resists, but reason frequently gives way.

In democratic times, enjoyments are more intense than in the ages of aristocracy, and the number of those who partake in them is vastly larger: but, on the other hand, it must be admitted that man's hopes and desires are oftener blasted, the soul is more stricken and perturbed, and care itself more keen.

EDUCATION OF YOUNG WOMEN IN THE UNITED STATES.

No free communities ever existed without morals; and, as I observed in the former part of this work, morals are the work of woman. Consequently, whatever affects the condition of women, their habits and their opinions, has great political importance in my eyes.

Amongst almost all Protestant nations, young women are far more the mistresses of their own actions than they are in Catholic countries. This independence is still greater in Protestant countries like England, which have retained or acquired the right of self-government; freedom is then infused into the domestic circle by political habits and by religious opinions. In the United States, the doctrines of Protestantism are combined with great political liberty and a most democratic state of society; and nowhere are young women surrendered so early or so completely to their own guidance.

Long before an American girl arrives at the marriageable age, her emancipation from maternal control begins: she has scarcely ceased to be a child, when she already thinks for herself, speaks with freedom, and acts on her own impulse. The great scene of the world is constantly open to her view: far from seeking to conceal it from her, it is every day disclosed more completely, and she is taught to survey it with a firm and calm gaze. Thus the vices and dangers of society are early revealed to her; as she sees them clearly, she views them without illusion, and braves them without fear; for she is full of reliance on her own strength, and her confidence seems to be shared by all around her.

An American girl scarcely ever displays that virginal softness in the midst of young desires, or that innocent and ingenuous grace, which usually attend the European woman in the transition from girlhood to youth. It is rare that an American woman, at any age, displays childish timidity or ignorance. Like the young women of Europe, she seeks to please, but she knows precisely the cost of pleasing. If she does not abandon herself to evil, at least she knows that it exists; and she is remarkable rather for purity of manners than for chastity of mind.

I have been frequently surprised, and almost frightened, at the singular address and happy boldness with which young women in America contrive to manage their thoughts and their language, amidst all the difficulties of free conversation; a philosopher would have stumbled at every step along the narrow path which they trod without accident and without effort. It is easy, indeed, to perceive that, even amidst the independence of early youth, an American woman is always mistress of herself: she indulges in all permitted pleasures, without yielding herself up to any of them; and her reason never allows the reins of self-guidance to drop, though it often seems to hold them loosely.

In France, where traditions of every age are still so strangely mingled in the opinions and tastes of the people, women commonly receive a reserved, retired, and almost conventual education, as they did in aristocratic times; and then they are suddenly abandoned, without a guide and without assistance, in the midst of all the irregularities inseparable from democratic society.

The Americans are more consistent. They have found out that, in a democracy, the independence of individuals cannot fail to be very great, youth premature, tastes ill-restrained, customs fleeting, public opinion often unsettled and powerless, paternal authority weak, and marital authority contested. Under these circumstances, believing that they had little chance of repressing in woman the most vehement passions of the human heart, they held that the surer way was to teach her the art of combating those passions for herself. As they could not prevent her virtue from being exposed to frequent danger, they determined that she should know how best to defend it; and more reliance was placed on the free vigor of her will than on safeguards which have been shaken or overthrown. Instead then of inculcating mistrust of herself, they constantly seek to enhance her confidence in her own strength of character. As it is neither possible nor desirable to keep a young woman in perpetual and complete ignorance, they hasten to give her a precocious knowledge on all subjects. Far from hiding the corruptions of the world from her, they prefer that she should see them at once, and train herself to shun them; and they hold it of more importance to protect her conduct, than to be over-scrupulous of the innocence of her thoughts.

Although the Americans are a very religious people, they do not rely on religion alone to defend the virtue of woman; they seek to arm her reason also. In this respect they have followed the same method as in several others: they first make vigorous efforts to cause individual independence to control itself, and they do not call in the aid of religion until they have reached the utmost limits of human strength.

I am aware that an education of this kind is not without danger; I am sensible that it tends to invigorate the judgment at the expense of the imagination, and to make cold and virtuous women instead of affectionate wives and agreeable companions to man. Society may be more tranquil and better regulated, but domestic life has often fewer charms. These, however, are secondary evils, which may be braved for the sake of higher interests. At the stage at which we are now arrived, the choice is no longer left to us; a democratic education is indispensable to protect women from the dangers with which democratic institutions and manners surround them.

HERMAN MELVILLE (1819-91)

Descended on both sides of his family from distinguished and wealthy ancestors, Melville was nevertheless forced to find work as a clerk in a New York bank at the age of fifteen. For Melville's father was a merchant who had gone bankrupt and then died, leaving his family in drastically reduced circumstances.

After clerking for a time, Melville tried his hand at farming and teaching, but in 1837 he gave up all land-bound occupations and went to sea as a cabin boy in a ship bound for Liverpool. Upon his return he again taught school—and again shipped out, this time on the whaler, Acushnet, bound for the South Seas. In the Marquesas Islands, Melville and a friend jumped ship and lived for a month among man-eating savages. Escaping on an Australian whaler, Melville finally reached Tahiti. From 1843 to 1844, he served as a sailor in the United States Navy.

The voyages to England and the South Seas became the raw material of the most important of Melville's subsequent writings. Typee *(1846), which made him famous, and* Omoo *(1847) are based on his life among South Seas savages and on his stay in Tahiti.* Redburn *(1849) tells the story of a young boy's trip to England.* White Jacket *(1850) pictures life aboard a man-of-war.*

In 1847, Melville married, and eventually he and his wife settled on a farm near Pittsfield, Massachusetts. While living in Pittsfield, he became the friend of Nathaniel Hawthorne, to whom he dedicated Moby Dick *(1851). One of the great sea-tales of literature,* Moby Dick *is also a book which deals with man's doomed quest to fathom the mystery of an inscrutable universe. When* Moby Dick *was misunderstood and ignored, Melville immediately began writing* Pierre; or, The Ambiguities *(1852), which tells of the fall of a young man from idyllic happiness to disillusioned despair. If* Moby Dick *was a*

82

failure with the critics, Pierre *was a disaster. Nevertheless, Melville continued to write for another decade and a half.* Israel Potter *appeared in 1855,* The Piazza Tales *in 1856,* Battle-Pieces and Aspects of the War *in 1866. In the latter year, Melville was appointed a customs inspector in New York, and the last twenty-five years of his life were spent in quiet anonymity. A final tale of the sea,* Billy Budd, *was written at the very end of his life.*

The following two selections are from Moby Dick *and* Israel Potter. *"Nantucket" describes the inhabitants of the island whence Captain Ahab sets out in pursuit of the White Whale. In the episode from* Israel Potter, *the hero of the novel sees Ethan Allen, of Revolutionary War fame, in chains; Melville exploits the occasion to say something about the American character.*

Nantucket

Nothing more happened on the passage worthy the mentioning; so, after a fine run, we safely arrived in Nantucket.

Nantucket! Take out your map and look at it. See what a real corner of the world it occupies; how it stands there, away off shore, more lonely than the Eddystone lighthouse. Look at it—a mere hillock, and elbow of sand; all beach, without a background. There is more sand there than you would use in twenty years as a substitute for blotting paper. Some gamesome wights will tell you that they have to plant weeds there, they don't grow naturally; that they import Canada thistles; that they have to send beyond seas for a spile to stop a leak in an oil cask; that pieces of wood in Nantucket are carried about like bits of the true cross in Rome; that people there plant toadstools before their houses, to get under the shade in summer time; that one blade of grass makes an oasis, three blades in a day's walk a prairie; that they wear quicksand shoes, something like Laplander snowshoes; that they are so shut up, belted about, every way inclosed, surrounded, and made an utter island of by the ocean, that

From Herman Melville, *Moby Dick,* 1851.

to their very chairs and tables small clams will sometimes be found adhering, as to the backs of sea turtles. But these extravaganzas only show that Nantucket is no Illinois.

Look now at the wondrous traditional story of how this island was settled by the red-men. Thus goes the legend. In olden times an eagle swooped down upon the New England coast, and carried off an infant Indian in his talons. With loud lament the parents saw their child borne out of sight over the wide waters. They resolved to follow in the same direction. Setting out in their canoes, after a perilous passage they discovered the island, and there they found an empty ivory casket,—the poor little Indian's skeleton.

What wonder, then, that these Nantucketers, born on a beach, should take to the sea for a livelihood! They first caught crabs and quohogs in the sand; grown bolder, they waded out with nets for mackerel; more experienced, they pushed off in boats and captured cod; and at last, launching a navy of great ships on the sea, explored this watery world; put an incessant belt of circumnavigations round it; peeped in at Behring's Straits; and in all seasons and all oceans declared everlasting war with the mightiest animated mass that has survived the flood; most monstrous and most mountainous! That Himmalehan, salt-sea Mastodon, clothed with such portentousness of unconscious power, that his very panics are more to be dreaded than his most fearless and malicious assaults!

And thus have these naked Nantucketers, these sea hermits, issuing from their ant-hill in the sea, overrun and conquered the watery world like so many Alexanders; parcelling out among them the Atlantic, Pacific, and Indian oceans, as the three pirate powers did Poland. Let America add Mexico to Texas, and pile Cuba upon Canada; let the English overswarm all India, and hang out their blazing banner from the sun; two thirds of this terraqueous globe are the Nantucketer's. For the sea is his; he owns it, as Emperors own empires; other seamen having but a right of way through it. Merchant ships are but extension bridges; armed ones but floating forts; even pirates and privateers, though following the sea as highwaymen the road, they but plunder other ships, other fragments of the land like themselves, without seeking to draw their living from the bottomless deep itself. The Nantucketer, he alone resides and riots on the sea; he alone, in Bible language, goes down to it in ships; to and fro ploughing it as his own special plantation. *There* is his home; *there* lies his business which a Noah's flood would not interrupt, though it overwhelmed all the millions in China. He lives on the sea, as prairie cocks in the prairie; he hides among the waves, he climbs them as chamois hunters climb the Alps. For years he knows not the land; so that when he comes to it at last, it smells like another world, more strangely than the moon would to an Earthsman. With the landless gull, that at sunset folds her wings and is rocked to sleep between billows; so at nightfall, the Nantucketer, out of sight of land, furls his sails and lays him to his rest, while under his very pillow rush herds of walruses and whales.

Ethan Allen

*A*MONG the episodes of the Revolutionary War, none is stranger than that of Ethan Allen in England; the event and the man being equally uncommon.

Allen seems to have been a curious combination of a Hercules, a Joe Miller, a Bayard, and a Tom Hyer; had a person like the Belgian giants; mountain music in him like a Swiss; a heart plump as Cœur de Lion's. Though born in New England, he exhibited no trace of her character. He was frank, bluff, companionable as a Pagan, convivial, a Roman, hearty as a harvest. His spirit was essentially Western; and herein is his peculiar Americanism; for the Western spirit is, or will yet be (for no other is, or can be), the true American one.

For the most part, Allen's manner while in England was scornful and ferocious in the last degree; however, qualified by that wild, heroic sort of levity, which in the hour of oppression or peril seems inseparable from a nature like his; the mode whereby such a temper best evinces its barbaric disdain of adversity, and how cheaply and waggishly it holds the malice, even though triumphant, of its foes!

From Herman Melville, *Israel Potter*, 1855.

Aside from that inevitable egotism relatively pertaining to pine trees, spires, and giants, there were, perhaps, two special incidental reasons for the Titanic Vermonter's singular demeanor abroad. Taken captive while heading a forlorn hope before Montreal, he was treated with inexcusable cruelty and indignity; something as if he had fallen into the hands of the Dyaks. Immediately upon his capture he would have been deliberately suffered to have been butchered by the Indian allies in cold blood on the spot, had he not, with desperate intrepidity, availed himself of his enormous physical strength, by twitching a British officer to him, and using him for a living target, whirling him round and round against the murderous tomahawks of the savages. Shortly afterwards, led into the town, fenced about by bayonets of the guard, the commander of the enemy, one Colonel McCloud, flourished his cane over the captive's head, with brutal insults promising him a rebel's halter at Tyburn. During his passage to England in the same ship wherein went passenger Colonel Guy Johnson, the implacable tory, he was kept heavily ironed in the hold, and in all ways treated as a common mutineer; or, it may be, rather as a lion of Asia; which, though caged, was still too dreadful to behold without fear and trembling, and consequent cruelty. And no wonder, at least for the fear; for on one occasion, when chained hand and foot, he was insulted on shipboard by an officer; with his teeth he twisted off the nail that went through the mortise of his handcuffs, and so, having his arms at liberty, challenged his insulter to combat. Often, as at Pendennis Castle, when no other avengement was at hand, he would hurl on his foes such howling tempests of anathema as fairly to shock them into retreat. Prompted by somewhat similar motives, both on shipboard and in England, he would often make the most vociferous allusions to Ticonderoga, and the part he played in its capture, well knowing, that of all American names, Ticonderoga was, at that period, by far the most famous and galling to Englishmen.

Parlor-men, dancing-masters, the graduates of the Albe Bellgarde, may shrug their laced shoulders at the boisterousness of Allen in England. True, he stood upon no punctilios with his jailers; for where modest gentlemanhood is all on one side, it is a losing affair; as if my Lord Chesterfield should take off his hat, and smile, and bow, to a mad bull, in hopes of a reciprocation of politeness. When among wild beasts, if they menace you, be a wild beast. Neither is it unlikely that this was the view taken by Allen. For, besides the exasperating tendency to self-assertion which such treatment as his must have bred on a man like him, his experience must have taught him, that by assuming the part of a jocular, reckless, and even braggart barbarian, he would better sustain himself against bullying turnkeys than by submissive quietude. Nor should it be forgotten, that besides the petty details of personal malice, the enemy violated every international usage of right and decency, in treating a distinguished prisoner of war as if he had been a Botany-Bay convict. If, at the present day, in any similar case between the same States, the repetition of such outrages would be more than unlikely, it is only because it is among nations as among individuals: imputed indigence provokes oppression and scorn; but that same indigence being risen to opulence, receives a polite consideration even from its former insulters.

As the event proved, in the course Allen pursued, he was right. Because, though at first nothing was talked of by his captors, and nothing anticipated by himself, but his ignominious execution, or at the least, prolonged and squalid incarceration, nevertheless, these threats and prospects evaporated, and by his facetious scorn for scorn, under the extremest sufferings, he finally wrung repentant usage from his foes; and in the end, being liberated from his irons, and walking the quarter-deck where before he had been thrust into the hold, was carried back to America, and in due time, at New York, honorably included in a regular exchange of prisoners.

III.   Out of the Cradle Endlessly Rocking

GEORGE FITZHUGH (1806-81)

*Fitzhugh grew up on a plantation in Virginia. Although he re-
ceived little formal education, he read a good deal, and after settling
with his large family in Port Royal, Caroline County, he began a
successful career as a lawyer.*

*Like many other Southerners of his generation, Fitzhugh as a
young man was a Jeffersonian liberal who looked forward to the day
when slavery would no longer exist in the South. However, the rise
of cotton culture made slavery a greater advantage than ever before
in the successful management of the big plantations. As abolitionist
agitation mounted in the North, Southern leaders felt more and
more impelled to defend slavery not only as a necessary evil, but as a
positive good which was in complete accord with the ideal human
community described in the Bible.*

Fitzhugh's two famous books, Sociology for the South; or, The
Failure of Free Society (1854) *and* Cannibals All! or, Slaves Without Masters (1857), *from which the following selection is taken,
carry the intersectional conflict home to the North by arguing that
Northern industrial society exploited workers far more ruthlessly
than did the slavocracy, in which owner and owned were both parts
of one big happy family.*

The Universal Trade

WE ARE, all, North and South, engaged in the White Slave Trade,
and he who succeeds best, is esteemed most respectable. It is far more
cruel than the Black Slave Trade, because it exacts more of its slaves,

From George Fitzhugh, *Cannibals All!*, 1857.

and neither protects nor governs them. We boast, that it exacts more
when we say, "that the *profits* made from employing free labor are
greater than those from slave labor." The profits, made from free
labor, are the amount of the products of such labor, which the employer, by means of the command which capital or skill gives him,
takes away, exacts or "exploitates" from the free laborer. The profits
of slave labor are that portion of the products of such labor which the
power of the master enables him to appropriate. These profits are
less, because the master allows the slave to retain a larger share of
the results of his own labor, than do the employers of free labor. But
we not only boast that the White Slave Trade is more exacting and
fraudulent (in fact, though not in intention,) than Black Slavery;
but we also boast, that it is more cruel, in leaving the laborer to take
care of himself and family out of the pittance which skill or capital
have allowed him to retain. When the day's labor is ended, he is free,
but is overburdened with the cares of family and household, which
make his freedom an empty and delusive mockery. But his employer
is really free, and may enjoy the profits made by others' labor, without a care, or a trouble, as to their well-being. The negro slave is
free, too, when the labors of the day are over, and free in mind as
well as body; for the master provides food, raiment, house, fuel,
and everything else necessary to the physical well-being of himself
and family. The master's labors commence just when the slave's end.
No wonder men should prefer white slavery to capital, to negro
slavery, since it is more profitable, and is free from all the cares and
labors of black slave-holding.

Now, reader, if you wish to know yourself—to "descant on your
own deformity"—read on. But if you would cherish self-conceit, self-
esteem, or self-appreciation, throw down our book; for we will dispel
illusions which have promoted your happiness, and shew you that
what you have considered and practiced as virtue, is little better than
moral Cannibalism. But you will find yourself in numerous and respectable company; for all good and respectable people are "Cannibals all," who do not labor, or who are successfully trying to live
without labor, on the unrequited labor of other people:—Whilst low
bad, and disreputable people, are those who labor to support themselves, and to support said respectable people besides. Throwing the

negro slaves out of the account, and society is divided in Christendom into four classes: The rich, or independent respectable people, who live well and labor not at all; the professional and skillful respectable people, who do a little light work, for enormous wages; the poor hard-working people, who support every body, and starve themselves; and the poor thieves, swindlers and sturdy beggars, who live like gentlemen, without labor, on the labor of other people. The gentlemen exploitate, which being done on a large scale, and requiring a great many victims, is highly respectable—whilst the rogues and beggars take so little from others, that they fare little better than those who labor.

But, reader, we do not wish to fire into the flock. "Thou art the man!" You are a Cannibal! and if a successful one, pride yourself on the number of your victims, quite as much as any Feejee chieftain, who breakfasts, dines and sups on human flesh.—And your conscience smites you, if you have failed to succeed, quite as much as his, when he returns from an unsuccessful foray.

Probably, you are a lawyer, or a merchant, or a doctor, who have made by your business fifty thousand dollars, and retired to live on your capital. But, mark! not to spend your capital. That would be vulgar, disreputable, criminal. That would be, to live by your own labor; for your capital is your amassed labor. That would be, to do as common working men do; for they take the pittance which their employers leave them, to live on. They live by labor; for they exchange the results of their own labor for the products of other people's labor. It is, no doubt, an honest, vulgar way of living; but not at all a respectable way. The respectable way of living is, to make other people work for you, and to pay them nothing for so doing—and to have no concern about them after their work is done. Hence, white slaveholding is much more respectable than negro slavery—for the master works nearly as hard for the negro, as he for the master. But you, my virtuous, respectable reader, exact three thousand dollars per annum from white labor, (for your income is the product of white labor,) and make not one cent of return in any form. You retain your capital, and never labor, and yet live in luxury on the labor of others. Capital commands labor, as the master does the slave. Neither pays for labor; but the master permits the slave to retain a larger allowance from the proceeds of his own labor, and hence "free labor is cheaper than slave labor." You, with the command over labor which your capital gives you, are a slave owner—a master, without the obligations of a master. They who work for you, who create your income, are slaves, without the rights of slaves. Slaves without a master! Whilst you were engaged in amassing your capital, in seeking to become independent, you were in the White Slave Trade. To become independent, is to be able to make other people support you, without being obliged to labor for *them.* Now, what man in society is not seeking to attain this situation? He who attains it, is a slave owner, in the worst sense. He who is in pursuit of it, is engaged in the slave trade. You, reader, belong to the one or other class. The men without property, in free society, are theoretically in a worse condition than slaves. Practically, their condition corresponds with this theory, as history and statistics every where demonstrate. The capitalists, in free society, live in ten times the luxury and show that Southern masters do, because the slaves to capital work harder and cost less, than negro slaves.

The negro slaves of the South are the happiest, and, in some sense, the freest people in the world. The children and the aged and infirm work not at all, and yet have all the comforts and necessaries of life provided for them. They enjoy liberty, because they are oppressed neither by care nor labor. The women do little hard work, and are protected from the despotism of their husbands by their masters. The negro men and stout boys work, on the average, in good weather, not more than nine hours a day. The balance of their time is spent in perfect abandon. Besides, they have their Sabbaths and holidays. White men, with so much of license and liberty, would die of ennui; but negroes luxuriate in corporeal and mental repose. With their faces upturned to the sun, they can sleep at any hour; and quiet sleep is the greatest of human enjoyments. "Blessed be the man who invented sleep." 'Tis happiness in itself—and results from contentment with the present, and confident assurance of the future. We do not know whether free laborers ever sleep. They are fools to do so; for, whilst they sleep, the wily and watchful capitalist is devising means to ensnare and exploitate them. The free laborer must work or starve. He is more of a slave than the negro, because he works longer and harder for less allowance than the slave, and has no holiday, because the cares of life with him begin when its labors end. He has no liberty, and not a single right. We know, 'tis often said, air and water are common property, which all have equal right to participate and enjoy; but this is utterly false. The appropriation of the lands carries with it the appropriation of all on or above the lands, *usque ad cœlum, aut ad inferos.* A man cannot breathe the air, without a place to breathe it from, and all places are appropriated. All water is private property "to the middle of the stream," except the ocean, and that is not fit to drink.

Free laborers have not a thousandth part of the rights and liberties of negro slaves. Indeed, they have not a single right or a single liberty, unless it be the right or liberty to die. But the reader may think that he and other capitalists and employers are freer than negro slaves. Your capital would soon vanish, if you dared indulge in the liberty and abandon of negroes. You hold your wealth and position by the tenure of constant watchfulness, care and circumspection. You never labor; but you are never free.

Where a few own the soil, they have unlimited power over the balance of society, until domestic slavery comes in, to compel them to permit this balance of society to draw a sufficient and comfortable living from "terra mater." Free society, asserts the right of a few to the earth—slavery, maintains that it belongs, in different degrees, to all.

But, reader, well may you follow the slave trade. It is the only trade worth following, and slaves the only property worth owning. All other is worthless, a mere *caput mortuum*, except in so far as it vests the owner with the power to command the labors of others—to enslave them. Give you a palace, ten thousand acres of land, sumptuous clothes, equipage and every other luxury; and with your artificial wants, you are poorer than Robinson Crusoe, or the lowest working man, if you have no slaves to capital, or domestic slaves. Your capital will not bring you an income of a cent, nor supply one of your wants, without labor. Labor is indispensable to give value to property, and if you owned every thing else, and did not own labor, you would be poor. But fifty thousand dollars means, and is, fifty thousand dollars worth of slaves. You can command, without touching on that capital, three thousand dollars' worth of labor per annum. You could do no more were you to buy slaves with it, and then you would be cumbered with the cares of governing and providing for them. You are a slaveholder now, to the amount of fifty thousand dollars, with all the advantages, and none of the cares and responsibilities of a master.

"Property in man" is what all are struggling to obtain. Why should they not be obliged to take care of man, their property, as they do of their horses and their hounds, their cattle and their sheep. Now, under the delusive name of liberty, you work him, "from morn to dewy eve"—from infancy to old age—then turn him out to starve. You treat your horses and hounds better. Capital is a cruel master. The free slave trade, the commonest, yet the cruellest of trades.

HARRIET BEECHER STOWE (1811–96)

A daughter of the most prominent Congregationalist minister of the Jacksonian era, Harriet Beecher was raised in a household in which moral self-scrutiny was continuously practiced.

In 1832, the Beecher family moved to Cincinnati, Ohio, from Litchfield, Connecticut, where Harriet had been born. Four years later, Harriet Beecher married Calvin Stowe, a professor of theology at Lane Theological Seminary, of which her father, Lyman Beecher, was president. In 1850, the Stowes moved to Brunswick, Maine, where Calvin took up a professorship at Bowdoin College. Upon their arrival in Maine, Mrs. Stowe discovered that all New England was up in arms about the slavery controversy, particularly about the placatory role Daniel Webster had assumed in working out the celebrated political "Compromise" of that year between the sections. Urged by friends to contribute her imaginative talents to the cause of human freedom and justice, Mrs. Stowe began Uncle Tom's Cabin. *When the novel was published in book form in 1852, it became an international best seller. The most important of Mrs. Stowe's later fictions are a series of novels dealing with the New England past:* The Minister's Wooing *(1859),* The Pearl of Orr's Island *(1862), and* Oldtown Folks *(1869). None of these works, however, has the sweep and power of her masterpiece.*

Dark Places

"THE DARK PLACES OF THE EARTH ARE FULL OF THE HABITATIONS OF CRUELTY."

TRAILING wearily behind a rude wagon, and over a ruder road, Tom and his associates faced onward.

From Harriet Beecher Stowe, *Uncle Tom's Cabin*, 1852.

In the wagon was seated Simon Legree; and the two women, still fettered together, were stowed away with some baggage in the back part of it, and the whole company were seeking Legree's plantation, which lay a good distance off.

It was a wild, forsaken road, now winding through dreary pine barrens, where the wind whispered mournfully, and now over log causeways, through long cypress swamps, the doleful trees rising out of the slimy, spongy ground, hung with long wreaths of funeral black moss, while ever and anon the loathsome form of the moccasin snake might be seen sliding among broken stumps and shattered branches that lay here and there, rotting in the water.

It is disconsolate enough, this riding, to the stranger, who, with well-filled pocket and well-appointed horse, threads the lonely way on some errand of business; but wilder, drearier, to the man enthralled, whom every weary step bears further from all that man loves and prays for.

So one should have thought, that witnessed the sunken and dejected expression on those dark faces; the wistful, patient weariness with which those sad eyes rested on object after object that passed them in their sad journey.

Simon rode on, however, apparently well pleased, occasionally pulling away at a flask of spirit, which he kept in his pocket.

"I say, *you!*" he said, as he turned back and caught a glance at the dispirited faces behind him. "Strike up a song, boys,—come!"

The men looked at each other, and the *"come"* was repeated, with a smart crack of the whip which the driver carried in his hands. Tom began a Methodist hymn.

> *"Jerusalem, my happy home,*
> *Name ever dear to me!*
> *When shall my sorrows have an end,*
> *Thy joys when shall—"*

"Shut up, you black cuss!" roared Legree; "did ye think I wanted any o' yer infernal old Methodism? I say, tune up, now, something real rowdy,—quick!"

One of the other men struck up one of those unmeaning songs, common among the slaves.

> *"Mas'r see'd me cotch a coon,*
> *High boys, high!*
> *He laughed to split,—d'ye see the moon,*
> *Ho! ho! ho! boys, ho!*
> *Ho! yo! hi—e! oh!"*

The singer appeared to make up the song to his own pleasure, generally hitting on rhyme, without much attempt at reason; and the party took up the chorus, at intervals,

> *"Ho! ho! ho! boys, ho!*
> *High—e—oh! high—e—oh!"*

It was sung very boisterously, and with a forced attempt at merriment; but no wail of despair, no words of impassioned prayer, could have had such a depth of woe in them as the wild notes of the chorus. As if the poor, dumb heart, threatened,—prisoned,—took refuge in that inarticulate sanctuary of music, and found there a language in which to breathe its prayer to God! There was a prayer in it, which Simon could not hear. He only heard the boys singing noisily, and was well pleased; he was making them "keep up their spirits."

"Well, my little dear," said he, turning to Emmeline, and laying his hand on her shoulder, "we're almost home!"

When Legree scolded and stormed, Emmeline was terrified; but when he laid his hand on her, and spoke as he now did, she felt as if she had rather he would strike her. The expression of his eyes made her soul sick, and her flesh creep. Involuntarily she clung closer to the mulatto woman by her side, as if she were her mother.

"You didn't ever wear ear-rings," he said, taking hold of her small ear with his coarse fingers.

"No, Mas'r!" said Emmeline, trembling and looking down.

"Well, I'll give you a pair, when we get home, if you're a good girl. You needn't be so frightened; I don't mean to make you work very hard. You'll have fine times with me, and live like a lady,— only be a good girl."

Legree had been drinking to that degree that he was inclining to be very gracious; and it was about this time that the enclosures of the plantation rose to view. The estate had formerly belonged to a gentleman of opulence and taste, who had bestowed some consider-

able attention to the adornment of his grounds. Having died insol-
vent, it had been purchased, at a bargain, by Legree, who used it, as
he did everything else, merely as an implement for money-making.
The place had that ragged, forlorn appearance, which is always produced by the evidence that the care of the former owner has been
left to go to utter decay.

What was once a smooth-shaven lawn before the house, dotted here
and there with ornamental shrubs, was now covered with frowsy
tangled grass, with horse-posts set up, here and there, in it, where
the turf was stamped away, and the ground littered with broken
pails, cobs of corn, and other slovenly remains. Here and there, a
mildewed jessamine or honeysuckle hung raggedly from some ornamental support, which had been pushed to one side by being used as
a horse-post. What once was a large garden was now all grown over
with weeds, through which, here and there, some solitary exotic
reared its forsaken head. What had been a conservatory had now no
window-shades, and on the mouldering shelves stood some dry, forsaken flower-pots, with sticks in them, whose dried leaves showed
they had once been plants.

The wagon rolled up a weedy gravel walk, under a noble avenue
of China trees, whose graceful forms and ever-springing foliage
seemed to be the only things there that neglect could not daunt or
alter,—like noble spirits, so deeply rooted in goodness, as to flourish
and grow stronger amid discouragement and decay.

The house had been large and handsome. It was built in a manner
common at the South; a wide verandah of two stories running round
every part of the house, into which every outer door opened, the
lower tier being supported by brick pillars.

But the place looked desolate and uncomfortable; some windows
stopped up with boards, some with shattered panes, and shutters
hanging by a single hinge,—all telling of coarse neglect and discom-
fort.

Bits of board, straw, old decayed barrels and boxes, garnished the
ground in all directions; and three or four ferocious-looking dogs,
roused by the sound of the wagon-wheels, came tearing out, and were
with difficulty restrained. from laying hold of Tom and his companions, by the effort of the ragged servants who came after them.

"Ye see what ye'd get!" said Legree, caressing the dogs with grim satisfaction, and turning to Tom and his companions. "Ye see what ye'd get, if ye try to run off. These yer dogs has been raised to track niggers; and they'd jest as soon chaw one on ye up as eat their supper. So, mind yerself! How now, Sambo!" he said, to a ragged fellow, without any brim to his hat, who was officious in his attentions. "How have things been going?"

"Fust rate, Mas'r."

"Quimbo," said Legree to another, who was making zealous demonstrations to attract his attention, "ye minded what I telled ye?"

"Guess I did, didn't I?"

These two colored men were the two principal hands on the plantation. Legree had trained them in savageness and brutality as systematically as he had his bull-dogs; and, by long practice in hardness and cruelty, brought their whole nature to about the same range of capacities. It is a common remark, and one that is thought to militate strongly against the character of the race, that the negro overseer is always more tyrannical and cruel than the white one. This is simply saying that the negro mind has been more crushed and debased than the white. It is no more true of this race than of every oppressed race, the world over. The slave is always a tyrant, if he can get a chance to be one.

Legree, like some potentates we read of in history, governed his plantation by a sort of resolution of forces. Sambo and Quimbo cordially hated each other; the plantation hands, one and all, cordially hated them; and, by playing off one against another, he was pretty sure, through one or the other of the three parties, to get informed of whatever was on foot in the place.

Nobody can live entirely without social intercourse; and Legree encouraged his two black satellites to a kind of coarse familiarity with him,—a familiarity, however, at any moment liable to get one or the other of them into trouble; for, on the slightest provocation, one of them always stood ready, at a nod, to be a minister of his vengeance on the other.

As they stood there now by Legree, they seemed an apt illustration of the fact that brutal men are lower even than animals. Their coarse, dark, heavy features; their great eyes, rolling enviously on each other; their barbarous, guttural, half-brute intonation; their dilapidated garments fluttering in the wind,—were all in admirable keeping with the vile and unwholesome character of everything about the place.

"Here, you Sambo," said Legree, "take these yer boys down to the quarters; and here's a gal I've got for *you*," said he, as he separated the mulatto woman from Emmeline, and pushed her towards him;— "I promised to bring you one, you know."

The woman gave a start, and drawing back, said, suddenly,

"O, Mas'r! I left my old man in New Orleans."

"What of that, you ——; won't you want one here? None o' your words,—go long!" said Legree, raising his whip.

"Come, mistress," he said to Emmeline, "you go in here with me."

A dark, wild face was seen, for a moment, to glance at the window of the house; and, as Legree opened the door, a female voice said something, in a quick, imperative tone. Tom, who was looking, with anxious interest, after Emmeline, as she went in, noticed this, and heard Legree answer, angrily, "You may hold your tongue! I'll do as I please, for all you!"

Tom heard no more; for he was soon following Sambo to the quarters. The quarters was a little sort of street of rude shanties, in a row, in a part of the plantation, far off from the house. They had a forlorn, brutal, forsaken air. Tom's heart sunk when he saw them. He had been comforting himself with the thought of a cottage, rude, indeed, but one which he might make neat and quiet, and where he might have a shelf for his Bible, and a place to be alone out of his laboring hours. He looked into several; they were mere rude shells, destitute of any species of furniture, except a heap of straw, foul with dirt, spread confusedly over the floor, which was merely the bare ground, trodden hard by the tramping of innumerable feet.

"Which of these will be mine?" said he, to Sambo, submissively.

"Dunno; ken turn in here, I spose," said Sambo; "spects thar's room for another thar; thar's a pretty smart heap o' niggers to each on 'em, now; sure, I dunno what I's to do with more."

WALT WHITMAN (1819–92)

Whitman was born on Long Island in 1819 and grew up in Brooklyn—where he worked as an office boy, printer's devil, and journeyman compositor. After a fling at schoolteaching and free-lance writing for magazines and newspapers, he became editor, in 1846, of the Brooklyn Eagle, *a Democratic newspaper. Two years later, when he switched his support to the Free Soil party, he resigned from the* Eagle. *After a trip to New Orleans, Whitman came back to New York and became editor of the liberal* Freeman, *but his tenure here was also short.*

The first edition of Leaves of Grass *was published in 1855. It contained a preface and twelve poems, including* Song of Myself. *The poems were too startling in their subject matter and too untraditional in form to be widely accepted, but Emerson wrote to Whitman an appreciative letter in which he said, "I greet you at the beginning of a great career, which yet must have had a long foreground somewhere for such a start."*

The "foreground" for Leaves of Grass *included Whitman's Quaker heritage, his trip down the Mississippi to New Orleans, his life in New York at a time when the city's exuberant atmosphere caught the excitement of a nation that was fulfilling a continental destiny, and his excited response to the writings of Emerson, Shakespeare, Carlyle, and Goethe. For Whitman as for Emerson, the poet was a seer, who could discern divinity in all things.*

The 1860 edition of Leaves of Grass *included two new sections,* Children of Adam *and* Calamus. *In this edition, Whitman probed at the darker side of his experience, revealing a fascination with death that rivaled Emily Dickinson's. In 1862, Whitman went to Washington and for the remainder of the Civil War worked as a nurse in army hospitals. These wartime experiences are embodied in* Drum-Taps *(1865) and* Sequel to Drum-Taps *(1865–66).*

After the war, Whitman was made a clerk in the Department of the Interior, but was dismissed because Leaves of Grass *was considered to be an immoral book. In 1871, he published* Democratic Vistas, *which deplored the brute materialism of the Gilded Age.*

In 1873, Whitman suffered a stroke and retired to Camden, New Jersey. He continued to revise and add to Leaves of Grass *until his death in 1891.*

Crossing Brooklyn Ferry

I

Flood-tide below me! I see you face to face!
Clouds of the west—sun there half an hour high—I see you also
    face to face.

Crowds of men and women attired in the usual costumes, how curious
    you are to me!
On the ferry-boats the hundreds and hundreds that cross, returning
    home, are more curious to me than you suppose,
And you that shall cross from shore to shore years hence are more to
    me, and more in my meditations, than you might suppose.

2

The impalpable sustenance of me from all things at all hours of the
    day,
The simple, compact, well-join'd scheme, myself disintegrated, every
    one disintegrated yet part of the scheme,
The similitudes of the past and those of the future,
The glories strung like beads on my smallest sights and hearings, on
    the walk in the street and the passage over the river,
The current rushing so swiftly and swimming with me far away,

From Walt Whitman, *Leaves of Grass,* 1891-92.

The others that are to follow me, the ties between me and them,
The certainty of others, the life, love, sight, hearing of others.

Others will enter the gates of the ferry and cross from shore to
    shore,
Others will watch the run of the flood-tide,
Others will see the shipping of Manhattan north and west, and the
    heights of Brooklyn to the south and east,
Others will see the islands large and small;
Fifty years hence, others will see them as they cross, the sun half an
    hour high,
A hundred years hence, or ever so many hundred years hence, others
    will see them,
Will enjoy the sunset, the pouring-in of the flood-tide, the falling-
    back to the sea of the ebb-tide.

3

It avails not, time nor place—distance avails not,
I am with you, you men and women of a generation, or ever so many
    generations hence,
Just as you feel when you look on the river and sky, so I felt,
Just as any of you is one of a living crowd, I was one of a crowd,
Just as you are refresh'd by the gladness of the river and the bright
    flow, I was refresh'd,
Just as you stand and lean on the rail, yet hurry with the swift cur-
    rent, I stood yet was hurried,
Just as you look on the numberless masts of ships and the thick-
    stemm'd pipes of steamboats, I look'd.

I too many and many a time cross'd the river of old,
Watched the Twelfth-month sea-gulls, saw them high in the air float-
    ing with motionless wings, oscillating their bodies,
Saw how the glistening yellow lit up parts of their bodies and left the
    rest in strong shadow,
Saw the slow-wheeling circles and the gradual edging toward the
    south,

Saw the reflection of the summer sky in the water,
Had my eyes dazzled by the shimmering track of beams,
Look'd at the fine centrifugal spokes of light round the shape of my
     head in the sunlit water,
Look'd on the haze on the hills southward and south-westward,
Look'd on the vapor as it flew in fleeces tinged with violet,
Look'd toward the lower bay to notice the vessels arriving,
Saw their approach, saw aboard those that were near me,
Saw the white sails of schooners and sloops, saw the ships at anchor,
The sailors at work in the rigging or out astride the spars,
The round masts, the swinging motion of the hulls, the slender ser-
     pentine pennants,
The large and small steamers in motion, the pilots in their pilot-
     houses,
The white wake left by the passage, the quick tremulous whirl of the
     wheels,
The flags of all nations, the falling of them at sunset,
The scallop-edged waves in the twilight, the ladled cups, the frolic-
     some crests and glistening.
The stretch afar growing dimmer and dimmer, the gray walls of the
     granite storehouses by the docks,
On the river the shadowy group, the big steam-tug closely flank'd on
     each side by the barges, the hay-boat, the belated lighter,
On the neighboring shore the fires from the foundry chimneys burn-
     ing high and glaringly into the night,
Casting their flicker of black contrasted with wild red and yellow
     light over the tops of houses, and down into the clefts of streets.

4

These and all else were to me the same as they are to you,
I loved well those cities, loved well the stately and rapid river,
The men and women I saw were all near to me,
Others the same—others who look back on me because I look'd for-
     ward to them,
(The time will come, though I stop here to-day and to-night.)

5

What is it then between us?

What is the count of the scores or hundreds of years between us?

Whatever it is, it avails not—distance avails not, and place avails not,
I too lived, Brooklyn of ample hills was mine,
I too walk'd the streets of Manhattan island, and bathed in the waters
    around it,
I too felt the curious abrupt questionings stir within me.
In the day among crowds of people sometimes they came upon me,
In my walks home late at night or as I lay in my bed they came upon
    me,
I too had been struck from the float forever held in solution,
I too had receiv'd identity by my body,
That I was I knew was of my body, and what I should be I knew I
    should be of my body.

6

It is not upon you alone the dark patches fall,
The dark threw its patches down upon me also,
The best I had done seem'd to me blank and suspicious,
My great thoughts as I supposed them, were they not in reality
    meagre?
Nor is it you alone who know what it is to be evil,
I am he who knew what it was to be evil,
I too knitted the old knot of contrariety,
Blabb'd, blush'd, resented, lied, stole, grudg'd,
Had guile, anger, lust, hot wishes I dared not speak,
Was wayward, vain, greedy, shallow, sly, cowardly, malignant,
The wolf, the snake, the hog, not wanting in me,
The cheating look, the frivolous word, the adulterous wish, not
    wanting,
Refusals, hates, postponements, meanness, laziness, none of these
    wanting,
Was one with the rest, the days and haps of the rest,
Was call'd by my nighest name by clear loud voices of young men
    as they saw me approaching or passing,
Felt their arms on my neck as I stood, or the negligent leaning of
    their flesh against me as I sat,

Saw many I loved in the street or ferry-boat or public assembly, yet
    never told them a word,
Lived the same life with the rest, the same old laughing, gnawing,
    sleeping,
Play'd the part that still looks back on the actor or actress,
The same old role, the role that is what we make it, as great as we
    like,
Or as small as we like, or both great and small.

7

Closer yet I approach you,
What thought you have of me now, I had as much of you—I laid in
    my stores in advance,
I consider'd long and seriously of you before you were born.

Who was to know what should come home to me?
Who knows but I am enjoying this?
Who knows, for all the distance, but I am as good as looking at you
    now, for all you cannot see me?

8

Ah, what can ever be more stately and admirable to me than mast-
    hemm'd Manhattan?
River and sunset and scallop-edg'd waves of flood-tide?
The sea-gulls oscillating their bodies, the hay-boat in the twilight,
    and the belated lighter?
What gods can exceed these that clasp me by the hand, and with
    voices I love call me promptly and loudly by my nighest name
    as I approach?

What is more subtle than this which ties me to the woman or man
    that looks in my face?
Which fuses me into you now, and pours my meaning into you?

We understand then do we not?
What I promis'd without mentioning it, have you not accepted?
What the study could not teach—what the preaching could not
    accomplish is accomplish'd, is it not?

9

Flow on, river! flow with the flood-tide, and ebb with the ebb-tide!
Frolic on, crested and scallop-edg'd waves!
Gorgeous clouds of the sunset! drench with your splendor me, or the
    men and women generations after me!
Cross from shore to shore, countless crowds of passengers!
Stand up, tall masts of Mannahatta! stand up, beautiful hills of
    Brooklyn!
Throb, baffled and curious brain! throw out questions and answers!
Suspend here and everywhere, eternal float of solution!
Gaze, loving and thirsting eyes, in the house or street or public
    assembly!
Sound out, voices of young men! loudly and musically call me by my
    nighest name!
Live, old life! play the part that looks back on the actor or actress!
Play the old role, the role that is great or small according as one
    makes it!
Consider, you who peruse me, whether I may not in unknown ways
    be looking upon you;
Be firm, rail over the river, to support those who lean idly, yet haste
    with the hasting current;
Fly on, sea-birds! fly sideways, or wheel in large circles high in the
    air;
Receive the summer sky, you water, and faithfully hold it till all
    downcast eyes have time to take it from you!
Diverge, fine spokes of light, from the shape of my head, or any one's
    head, in the sunlit water!
Come on, ships from the lower bay! pass up or down, white-sail'd
    schooners, sloops, lighters!
Flaunt away, flags of all nations! be duly lower'd at sunset!
Burn high your fires, foundry chimneys! cast black shadows at night-
    fall! cast red and yellow light over the tops of the houses!
Appearances, now or henceforth, indicate what you are,
You necessary film, continue to envelop the soul,
About my body for me, and your body for you, be hung our divinest
    aromas,

Thrive, cities—bring your freight, bring your shows, ample and
    sufficient rivers,
Expand, being than which none else is perhaps more spiritual,
Keep your places, objects than which none else is more lasting.
You have waited, you always wait, you dumb, beautiful ministers,
We receive you with free sense at last, and are insatiate hence-
    forward,
Not you any more shall be able to foil us, or withhold yourselves
    from us,
We use you, and do not cast you aside—we plant you permanently
    within us,
We fathom you not—we love you—there is perfection in you also,
You furnish your parts toward eternity,
Great or small, you furnish your parts toward the soul.

JOHN W. DE FOREST (1826-1906)

A native of Seymour, Connecticut, De Forest was the son of a wealthy cotton manufacturer. His father's early death and his own serious illness prevented him from going to college, but De Forest widened his horizons in other ways. In 1846, he went to Syria to visit his brother who was a medical missionary in Beirut. From 1850 to 1855 he lived on the Continent, reading widely in European literature, especially English and French.

On his return to America, he began his writing career with accounts of his foreign travels, Oriental Acquaintance *(1856) and* European Acquaintance *(1858). Two early novels,* Witching Times *(1856) and* Seacliff *(1859), were De Forest's first attempts to write fiction in the Balzacian vein.*

When the Civil War broke out, De Forest recruited a company of volunteers, of which he became captain. After the war, he worked with the Bureau of Freedmen in South Carolina, but in 1868 he retired to devote his life to writing.

The year before his retirement, De Forest had published Miss Ravenel's Conversion from Secession to Loyalty, *which in its brutally candid depiction of war, its criticism of social corruption, and its frank treatment of sexual relationships was the most realistic novel published in America up to that time. Yet* Miss Ravenel *was not received favorably by a public which wanted to forget the tragedy of the war. In consequence, his subsequent novels are marked by a tension between his own realistic view of life and his anxiety to conform to the public demand for sentimentality. Among the best of the later novels are* Kate Beaumont *(1872) and* The Bloody Chasm *(1881), which deal with life in the South, and* Honest John Vane *(1875), which depicts the corruption of Washington politics in the Gilded Age.*

The following selection is taken from Miss Ravenel's Conversion *and is based on De Forest's own experiences in the Civil War.*

Experience Under Fire

$\mathcal{E}$VERY MORNING at dawn, Carter, who had his quarters in the midst of the Tenth, was awakened by a spattering of musketry and the singing of Minie-balls through the branches above him, or even through the dry foliage of his own sylvan shanty. Now and then a shriek or oath indicated that a bullet had done its brutal work on some human frame. No crowd collected; the men were hardened to such tragedies; four or five bore the victim away; the rest asked, "Who is it?" One death which Carter witnessed was of so remarkable a character that he wrote an account of it to his wife, although not given to noting with much interest the minor and personal incidents of war.

"I had just finished breakfast, and was lying on my back smoking. A bullet whistled so unusually low as to attract my attention and struck with a loud smack, apparently in a tree about twenty feet from me. Between me and the tree a soldier, with his great coat rolled under his head for a pillow, lay on his back reading a newspaper which he held in both hands. I remember smiling to myself to see this man start as the bullet passed. Some of his comrades left off playing cards and looked for it. The man who was reading remained perfectly still, his eyes fixed on the paper with a steadiness which I thought curious, considering the bustle around him. Presently I noticed that there were a few drops of blood on his neck, and that his face was paling. Calling to the card-players, who had resumed their game, I said, 'See to that man with the paper.' They went to him, spoke to him, touched him, and found him perfectly dead. The ball had struck him under the chin, traversed the neck, and cut the spinal column where it joins the brain, making a fearful hole through which the blood had already soaked his great-coat. It was this man's head,

From John W. De Forest, *Miss Ravenel's Conversion from Secession to Loyalty*, 1867.

and not the tree, which had been hit with such a report. There he lay, still holding the New York Independent, with his eyes fixed on a sermon by Henry Ward Beecher. It was really quite a remarkable circumstance.

"By the way, you must not suppose, my dear little girl, that bullets often come so near me. I am as careful of myself as you exhort me to be."

Not quite true, this soothing story; and the Colonel knew it to be false as he wrote it. He knew that he was in danger of death at any moment, but he had not the heart to tell his wife so, and make her unhappy.

ABRAHAM LINCOLN (1809–65)

Lincoln's role in American history and his hold on the national imagination are unsurpassed by any other president. His birth on the Kentucky frontier, the rail-splitting feats of his young manhood in New Salem, Illinois, his success as a lawyer, his election and re-election to the Presidency in the two most bitterly fought campaigns in American history are all part of the Lincoln legend. But more important, and far harder to grasp, is the overwhelming impression Lincoln gives us of being a haunted man, for whom every victory was a kind of defeat.

With Malice Toward None; with Charity for All

ADDRESS AT THE DEDICATION OF
THE GETTYSBURG NATIONAL CEMETERY

FOUR SCORE and seven years ago our fathers brought forth on this continent, a new nation, conceived in Liberty, and dedicated to the proposition that all men are created equal.

Now we are engaged in a great civil war; testing whether that nation, or any nation so conceived and so dedicated, can long endure. We are met on a great battlefield of that war. We have come to dedicate a portion of that field as a final resting-place for those who here gave their lives that that nation might live. It is altogether fitting and proper that we should do this.

But, in a larger sense, we cannot dedicate—we cannot consecrate— we cannot hallow—this ground. The brave men, living and dead, who struggled here have consecrated it, far above our poor power to add or detract. The world will little note, nor long remember, what we say here, but it can never forget what they did here. It is for us the living, rather, to be dedicated here to the unfinished work which they who fought here have thus far so nobly advanced. It is rather for us to be here dedicated to the great task remaining before us— that from these honored dead we take increased devotion to that cause for which they gave the last full measure of devotion; that we here highly resolve that these dead shall not have died in vain; that this nation, under God, shall have a new birth of freedom; and that government of the people, by the people, for the people, shall not perish from the earth.

SECOND INAUGURAL ADDRESS

FELLOW-COUNTRYMEN:

At this second appearing to take the oath of the presidential office, there is less occasion for an extended address than there was at the first. Then a statement, somewhat in detail, of a course to be pursued, seemed fitting and proper. Now, at the expiration of four years, dur- ing which public declarations have been constantly called forth on every point and phase of the great contest which still absorbs the at- tention and engrosses the energies of the nation, little that is new could be presented. The progress of our arms, upon which all else chiefly depends, is as well known to the public as to myself; and it is, I trust, reasonably satisfactory and encouraging to all. With high hope for the future, no prediction in regard to it is ventured.

On the occasion corresponding to this four years ago, all thoughts were anxiously directed to an impending civil war. All dreaded it— all sought to avert it. While the inaugural address was being de- livered from this place, devoted altogether to saving the Union with- out war, insurgent agents were in the city seeking to destroy it without war—seeking to dissolve the Union, and divide effects, by negotiation. Both parties deprecated war; but one of them would make war rather than let the nation survive; and the other would accept war rather than let it perish. And the war came.

One-eighth of the whole population were colored slaves, not dis- tributed generally over the Union, but localized in the Southern part of it. These slaves constituted a peculiar and powerful interest. All knew that this interest was, somehow, the cause of the war. To strengthen, perpetuate, and extend this interest was the object for which the insurgents would rend the Union, even by war; while the government claimed no right to do more than to restrict the territorial enlargement of it.

Neither party expected for the war the magnitude or the duration which it has already attained. Neither anticipated that the cause of the conflict might cease with, or even before, the conflict itself should cease. Each looked for an easier triumph, and a result less fundamental and astounding. Both read the same Bible, and pray to the same God; and each invokes his aid against the other. It may seem strange that any men should dare to ask a just God's assistance in wringing their bread from the sweat of other men's faces; but let us judge not, that we be not judged. The prayers of both could not be answered—that of neither has been answered fully.

The Almighty has his own purposes. "Woe unto the world because of offences! for it must needs be that offences come; but woe to that man by whom the offence cometh." If we shall suppose that American slavery is one of those offences which, in the providence of God, must needs come, but which, having continued through his appointed time, he now wills to remove, and that he gives to both North and South this terrible war, as the woe due to those by whom the offence came, shall we discern therein any departure from those divine attributes which the believers in a living God always ascribe to him? Fondly do we hope—fervently do we pray—that this mighty scourge of war may speedily pass away. Yet, if God wills that it continue until all the wealth piled by the bondman's two hundred and fifty years of unrequited toil shall be sunk, and until every drop of blood drawn with the lash shall be paid by another drawn with the sword, as was said three thousand years ago, so still it must be said, "The judgments of the Lord are true and righteous altogether."

With malice toward none; with charity for all; with firmness in the right, as God gives us to see the right, let us strive on to finish the work we are in; to bind up the nation's wounds; to care for him who shall have borne the battle, and for his widow, and his orphan—to do all which may achieve and cherish a just and lasting peace among ourselves, and with all nations.

COWBOY SONGS

The cowboys of the West sang songs to relieve their boredom as they drove their cattle along the lonely trails to market, or as the tired men huddled close to their campfires at night. The songs had a practical purpose, too. They could quiet cattle which had been startled or frightened, and they were a means of letting your fellow cowboys know where you were when the dust was so thick that they couldn't see you. Many of the cowboy songs were work songs; others told adventure stories; still others revealed the singer's yearning for a woman's love, or his fear of death, or his enormous loneliness. Some of the tunes the cowboys themselves made up, but most of them were variations on old British ballads which the immigrant-ancestors of the cowboys had brought to America in the seventeenth century.

Sam Bass

Sam Bass was born in Indiana, it was his native home,
And at the age of seventeen young Sam began to roam,
Sam first came out to Texas a cowboy for to be,—
A kinder-hearted fellow you seldom ever see.

Sam used to deal in race stock, one called the Denton mare,
He matched her in scrub races, and took her to the fair.
Sam used to coin the money and spent it just as free,
He always drank good whiskey wherever he might be.

Sam left the Collins ranch in the merry month of May
With a herd of Texas cattle the Black Hills for to see,

Sold out in Custer City and then got on a spree,—
A harder set of cowboys you seldom ever see.

On their way back to Texas they robbed the U.P. train,
And then split up in couples and started out again.
Joe Collins and his partner were overtaken soon,
With all their hard-earned money they had to meet their doom.

Sam made it back to Texas all right side up with care;
Rode into the town of Denton with all his friends to share.
Sam's life was short in Texas; three robberies did he do,
He robbed all the passenger, mail, and express cars too.

Sam had four companions—four bold and daring lads—
They were Richardson, Jackson, Joe Collins, and Old Dad;
Four more bold and daring cowboys the rangers never knew,
They whipped the Texas rangers and ran the boys in blue.

Sam had another companion, called Arkansas for short,
Was shot by a Texas ranger by the name of Thomas Floyd;
Oh, Tom is a big six-footer and thinks he's mighty fly,
But I can tell you his racket,—he's a deadbeat on the sly.

Jim Murphy was arrested, and then released on bail;
He jumped his bond at Tyler and took the train for Terrell;
But Mayor Jones had posted Jim and that was all a stall,
'Twas only a plan to capture Sam before the coming fall.

Sam met his fate at Round Rock, July the twenty-first,
They pierced poor Sam with rifle balls and then emptied his purse.
Poor Sam he is a corpse and six foot under clay,
And Jackson's in the bushes trying to get away.

Jim had borrowed Sam's good gold and didn't want to pay,
The only shot he saw was to give poor Sam away.
He sold out Sam and Barnes and left their friends to mourn,—
Oh, what a scorching Jim will get when Gabriel blows his horn.

And so he sold out Sam and Barnes and left their friends to mourn,
Oh, what a scorching Jim will get when Gabriel blows his horn.
Perhaps he's got to heaven, there's none of us can say,
But if I'm right in my surmise he's gone the other way.

Good-By, Old Paint

My foot in the stirrup, my pony won't stan',
Good-by, old Paint, I'm a-leavin' Cheyenne.
I'm a-leavin' Cheyenne, I'm off for Montan';
Good-by, old Paint, I'm a-leavin' Cheyenne.

I'm a-ridin' old Paint, I'm a-leadin' old Dan;
Good-by, old Paint, I'm a-leavin' Cheyenne.
With my feet in the stirrups, my bridle in my hand;
Good-by, old Paint, I'm a-leavin' Cheyenne.

Old Paint's a good pony, he paces when he can;
Good-by, little Annie, I'm off for Cheyenne.
Oh, hitch up your horses and feed 'em some hay,
And seat yourself by me as long as you stay.

My hosses ain't hungry, they won't eat your hay;
My wagon is loaded and rollin' away.
I'm a-ridin', old Paint, I'm a-leadin' old Dan,
I'm a-goin' to Montan' to throw the hoolihan.

They feed in the coulees, they water in the draw,
Their tails are all matted, their backs are all raw.
Old Bill Jones had two daughters and a song;
One went to Denver, the other went wrong.

His wife died in a pool-room fight,
And still he sings from morning till night.
I'm a rambler and a gambler and far from my home,
And those that don't like me can leave me alone.

Oh, whiskey and beer, they are nothing to me,
They killed my old Dad, now they can try me.
I'll tell you the truth, not lyin' or jokin',
I'd rather be in jail than to be heart-broken.

Oh, when I die take my saddle from the wall,
Put it on my pony, lead him from the stall,
Tie my bones to his back, turn our faces to the west,
And we'll ride the prairie that we love the best.

Whoopee Ti Yi Yo, Git Along, Little Dogies

As I was a-walking one morning for pleasure,
I spied a cow-puncher a-riding along;
His hat was throwed back and his spurs were a-jinglin',
As he approached me a-singin' this song:

Chorus
        Whoopee ti yi yo, git along, little dogies,
        It's your misfortune and none of my own;
        Whoopee ti yi yo, git along, little dogies,
        For you know Wyoming will be your new home.

Early in the springtime we'll round up the dogies,
Slap on their brands, and bob off their tails;
Round up our horses, load up the chuck wagon,
Then throw those dogies upon the trail.

It's whooping and yelling and driving the dogies,
Oh, how I wish you would go on;
It's whooping and punching and go on, little dogies,
For you know Wyoming will be your new home.

Some of the boys goes up the trail for pleasure,
But that's where they git it most awfully wrong;

For you haven't any idea the trouble they give us
When we go driving them dogies along.

When the night comes on and we hold them on the bed-ground,
These little dogies that roll on so slow;
Roll up the herd and cut out the strays,
And roll the little dogies that never rolled before.

Your mother she was raised way down in Texas,
Where the jimson weed and sand-burrs grow;
Now we'll fill you up on prickly pear and cholla
Till you are ready for the trail to Idaho.

Oh, you'll be soup for Uncle Sam's Injuns;
"It's beef, heap beef," I hear them cry.
Git along, git along, git along, little dogies,
You're going to be beef steers by and by.

The Old Chisholm Trail

Come along, boys, and listen to my tale,
I'll tell you of my troubles on the old Chisholm trail.

Chorus
       Come ti yi youpy, youpy yea, youpy yea,
       Coma ti yi youpy, youpy yea.

I started up the trail October twenty-third,
I started up the trail with the 2-U herd.

Oh, a ten-dollar hoss and a forty-dollar saddle,
And I'm goin' to punchin' Texas cattle.

I woke up one morning on the old Chisholm trail,
Rope in my hand and a cow by the tail.

I'm up in the mornin' afore daylight
And afore I sleep the moon shines bright.

My hoss throwed me off at the creek called Mud,
My hoss throwed me off round the 2-U herd.

Last time I saw him he was going 'cross the level
A-kicking up his heels and a-running like the devil.

It's cloudy in the west, a-looking like rain,
And my damned old slicker's in the wagon again.

No chaps, no slicker, and it's pouring down rain,
And I swear, by God, I'll never night-herd again.

Last night I was on guard and the leader broke the ranks,
I hit my horse down the shoulders and I spurred him in the flanks.

The wind commenced to blow, and the rain began to fall,
Hit looked, by grab, like we was goin' to lose 'em all.

My slicker's in the wagon and I'm gittin' mighty cold,
And these longhorn sons-o'-guns are gittin' hard to hold.

Saddle up, boys, and saddle up well,
For I think these cattle have scattered to hell.

With my blanket and my gun and my rawhide rope,
I'm a-slidin' down the trail in a long, keen lope.

I don't give a damn if they never do stop;
I'll ride as long as an eight-day clock.

We rounded 'em up and put 'em on the cars,
And that was the last of the old Two Bars.

Oh, it's bacon and beans most every day—

I'd as soon be a-eatin' prairie hay.

I went to the boss to draw my roll,
He had it figgered out I was nine dollars in the hole.

I'll sell my outfit just as soon as I can,
I won't punch cattle for no damned man.

With my knees in the saddle and my seat in the sky,
I'll quit punching cows in the sweet by-and-by.

Fare you well, old trail-boss, I don't wish you any harm,
I'm quittin' this business to go on the farm.

Blood On The Saddle

There was bul-lud on the saddle—
And bul-lud all araound,
An' a great big puddle
Of bul-lud on the graound.

Oh, a cowboy lay in it,
All covered with gore,
An' he never will ride on
Any broncos no more.

Oh, pity the cowboy,
All bul-luddy and red;
Oh, a bronco fell on him,
An' mashed in his head.

There was bul-lud on the saddle—
And bul-lud all araound,
An' a great big puddle
Of bul-lud on the graound.

EMILY DICKINSON (1830–86)

Emily Dickinson was born, grew up, and died in her father's house on Main Street in Amherst, Massachusetts. She never married, and in her later years she withdrew from all but epistolary contact with the outside world.

Yet her poems reveal that the inner life of this inordinately shy woman trembled with passion and excitement. They record her daring revolt against the Calvinism of her ancestors, her desire to be loved, her delight in nature, and her obsession with death. Although they are deeply personal documents, her poems also tell us a great deal about the suffocatingly repressive, yet oddly rewarding life of the smalltown spinster in late nineteenth-century New England.

Three Poems

Wild Nights—Wild Nights!
Were I with thee
Wild Nights should be
Our luxury!

Futile—the Winds—
To a Heart in port—
Done with the Compass—
Done with the Chart!

From *The Poems of Emily Dickinson*, edited by Thomas H. Johnson. (Cambridge Mass., The Belknap Press of Harvard University Press, 1951, 1955) pp. 179, 392-393, 492-493.

Rowing in Eden—
Ah, the Sea!
Might I but moor—Tonight—
In Thee!

If you were coming in the Fall,
I'd brush the Summer by
With half a smile, and half a spurn,
As Housewives do, a Fly.

If I could see you in a year,
I'd wind the months in balls—
And put them each in separate Drawers,
For fear the numbers fuse—

If only Centuries, delayed,
I'd count them on my Hand,
Subtracting, till my fingers dropped
Into Van Dieman's Land.

If certain, when this life was out—
That yours and mine, should be
I'd toss it yonder, like a Rind,
And take Eternity—

But, now, uncertain of the length
Of this, that is between,
It goads me, like the Goblin Bee—
That will not state—its sting.

I cannot live with You—
It would be Life—
And Life is over there—
Behind the Shelf

The Sexton keeps the Key to—
Putting up
Our Life—His Porcelain—
Like a Cup—

Discarded of the Housewife—
Quaint—or Broke—
A newer Sevres pleases—
Old Ones crack—

I could not die—with You—
For One must wait
To shut the Other's Gaze down—
You—could not—

And I—Could I stand by
And see You—freeze—
Without my Right of Frost—
Death's privilege?

Nor could I rise—with You—
Because Your Face
Would put out Jesus'—
That New Grace

Glow plain—and foreign
On my homesick Eye—
Except that You than He
Shone closer by—

They'd judge Us—How—
For You—served Heaven—You know,
Or sought to—
I could not—

Because You saturated Sight—
And I had no more Eyes
For sordid excellence
As Paradise

And were You lost, I would be—
Though My Name
Rang loudest
On the Heavenly fame—

And were You—saved—
And I—condemned to be
Where You were not—
That self—were Hell to Me—

So We must meet apart—
You there—I—here—
With just the Door ajar
That Oceans are—and Prayer—
And that White Sustenance—
Despair—

MARK TWAIN (SAMUEL LANGHORNE CLEMENS) (1835-1910)

Twain was born in Florida, Missouri, but grew up in nearby Hannibal, Missouri, a river town on the Mississippi. When he was eighteen, Twain left Hannibal and worked as a journeyman printer in the East and Middle West. Deciding to seek his fortune in South America, Twain set out in 1856 to cross the Caribbean, but got no further than New Orleans, where he changed his mind in favor of a career as a steamboat pilot on the Mississippi. He was licensed in 1858, but the Civil War shortly destroyed steamboat traffic on the river.

After a few weeks as a Confederate soldier, Twain left for Nevada, where he became a journalist for a Virginia City newspaper. The publication of his famous "Jumping Frog" story in 1865 made Twain nationally known as a Western humorist. His irreverent sense of fun soon led him to join a religious pilgrimage to Europe and the Holy Land, an experience which he recorded in his first best seller, The Innocents Abroad *(1869).*

In 1870, Twain married and, after a brief sojourn in Buffalo, settled in Hartford, Connecticut, where he remained for most of his life. Roughing It *(1872),* The Gilded Age *(1873),* The Adventures of Tom Sawyer *(1876),* Life on the Mississippi *(1883),* The Adventures of Huckleberry Finn *(1885), and* A Connecticut Yankee in King Arthur's Court *(1889) are all products of his Hartford years. In his old age, Twain became increasingly disillusioned and embittered about American life.* Pudd'nhead Wilson *(1894),* What is Man? *(1906), and* The Mysterious Stranger *(1916) are works of despair. For Twain had grown up in the years when the idea of the spiritual design of the Union was still deeply ingrained in the Ameri-*

*can mind. After the Civil War, when the design seemed lost, he was
at first torn between the passionate idealism of the earlier generation
and the realism which the Civil War and the Industrial Revolution
created and necessitated. But in the closing years of his life, belea-
guered by personal tragedies, he gave way to a savage nihilism.*

The Boy's Ambition

W H E N I was a boy, there was but one permanent ambition among
my comrades in our village on the west bank of the Mississippi River.
That was, to be a steamboatman. We had transient ambitions of other
sorts, but they were only transient. When a circus came and went, it
left us all burning to become clowns; the first negro minstrel show
that came to our section left us all suffering to try that kind of life;
now and then we had a hope that if we lived and were good, God
would permit us to be pirates. These ambitions faded out, each in
its turn; but the ambition to be a steamboatman always remained.

Once a day a cheap, gaudy packet arrived upward from St. Louis,
and another downward from Keokuk. Before these events, the day
was glorious with expectancy; after them, the day was a dead and
empty thing. Not only the boys, but the whole village, felt this. After
all these years I can picture that old time to myself now, just as it was
then: the white town drowsing in the sunshine of a summer's morning; the streets empty, or pretty nearly so; one or two clerks sitting
in front of the Water Street stores, with their splint-bottomed chairs
tilted back against the wall, chins on breasts, hats slouched over their
faces, asleep—with shingle-shavings enough around to show what
broke them down; a sow and a litter of pigs loafing along the sidewalk, doing a good business in watermelon rinds and seeds; two or
three lonely little freight piles scattered about the "levee;" a pile of
"skids" on the slope of the stone-paved wharf, and the fragrant town
drunkard asleep in the shadow of them; two or three wood flats at
the head of the wharf, but nobody to listen to the peaceful lapping
of the wavelets against them; the great Mississippi, the majestic, the

From Mark Twain, *Life on the Mississippi*, 1883.

magnificent Mississippi, rolling its mile-wide tide along, shining in the sun; the dense forest away on the other side; the "point" above the town, and the "point" below, bounding the river-glimpse and turning it into a sort of sea, and withal a very still and brilliant and lonely one. Presently a film of dark smoke appears above one of those remote "points;" instantly a negro drayman, famous for his quick eye and prodigious voice, lifts up the cry, "S-t-e-a-m-boat a-comin'!" and the scene changes! The town drunkard stirs, the clerks wake up, a furious clatter of drays follows, every house and store pours out a human contribution, and all in a twinkling the dead town is alive and moving. Drays, carts, men, boys, all go hurrying from many quarters to a common centre, the wharf. Assembled there, the people fasten their eyes upon the coming boat as upon a wonder they are seeing for the first time. And the boat *is* rather a handsome sight, too. She is long and sharp and trim and pretty; she has two tall, fancy-topped chimneys, with a gilded device of some kind swung between them; a fanciful pilot-house, all glass and "ginger-bread," perched on top of the "texas" deck behind them; the paddle-boxes are gorgeous with a picture or with gilded rays above the boat's name; the boiler deck, the hurricane deck, and the texas deck are fenced and ornamented with clean white railings; there is a flag gallantly flying from the jack-staff; the furnace doors are open and the fires glaring bravely; the upper decks are black with passengers; the captain stands by the big bell, calm, imposing, the envy of all; great volumes of the blackest smoke are rolling and tumbling out of the chimneys—a husbanded grandeur created with a bit of pitch pine just before arriving at a town; and the crew are grouped on the fore-castle; the broad stage is run far out over the port bow, and an envied deck-hand stands picturesquely on the end of it with a coil of rope in his hand; the pent steam is screaming through the gauge-cocks; the captain lifts his hand, a bell rings, the wheels stop; then they turn back, churning the water to foam, and the steamer is at rest. Then such a scramble as there is to get aboard, and to get ashore, and to take in freight and to discharge freight, all at one and the same time; and such a yelling and cursing as the mates facilitate it all with! Ten minutes later the steamer is under way again, with no flag on the jack-staff and no black smoke issuing from the chimneys.

After ten more minutes the town is dead again, and the town drunkard asleep by the skids once more.

My father was a justice of the peace, and I supposed he possessed the power of life and death over all men and could hang anybody that offended him. This was distinction enough for me as a general thing; but the desire to be a steamboatman kept intruding, nevertheless. I first wanted to be a cabin-boy, so that I could come out with a white apron on and shake a table-cloth over the side, where all my old comrades could see me; later I thought I would rather be the deck-hand who stood on the end of the stage-plank with the coil of rope in his hand, because he was particularly conspicuous. But these were only day-dreams,—they were too heavenly to be contemplated as real possibilities. By and by one of our boys went away. He was not heard of for a long time. At last he turned up as apprentice engineer or "striker" on a steamboat. This thing shook the bottom out of all my Sunday-school teachings. That boy had been notoriously worldly, and I just the reverse; yet he was exalted to this eminence, and I left in obscurity and misery. There was nothing generous about this fellow in his greatness. He would always manage to have a rusty bolt to scrub while his boat tarried at our town, and he would sit on the inside guard and scrub it, where we could all see him and envy him and loathe him. And whenever his boat was laid up he would come home and swell around the town in his blackest and greasiest clothes, so that nobody could help remembering that he was a steamboatman; and he used all sorts of steamboat technicalities in his talk, as if he were so used to them that he forgot common people could not understand them. He would speak of the "labboard" side of a horse in an easy, natural way that would make one wish he was dead. And he was always talking about "St. Looy" like an old citizen; he would refer casually to occasions when he "was coming down Fourth Street," or when he was "passing by the Planter's House," or when there was a fire and he took a turn on the brakes of "the old Big Missouri;" and then he would go on and lie about how many towns the size of ours were burned down there that day. Two or three of the boys had long been persons of consideration among us because they had been to St. Louis once and had a vague general knowledge of its wonders, but the day of their glory was over now. They lapsed into a humble silence, and learned to disappear when the ruthless "cub"-engineer approached. This fellow had money, too, and hair oil. Also an ignorant silver watch and a showy brass watch chain. He wore a leather belt and used no suspenders. If ever a youth was cordially admired and hated by his comrades, this one was. No girl could withstand his charms. He "cut out" every boy in the village. When his boat blew up at last, it diffused a tranquil contentment among us such as we had not known for months. But when he came home the next week, alive, renowned, and appeared in church all battered up and bandaged, a shining hero, stared at and wondered over by everybody, it seemed to us that the partiality of Providence for an undeserving reptile had reached a point where it was open to criticism.

This creature's career could produce but one result, and it speedily followed. Boy after boy managed to get on the river. The minister's son became an engineer. The doctor's and the postmaster's sons became "mud clerks;" the wholesale liquor dealer's son became a barkeeper on a boat; four sons of the chief merchant, and two sons of the county judge, became pilots. Pilot was the grandest position of all. The pilot, even in those days of trivial wages, had a princely salary—from a hundred and fifty to two hundred and fifty dollars a month, and no board to pay. Two months of his wages would pay a preacher's salary for a year. Now some of us were left disconsolate. We could not get on the river—at least our parents would not let us.

So by and by I ran away. I said I never would come home again till I was a pilot and could come in glory. But somehow I could not manage it. I went meekly aboard a few of the boats that lay packed together like sardines at the long St. Louis wharf, and very humbly inquired for the pilots, but got only a cold shoulder and short words from mates and clerks. I had to make the best of this sort of treatment for the time being, but I had comforting day-dreams of a future when I should be a great and honored pilot, with plenty of money, and could kill some of these mates and clerks and pay for them.

The Cayote

THE CAYOTE is a long, slim, sick and sorry-looking skeleton, with a gray wolf-skin stretched over it, a tolerably bushy tail that forever sags down with a despairing expression of forsakenness and misery, a furtive and evil eye, and a long, sharp face, with slightly lifted lip and exposed teeth. He has a general slinking expression all over. The cayote is a living, breathing allegory of Want. He is *always* hungry. He is always poor, out of luck and friendless. The meanest creatures despise him, and even the fleas would desert him for a velocipede. He is so spiritless and cowardly that even while his exposed teeth are pretending a threat, the rest of his face is apologizing for it. And he is *so* homely!—so scrawny, and ribby, and coarse-haired, and pitiful. When he sees you he lifts his lip and lets a flash of his teeth out, and then turns a little out of the course he was pursuing, depresses his head a bit, and strikes a long, soft-footed trot through the sage-brush, glancing over his shoulder at you, from time to time, till he is about out of easy pistol range, and then he stops and takes a deliberate survey of you; he will trot fifty yards and stop again—another fifty and stop again; and finally the gray of his gliding body blends with the gray of the sage-brush, and he disappears. All this is when you make no demonstration against him; but if you do, he develops a livelier interest in his journey, and instantly electrifies his heels and puts such a deal of real estate between himself and your weapon, that by the time you have raised the hammer you see that you need a minie rifle, and by the time you have got him in line you need a rifled cannon, and by the time you have "drawn a bead" on him you see well enough that nothing but an unusually long-winded streak of lightning could reach him where he is now. But if you start a swift-footed dog after him, you will enjoy it ever so much—especially if it is a dog that has a good opinion of himself, and has been brought up to think he knows something about speed. The cayote will go swinging gently off on that deceitful trot of his, and every little while he will smile a fraudful smile over his shoulder that will

From Mark Twain, *Roughing It*, 1872.

fill that dog entirely full of encouragement and worldly ambition, and make him lay his head still lower to the ground, and stretch his neck further to the front, and pant more fiercely, and stick his tail out straighter behind, and move his furious legs with a yet wilder frenzy, and leave a broader and broader, and higher and denser cloud of desert sand smoking behind, and marking his long wake across the level plain! And all this time the dog is only a short twenty feet behind the cayote, and to save the soul of him he cannot understand why it is that he cannot get perceptibly closer; and he begins to get aggravated, and it makes him madder and madder to see how gently the cayote glides along and never pants or sweats or ceases to smile; and he grows still more and more incensed to see how shamefully he has been taken in by an entire stranger, and what an ignoble swindle that long, calm, soft-footed trot is; and next he notices that he is getting fagged, and that the cayote actually has to slacken speed a little to keep from running away from him—and *then* that town-dog is mad in earnest, and he begins to strain and weep and swear, and paw the sand higher than ever, and reach for the cayote with concentrated and desperate energy. This "spurt" finds him six feet behind the gliding enemy, and two miles from his friends. And then, in the instant that a wild new hope is lighting up his face, the cayote turns and smiles blandly upon him once more, and with a something about it which seems to say: "Well, I shall have to tear myself away from you, bub—business is business, and it will not do for me to be fooling along this way all day"—and forthwith there is a rushing sound, and the sudden splitting of a long crack through the atmosphere, and behold that dog is solitary and alone in the midst of a vast solitude!

It makes his head swim. He stops, and looks all around; climbs the nearest sand-mound, and gazes into the distance; shakes his head reflectively, and then, without a word, he turns and jogs along back to his train, and takes up a humble position under the hindmost wagon, and feels unspeakably mean, and looks ashamed, and hangs his tail at half-mast for a week. And for as much as a year after that, whenever there is a great hue and cry after a cayote, that dog will merely glance in that direction without emotion, and apparently observe to himself, "I believe I do not wish any of the pie."

IV.   New Beginnings

ANDREW CARNEGIE (1835–1919)

The son of a Scottish handloom weaver, Carnegie came to the United States in 1848, when the factory system forced his father out of work. Starting as a bobbin boy in a cotton factory in Pennsylvania, Carnegie advanced rapidly. He became a messenger in the Pittsburgh telegraph office when he was fourteen, and at the age of thirty he was named superintendent of the Pittsburgh Division of the Pennsylvania Railroad.

At the end of the Civil War, when the United States was emerging as the industrial giant of the world, Carnegie decided to go into the steel business. By superb organization and shrewd insight, he built his enterprises into one of the great industrial empires of the world.

It was Carnegie's belief that the wealth he had created should not be used for further selfish aggrandizement. Rather, he believed that he held the wealth in trust for the people, and should use it for the improvement of mankind. From 1901, when he sold his steel company, until his death in 1919, Carnegie spent more than 350 million dollars to put his belief into practice. Among his most significant contributions were those to public libraries, colleges, the Carnegie Corporation, and the Endowment for International Peace.

Carnegie was a prolific writer. His best-known books are Triumphant Democracy *(1886), which proclaims the vast superiority of the American republic to the British monarchy, and* The Gospel of Wealth *(1889), the title of which indicates Carnegie's desire to unite the individual's ambition for wealth with the demands of the public good.*

The following selection forms the first chapter of The Gospel of Wealth.

How I Served My Apprenticeship

*I*T IS a great pleasure to tell how I served my apprenticeship as a business man. But there seems to be a question preceding this: Why did I become a business man? I am sure that I should never have selected a business career if I had been permitted to choose.

The eldest son of parents who were themselves poor, I had, fortunately, to begin to perform some useful work in the world while still very young in order to earn an honest livelihood, and was thus shown even in early boyhood that my duty was to assist my parents and, like them, become, as soon as possible, a bread-winner in the family. What I could get to do, not what I desired, was the question.

When I was born my father was a well-to-do master weaver in Dunfermline, Scotland. He owned no less than four damask-looms and employed apprentices. This was before the days of steam-factories for the manufacture of linen. A few large merchants took orders, and employed master weavers, such as my father, to weave the cloth, the merchants supplying the materials.

As the factory system developed hand-loom weaving naturally declined, and my father was one of the sufferers by the change. The first serious lesson of my life came to me one day when he had taken in the last of his work to the merchant, and returned to our little home greatly distressed because there was no more work for him to do. I was then just about ten years of age, but the lesson burned into my heart, and I resolved then that the wolf of poverty should be driven from our door some day, if I could do it.

The question of selling the old looms and starting for the United States came up in the family council, and I heard it discussed from day to day. It was finally resolved to take the plunge and join relatives already in Pittsburg. I well remember that neither father nor mother thought the change would be otherwise than a great sacrifice for them, but that "it would be better for the two boys."

In after life, if you can look back as I do and wonder at the complete surrender of their own desires which parents make for the good

From Andrew Carnegie, *The Gospel of Wealth*, 1889.

of their children, you must reverence their memories with feelings akin to worship.

On arriving in Allegheny City (there were four of us: father, mother, my younger brother, and myself), my father entered a cotton factory. I soon followed, and served as a "bobbin-boy," and this is how I began my preparation for subsequent apprenticeship as a business man. I received one dollar and twenty cents a week, and was then just about twelve years old.

I cannot tell you how proud I was when I received my first week's own earnings. One dollar and twenty cents made by myself and given to me because I had been of some use in the world! No longer entirely dependent upon my parents, but at last admitted to the family partnership as a contributing member and able to help them! I think this makes a man out of a boy sooner than almost anything else, and a real man, too, if there be any germ of true manhood in him. It is everything to feel that you are useful.

I have had to deal with great sums. Many millions of dollars have since passed through my hands. But the genuine satisfaction I had from that one dollar and twenty cents outweighs any subsequent pleasure in money-getting. It was the direct reward of honest, manual labor; it represented a week of very hard work—so hard that, but for the aim and end which sanctified it, slavery might not be much too strong a term to describe it.

For a lad of twelve to rise and breakfast every morning, except the blessed Sunday morning, and go into the streets and find his way to the factory and begin to work while it was still dark outside, and not be released until after darkness came again in the evening, forty minutes' interval only being allowed at noon, was a terrible task.

But I was young and had my dreams, and something within always told me that this would not, could not, should not last—I should some day get into a better position. Besides this, I felt myself no longer a mere boy, but quite a little man, and this made me happy.

A change soon came, for a kind old Scotsman, who knew some of our relatives, made bobbins, and took me into his factory before I was thirteen. But here for a time it was even worse than in the cotton factory, because I was set to fire a boiler in the cellar, and actually to run the small steam-engine which drove the machinery. The firing of the boiler was all right, for fortunately we did not use coal, but the refuse wooden chips; and I always liked to work in wood. But the responsibility of keeping the water right and of running the engine, and the danger of my making a mistake and blowing the whole factory to pieces, caused too great a strain, and I often awoke and found myself sitting up in bed through the night, trying the steam-gauges. But I never told them at home that I was having a hard tussle. No, no! everything must be bright to them.

This was a point of honor, for every member of the family was working hard, except, of course, my little brother, who was then a child, and we were telling each other only all the bright things. Besides this, no man would whine and give up—he would die first.

There was no servant in our family, and several dollars per week were earned by the mother by binding shoes after her daily work was done! Father was also hard at work in the factory. And could I complain?

My kind employer, John Hay,—peace to his ashes!—soon relieved me of the undue strain, for he needed some one to make out bills and keep his accounts, and finding that I could write a plain school-boy hand and could "cipher," he made me his only clerk. But still I had to work hard upstairs in the factory, for the clerking took but little time.

You know how people moan about poverty as being a great evil, and it seems to be accepted that if people had only plenty of money and were rich, they would be happy and more useful, and get more out of life.

As a rule, there is more genuine satisfaction, a truer life, and more obtained from life in the humble cottages of the poor than in the palaces of the rich. I always pity the sons and daughters of rich men, who are attended by servants, and have governesses at a later age, but am glad to remember that they do not know what they have missed.

They have kind fathers and mothers, too, and think that they enjoy the sweetness of these blessings to the fullest: but this they cannot do; for the poor boy who has in his father his constant companion, tutor, and model, and in his mother—holy name!—his nurse, teacher, guardian angel, saint, all in one, has a richer, more precious fortune in life than any rich man's son who is not so favored can possibly know, and compared with which all other fortunes count for little.

It is because I know how sweet and happy and pure the home of honest poverty is, how free from perplexing care, from social envies and emulations, how loving and how united its members may be in the common interest of supporting the family, that I sympathize with the rich man's boy and congratulate the poor man's boy; and it is for these reasons that from the ranks of the poor so many strong, eminent, self-reliant men have always sprung and always must spring.

If you will read the list of the immortals who "were not born to die," you will find that most of them have been born to the precious heritage of poverty.

It seems, nowadays, a matter of universal desire that poverty should be abolished. We should be quite willing to abolish luxury, but to abolish honest, industrious, self-denying poverty would be to destroy the soil upon which mankind produces the virtues which enable our race to reach a still higher civilization than it now possesses.

I come now to the third step in my apprenticeship, for I had already taken two, as you see—the cotton factory and then the bobbin factory; and with the third—the third time is the chance, you know —deliverance came. I obtained a situation as messenger boy in the telegraph office of Pittsburg when I was fourteen. Here I entered a new world.

Amid books, newspapers, pencils, pens and ink and writing-pads, and a clean office, bright windows, and the literary atmosphere, I was the happiest boy alive.

My only dread was that I should some day be dismissed because I did not know the city; for it is necessary that a messenger boy should know all the firms and addresses of men who are in the habit of receiving telegrams. But I was a stranger in Pittsburg. However, I made up my mind that I would learn to repeat successively each business house in the principal streets, and was soon able to shut my eyes and begin at one side of Wood Street, and call every firm successively to the top, then pass to the other side and call every firm to the bottom. Before long I was able to do this with the business streets generally. My mind was then at rest upon that point.

Of course every messenger boy wants to become an operator, and before the operators arrive in the early mornings the boys slipped up to the instruments and practised. This I did, and was soon able to talk to the boys in the other offices along the line, who were also practising.

One morning I heard Philadelphia calling Pittsburg and giving the signal, "Death message." Great attention was then paid to "death messages," and I thought I ought to try to take this one. I answered and did so, and went off and delivered it before the operator came. After that the operators sometimes used to ask me to work for them.

Having a sensitive ear for sound, I soon learned to take messages by the ear, which was then very uncommon—I think only two persons in the United States could then do it. Now every operator takes by ear, so easy it is to follow and do what any other boy can—if you only have to. This brought me into notice, and finally I became an operator, and received the, to me, enormous recompense of twenty-five dollars per month—three hundred dollars a year!

This was a fortune—the very sum that I had fixed when I was a factory-worker as the fortune I wished to possess, because the family could live on three hundred dollars a year and be almost or quite independent. Here it was at last! But I was soon to be in receipt of extra compensation for extra work.

The six newspapers of Pittsburg received telegraphic news in common. Six copies of each despatch were made by a gentleman who received six dollars per week for the work, and he offered me a gold dollar every week if I would do it, of which I was very glad indeed, because I always liked to work with news and scribble for newspapers.

The reporters came to a room every evening for the news which I had prepared, and this brought me into most pleasant intercourse with these clever fellows, and besides, I got a dollar a week as pocket-money, for this was not considered family revenue by me.

I think this last step of doing something beyond one's task is fully entitled to be considered "business." The other revenue, you see, was just salary obtained for regular work; but here was a little business operation upon my own account, and I was very proud indeed of my gold dollar every week.

The Pennsylvania Railroad shortly after this was completed to Pittsburg, and that genius, Thomas A. Scott, was its superintendent.

He often came to the telegraph office to talk to his chief, the general superintendent, at Altoona, and I became known to him in this way.

When that great railway system put up a wire of its own, he asked me to be his clerk and operator; so I left the telegraph office—in which there is great danger that a young man may be permanently buried, as it were—and became connected with the railways.

The new appointment was accompanied by what was, to me, a tremendous increase of salary. It jumped from twenty-five to thirty-five dollars per month. Mr. Scott was then receiving one hundred and twenty-five dollars per month, and I used to wonder what on earth he could do with so much money.

I remained for thirteen years in the service of the Pennsylvania Railroad Company, and was at last superintendent of the Pittsburg division of the road, successor to Mr. Scott, who had in the meantime risen to the office of vice-president of the company.

One day Mr. Scott, who was the kindest of men, and had taken a great fancy to me, asked if I had or could find five hundred dollars to invest.

Here the business instinct came into play. I felt that as the door was opened for a business investment with my chief, it would be wilful flying in the face of providence if I did not jump at it; so I answered promptly:

"Yes, sir; I think I can."

"Very well," he said, "get it; a man has just died who owns ten shares in the Adams Express Company which I want you to buy. It will cost you fifty dollars per share, and I can help you with a little balance if you cannot raise it all."

Here was a queer position. The available assets of the whole family were not five hundred dollars. But there was one member of the family whose ability, pluck, and resource never failed us, and I felt sure the money could be raised somehow or other by my mother.

Indeed, had Mr. Scott known our position he would have advanced it himself; but the last thing in the world the proud Scot will do is to reveal his poverty and rely upon others. The family had managed by this time to purchase a small house and pay for it in order to save rent. My recollection is that it was worth eight hundred dollars.

The matter was laid before the council of three that night, and the oracle spoke: "Must be done. Mortgage our house. I will take the steamer in the morning for Ohio, and see uncle, and ask him to arrange it. I am sure he can." This was done. Of course her visit was successful—where did she ever fail?

The money was procured, paid over; ten shares of Adams Express Company stock was mine; but no one knew our little home had been mortgaged "to give our boy a start."

Adams Express stock then paid monthly dividends of one per cent, and the first check for five dollars arrived. I can see it now, and I well remember the signature of "J. C. Babcock, Cashier," who wrote a big "John Hancock" hand.

The next day being Sunday, we boys—myself and my ever-constant companions—took our usual Sunday afternoon stroll in the country, and sitting down in the woods, I showed them this check, saying, "Eureka! We have found it."

Here was something new to all of us, for none of us had ever received anything but from toil. A return from capital was something strange and new.

How money could make money, how, without any attention from me, this mysterious golden visitor should come, led to much speculation upon the part of the young fellows, and I was for the first time hailed as a "capitalist."

You see, I was beginning to serve my apprenticeship as a business man in a satisfactory manner.

A very important incident in my life occurred when, one day in a train, a nice, farmer-looking gentleman approached me, saying that the conductor had told him I was connected with the Pennsylvania Railroad, and he would like to show me something. He pulled from a small green bag the model of the first sleeping-car. This was Mr. Woodruff, the inventor.

Its value struck me like a flash. I asked him to come to Altoona the following week, and he did so. Mr. Scott, with his usual quickness, grasped the idea. A contract was made with Mr. Woodruff to put two trial cars on the Pennsylvania Railroad. Before leaving Altoona Mr. Woodruff came and offered me an interest in the venture, which I promptly accepted. But how I was to make my payments rather troubled me, for the cars were to be paid for in monthly instalments after delivery, and my first monthly payment was to be two hundred and seventeen dollars and a half.

I had not the money, and I did not see any way of getting it. But I finally decided to visit the local banker and ask him for a loan, pledging myself to repay at the rate of fifteen dollars per month. He promptly granted it. Never shall I forget his putting his arm over my shoulder, saying, "Oh, yes, Andy; you are all right!"

I then and there signed my first note. Proud day this; and surely now no one will dispute that I was becoming a "business man." I had signed my first note, and, most important of all,—for any fellow can sign a note,—I had found a banker willing to take it as "good."

My subsequent payments were made by the receipts from the sleeping-cars, and I really made my first considerable sum from this investment in the Woodruff Sleeping-car Company, which was afterward absorbed by Mr. Pullman—a remarkable man whose name is now known over all the world.

Shortly after this I was appointed superintendent of the Pittsburg division, and returned to my dear old home, smoky Pittsburg. Wooden bridges were then used exclusively upon the railways, and the Pennsylvania Railroad was experimenting with a bridge built of cast-iron. I saw that wooden bridges would not do for the future, and organized a company in Pittsburg to build iron bridges.

Here again I had recourse to the bank, because my share of the capital was twelve hundred and fifty dollars, and I had not the money; but the bank lent it to me, and we began the Keystone Bridge Works, which proved a great success. This company built the first great bridge over the Ohio River, three hundred feet span, and has built many of the most important structures since.

This was my beginning in manufacturing; and from that start all our other works have grown, the profits of one building the other. My "apprenticeship" as a business man soon ended, for I resigned my position as an officer of the Pennsylvania Railroad Company to give exclusive attention to business.

I was no longer merely an official working for others upon a salary, but a full-fledged business man working upon my own account.

I never was quite reconciled to working for other people. At the most, the railway officer has to look forward to the enjoyment of a stated salary, and he has a great many people to please; even if he gets to be president, he has sometimes a board of directors who cannot know what is best to be done; and even if this board be satisfied, he has a board of stockholders to criticize him, and as the property is not his own he cannot manage it as he pleases.

I always liked the idea of being my own master, of manufacturing something and giving employment to many men. There is only one thing to think of manufacturing if you are a Pittsburger, for Pittsburg even then had asserted her supremacy as the "Iron City," the leading iron-and-steel-manufacturing city in America.

So my indispensable and clever partners, who had been my boy companions, I am delighted to say,—some of the very boys who had met in the grove to wonder at the five-dollar check,—began business, and still continue extending it to meet the ever-growing and ever-changing wants of our most progressive country, year after year.

Always we are hoping that we need expand no farther; yet ever we are finding that to stop expanding would be to fall behind; and even to-day the successive improvements and inventions follow each other so rapidly that we see just as much yet to be done as ever.

When the manufacturer of steel ceases to grow he begins to decay, so we must keep on extending. The result of all these developments is that three pounds of finished steel are now bought in Pittsburg for two cents, which is cheaper than anywhere else on the earth, and that our country has become the greatest producer of iron in the world.

And so ends the story of my apprenticeship and graduation as a business man.

HAMLIN GARLAND (1860–1940)

Garland was the son of a farmer who had emigrated from Maine to Wisconsin in hopes of making a fortune. But instead of gaining easy wealth, the elder Garland found life on the middle border a dull, bitter, and tiresome struggle with a hostile land.

While still a young man, Hamlin Garland left the Middle West for Boston, where he studied and taught at the Boston School of Oratory. In 1887, Garland paid a visit to his parents, who had moved to South Dakota; on his return to Boston, he began to write a series of short stories as a way of expressing his anger at the hardships and injustices which farm life on the middle border inflicted on its people. These stories were later collected in Main-Travelled Roads *(1891),* Prairie Folks *(1893), and* Wayside Courtships *(1897). Except for his autobiography,* A Son of the Middle Border *(1917), none of his later work has the power of his first stories.*

Under the Lion's Paw

"Along this main-travelled road trailed an endless line of prairie-schooners, coming into sight at the east, and passing out of sight over the swell to the west. We children used to wonder where they were going and why they went."

I

IT WAS the last of autumn and first day of winter coming together. All day long the ploughmen on their prairie farms had moved to and fro in their wide level fields through the falling snow, which melted

From Hamlin Garland, *Main-Travelled Roads*, 1891.

as it fell, wetting them to the skin—all day, notwithstanding the frequent squalls of snow, the dripping, desolate clouds, and the muck of the furrows, black and tenacious as tar.

Under their dripping harness the horses swung to and fro silently, with that marvellous uncomplaining patience which marks the horse. All day the wild geese, honking wildly, as they sprawled sidewise down the wind, seemed to be fleeing from an enemy behind, and with neck outthrust and wings extended, sailed down the wind, soon lost to sight.

Yet the ploughman behind his plough, though the snow lay on his ragged great-coat, and the cold clinging mud rose on his heavy boots, fettering him like gyves, whistled in the very beard of the gale. As day passed, the snow, ceasing to melt, lay along the ploughed land, and lodged in the depth of the stubble, till on each slow round the last furrow stood out black and shining as jet between the ploughed land and the gray stubble.

When night began to fall, and the geese, flying low, began to alight invisibly in the near corn-field, Stephen Council was still at work "finishing a land." He rode on his sulky plough when going with the wind, but walked when facing it. Sitting bent and cold but cheery under his slouch hat, he talked encouragingly to his four-in-hand.

"Come round there, boys!—Round agin! We got t' finish this land. Come in there, Dan! *Stiddy*, Kate,—stiddy! None o'y'r tantrums, Kittie. It's purty tuff, but got a be did. *Tchk! tchk!* Step along, Pete! Don't let Kate git y'r single-tree on the wheel. *Once more!*"

They seemed to know what he meant, and that this was the last round, for they worked with greater vigor than before.

"Once more, boys, an' then, sez I, oats an' a nice warm stall, an' sleep f'r all."

By the time the last furrow was turned on the land it was too dark to see the house, and the snow was changing to rain again. The tired and hungry man could see the light from the kitchen shining through the leafless hedge, and lifting a great shout, he yelled, "Sup*per* f'r a half a dozen!"

It was nearly eight o'clock by the time he had finished his chores and started for supper. He was picking his way carefully through the mud, when the tall form of a man loomed up before him with a premonitory cough.

"Whaddy ye want?" was the rather startled question of the farmer.

"Well, ye see," began the stranger, in a deprecating tone, "we'd like t' git in f'r the night. We've tried every house f'r the last two miles, but they hadn't any room f'r us. My wife's jest about sick, 'n' the children are cold and hungry——"

"Oh, y' want a stay all night, eh?"

"Yes, sir; it 'ud be a great accom——"

"Waal, I don't make it a practice t' turn anybody way hungry, not on sech nights as this. Drive right in. We ain't got much, but sech as it is——"

But the stranger had disappeared. And soon his steaming, weary team, with drooping heads and swinging single-trees, moved past the well to the block beside the path. Council stood at the side of the "schooner" and helped the children out—two little half-sleeping children—and then a small woman with a babe in her arms.

"There ye go!" he shouted jovially, to the children. "*Now* we're all right! Run right along to the house there, an' tell Mam' Council you wants sumpthin' t' eat. Right this way, Mis'—keep right off t' the right there. I'll go an' git a lantern. Come," he said to the dazed and silent group at his side.

"Mother," he shouted, as he neared the fragrant and warmly lighted kitchen, "here are some wayfarers an' folks who need sumpin' t' eat an' a place t' snooze." He ended by pushing them all in.

Mrs. Council, a large, jolly, rather coarse-looking woman, took the children in her arms. "Come right in, you little rabbits. 'Most asleep, hey? Now here's a drink o' milk f'r each o' ye. I'll have s'm tea in a minute. Take off y'r things and set up t' the fire."

While she set the children to drinking milk, Council got out his lantern and went out to the barn to help the stranger about his team, where his loud, hearty voice could be heard as it came and went between the haymow and the stalls.

The woman came to light as a small, timid, and discouraged-looking woman, but still pretty, in a thin and sorrowful way.

"Land sakes! An' you've travelled all the way from Clear Lake t'-day in this mud! Waal! waal! No wonder you're all tired out.

Don't wait f'r the men, Mis'——" She hesitated, waiting for the name.

"Haskins."

"Mis' Haskins, set right up to the table an' take a good swig o' tea whilst I make y' s'm toast. It's green tea, an' it's good. I tell Council as I git older I don't seem to enjoy Young Hyson n'r Gunpowder. I want the reel green tea, jest as it comes off'n the vines. Seems t' have more heart in it, some way. Don't s'pose it has. Council says it's all in m' eye."

Going on in this easy way, she soon had the children filled with bread and milk and the woman thoroughly at home, eating some toast and sweet-melon pickles, and sipping the tea.

"See the little rats!" she laughed at the children. "They're full as they can stick now, and they want to go to bed. Now, don't git up, Mis' Haskins; set right where you are an' let me look after 'em. I know all about young ones, though I'm all alone now. Jane went an' married last fall. But, as I tell Council, it's lucky we keep our health. Set right there, Mis' Haskins; I won't have you stir a finger."

It was an unmeasured pleasure to sit there in the warm, homely kitchen, the jovial chatter of the housewife driving out and holding at bay the growl of the impotent, cheated wind.

The little woman's eyes filled with tears which fell down upon the sleeping baby in her arms. The world was not so desolate and cold and hopeless, after all.

"Now I hope Council won't stop out there and talk politics all night. He's the greatest man to talk politics an' read the *Tribune*. How old is it?"

She broke off and peered down at the face of the babe.

"Two months 'n' five days," said the mother, with a mother's exactness.

"Ye don't say! I want 'o know! The dear little pudzy-wudzy!" she went on, stirring it up in the neighborhood of the ribs with her fat forefinger.

"Pooty tough on 'oo to go gallivant'n' 'cross lots this way——"

"Yes, that's so; a man can't lift a mountain," said Council, entering the door. "Mother, this is Mr. Haskins, from Kansas. He's been eat up 'n' drove out by grasshoppers."

"Glad t' see yeh!—Pa, empty that wash-basin 'n' give him a chance t' wash."

Haskins was a tall man, with a thin, gloomy face. His hair was a reddish brown, like his coat, and seemed equally faded by the wind and sun. And his sallow face, though hard and set, was pathetic somehow. You would have felt that he had suffered much by the line of his mouth showing under his thin, yellow mustache.

"Hain't Ike got home yet, Sairy?"

"Hain't seen 'im."

"W-a-a-l, set right up, Mr. Haskins; wade right into what we've got; 'taint much, but we manage to live on it—she gits fat on it," laughed Council, pointing his thumb at his wife.

After supper, while the women put the children to bed, Haskins and Council talked on, seated near the huge cooking-stove, the steam rising from their wet clothing. In the Western fashion Council told as much of his own life as he drew from his guest. He asked but few questions; but by and by the story of Haskins' struggles and defeat came out. The story was a terrible one, but he told it quietly, seated with his elbows on his knees, gazing most of the time at the hearth.

"I didn't like the looks of the country, anyhow," Haskins said, partly rising and glancing at his wife. "I was ust t' northern Ingy-annie, where we have lots o' timber 'n' lots o' rain, 'n' I didn't like the looks o' that dry prairie. What galled me the worst was goin' s' far away acrosst so much fine land layin' all through here vacant."

"And the 'hoppers eat ye four years hand running', did they?"

"Eat! They wiped us out. They chawed everything that was green. They jest set around waitin' f'r us to die t' eat us, too. My God! I ust t'dream of 'em sittin' 'round on the bedpost, six feet long, workin' their jaws. They eet the fork-handles. They got worse 'n' worse till they jest rolled on one another, piled up like snow in winter. Well, it ain't no use. If I was t' talk all winter I couldn't tell nawthin'. But all the while I couldn't help thinkin' of all that land back here that nobuddy was usin' that I ought 'o had 'stead o' bein' out there in that cussed country."

"Wall, why didn't ye stop an' settle here?" asked Ike, who had come in and was eating his supper.

"Fer the simple reason that you fellers wantid ten 'r fifteen dollars an acre fer the bare land, and I hadn't no money fer that kind o' thing."

"Yes, I do my own work," Mrs. Council was heard to say in the pause which followed. "I'm a gettin' purty heavy t' be on m' laigs all day, but we can't afford t' hire, so I keep rackin' around somehow, like a foundered horse. S'lame—I tell Council he can't tell how lame I am, f'r I'm jest as lame in one laig as t' other." And the good soul laughed at the joke on herself as she took a handful of flour and dusted the biscuit-board to keep the dough from sticking.

"Well, I haint *never* been very strong," said Mrs. Haskins. "Our folks was Canadians an' small-boned, and then since my last child I hain't got up again fairly. I don't like t' complain. Tim has about all he can bear now—but they was days this week when I jest wanted to lay right down an' die."

"Waal, now, I'll tell ye," said Council, from his side of the stove, silencing everybody with his good-natured roar, "I'd go down and *see* Butler, *anyway*, if I was you. I guess he'd let you have his place purty cheap; the farm's all run down. He's been anxious t' let t' somebuddy next year. It 'ud be a good chance fer you. Anyhow, you go to bed and sleep like a babe. I've got some ploughing t' do, anyhow, an' we'll see if somethin' can't be done about your case. Ike, you go out an' see if the horses is all right, an' I'll show the folks t' bed."

When the tired husband and wife were lying under the generous quilts of the spare bed, Haskins listened a moment to the wind in the eaves, and then said with a slow and solemn tone:

"There are people in this world who are good enough t' be angels, an' only haff t' die to *be* angels."

II

Jim Butler was one of those men called in the West "land poor." Early in the history of Rock River he had come into the town and started in the grocery business in a small way, occupying a small building in a mean part of the town. At this period of his life he earned all he got, and was up early and late sorting beans, working over butter, and carting his goods to and from the station. But a change came over him at the end of the second year, when he sold a lot of land for four times what he paid for it. From that time forward he believed in land speculation as the surest way of getting rich. Every cent he could save or spare from his trade he put into land at forced sale, or mortgages on land, which were "just as good as the wheat," he was accustomed to say.

Farm after farm fell into his hands, until he was recognized as one of the leading landowners of the county. His mortgages were scattered all over Cedar County, and as they slowly but surely fell in he sought usually to retain the former owner as tenant.

He was not ready to foreclose; indeed, he had the name of being one of the "easiest" men in the town. He let the debtor off again and again, extending the time whenever possible.

"I don't want y'r land," he said. "All I'm after is the int'rest on my money—that's all. Now, if y' want 'o stay on the farm, why, I'll give y' a good chance. I can't have the land layin' vacant." And in many cases the owner remained as tenant.

In the meantime he had sold his store; he couldn't spend time in it; he was mainly occupied now with sitting around town on rainy days smoking and "gassin' with the boys," or in riding to and from his farms. In fishing-time he fished a good deal. Doc Grimes, Ben Ashley, and Cal Cheatham were his cronies on these fishing excursions or hunting trips in the time of chickens or partridges. In winter they went to Northern Wisconsin to shoot deer.

In spite of all these signs of easy life Butler persisted in saying he hadn't enough money to pay taxes on his land," and was careful to convey the impression that he was poor in spite of his twenty farms. At one time he was said to be worth fifty thousand dollars, but land had been a little slow of sale of late, so that he was not worth so much. A fine farm, known as the Higley place, had fallen into his hands in the usual way the previous year, and he had not been able to find a tenant for it. Poor Higley, after working himself nearly to death on it in the attempt to lift the mortgage, had gone off to Dakota, leaving the farm and his curse to Butler.

This was the farm which Council advised Haskins to apply for; and the next day Council hitched up his team and drove down to see Butler.

"You jest let *me* do the talkin'," he said. "We'll find him wearin' out his pants on some salt barrel somew'ers; and if he thought you *wanted* the place he'd sock it to you hot and heavy. You jest keep quiet; I'll fix 'im."

Butler was seated in Ben Ashley's store telling fish yarns when Council sauntered in casually.

"Hello, But; lyin' agin, hey?"

"Hello, Steve! How goes it?"

"Oh, so-so. Too dang much rain these days. I thought it was gon t' freeze up f'r good last night. Tight squeak if I get m' ploughin done. How's farmin' with *you* these days?"

"Bad. Ploughin' ain't half done."

"It 'ud be a religious idee f'r you t' go out an' take a hand y'rself."

"I don't haff to," said Butler, with a wink.

"Got anybody on the Higley place?"

"No. Know of anybody?"

"Waal, no; not eggsackly. I've got a relation back t' Michigan who's ben hot an' cold on the idee o' comin' West f'r some time Might come if he could get a good lay-out. What do you talk on the farm?"

"Well, I d' know. I'll rent it on shares or I'll rent it money rent."

"Wall, how much money, say?"

"Well, say ten per cent, on the price—two-fifty."

"Wall, that ain't bad. Wait on 'im till 'e thrashes?"

Haskins listened eagerly to this important question, but Council was coolly eating a dried apple which he had speared out of a barrel with his knife. Butler studied him carefully.

"Well, knocks me out of twenty-five dollars interest."

"My relation'll need all he's got t' git his crops in," said Council in the same, indifferent way.

"Well, all right; *say* wait," concluded Butler.

"All right; this is the man. Haskins, this is Mr. Butler—no relation to Ben—the hardest-working man in Cedar County."

On the way home Haskins said: "I ain't much better off. I'd like that farm; it's a good farm, but it's all run down, an' so 'm I. I could make a good farm of it if I had half a show. But I can't stock it n'r seed it."

"Waal, now, don't you worry," roared Council in his ear. "We'll pull y' through somehow till next harvest. He's agreed t' hire it ploughed, an' you can earn a hundred dollars ploughin' an' y' c'n git the seed o' me, an' pay me back when y' can."

Haskins was silent with emotion, but at last he said, "I ain't got nothin' t' live on."

"Now, don't you worry 'bout that. You jest make your headquarters at o' Steve Council's. Mother'll take a pile o' comfort in havin' y'r wife an' children 'round. Y' see, Jane's married off lately, an' Ike's away a good 'eal, so we'll be darn glad t' have y' with us this winter. Nex' spring we'll see if y' can't git a start agin." And he chirruped to the team, which sprang forward with the rumbling, clattering wagon.

"Say, looky here, Council, you can't do this. I never saw——" shouted Haskins in his neighbor's ear.

Council moved about uneasily in his seat and stopped his stammering gratitude by saying: "Hold on, now; don't make such a fuss over a little thing. When I see a man down, an' things all on top of 'm, I jest like t' kick 'em off an' help 'm up. That's the kind of religion I got, an' it's about the *only* kind."

They rode the rest of the way home in silence. And when the red light of the lamp shone out into the darkness of the cold and windy night, and he thought of this refuge for his children and wife, Haskins could have put his arm around the neck of his burly companion and squeezed him like a lover. But he contented himself with saying, "Steve Council, you'll git y'r pay f'r this some day."

"Don't want any pay. My religion ain't run on such business principles."

The wind was growing colder, and the ground was covered with a white frost, as they turned into the gate of the Council farm, and the children came rushing out, shouting, "Papa's come!" They hardly looked like the same children who had sat at the table the night before. Their torpidity, under the influence of sunshine and Mother Council, had given way to a sort of spasmodic cheerfulness, as insects in winter revive when laid on the hearth.

III

Haskins worked like a fiend, and his wife, like the heroic woman that she was, bore also uncomplainingly the most terrible burdens.

They rose early and toiled without intermission till the darkness fell on the plain, then tumbled into bed, every bone and muscle aching with fatigue, to rise with the sun next morning to the same round of the same ferocity of labor.

The eldest boy, now nine years old, drove a team all through the spring, ploughing and seeding, milked the cows, and did chores innumerable, in most ways taking the place of a man; an infinitely pathetic but common figure—this boy—on the American farm, where there is no law against child labor. To see him in his coarse clothing, his huge boots, and his ragged cap, as he staggered with a pail of water from the well, or trudged in the cold and cheerless dawn out into the frosty field behind his team, gave the city-bred visitor a sharp pang of sympathetic pain. Yet Haskins loved this boy, and would have saved him from this if he could, but he could not.

By June the first year the result of such herculean toil began to show on the farm. The yard was cleaned up and sown to grass, the garden ploughed and planted, and the house mended. Council had given them four of his cows.

"Take 'em an' run 'em on shares. I don't want a milk s' many Ike's away s' much now, Sat'd'ys an' Sund'ys, I can't stand the bother anyhow."

Other men, seeing the confidence of Council in the newcomer, had sold him tools on time; and as he was really an able farmer, he soon had round him many evidences of his care and thrift. At the advice of Council he had taken the farm for three years, with the privilege of re-renting or buying at the end of the term.

"It's a good bargain, an' y' want 'o nail it," said Council. "If you have any kind ov a crop, you c'n pay y'r debts, an' keep seed an' bread."

The new hope which now sprang up in the heart of Haskins and his wife grew almost as a pain by the time the wide field of wheat began to wave and rustle and swirl in the winds of July. Day after day he would snatch a few moments after supper to go and look at it.

"Have ye seen the wheat t'-day, Nettie?" he asked one night as he rose from supper.

"No, Tim, I ain't had time."

"Well, take time now. Le's go look at it."

She threw an old hat on her head—Tommy's hat—and looking

almost pretty in her thin, sad way, went out with her husband to the hedge.

"Ain't it grand, Nettie? Just look at it."

It was grand. Level, russet here and there, heavy-headed, wide as a lake, and full of multitudinous whispers and gleams of wealth, it stretched away before the gazers like the fabled field of the cloth of gold.

"Oh, I think—I *hope* we'll have a good crop, Tim; and oh, how good the people have been to us!"

"Yes; I don't know where we'd be t'-day if it hadn't ben f'r Council and his wife."

"They're the best people in the world," said the little woman, with a great sob of gratitude.

"We'll be in the field on Monday, sure," said Haskins, gripping the rail on the fences as if already at the work of the harvest.

The harvest came, bounteous, glorious, but the winds came and blew it into tangles, and the rain matted it here and there close to the ground, increasing the work of gathering it threefold.

Oh, how they toiled in those glorious days! Clothing dripping with sweat, arms aching, filled with briers, fingers raw and bleeding, backs broken with the weight of heavy bundles, Haskins and his man toiled on. Tommy drove the harvester, while his father and a hired man bound on the machine. In this way they cut ten acres every day, and almost every night after supper, when the hand went to bed, Haskins returned to the field shocking the bound grain in the light of the moon. Many a night he worked till his anxious wife came out at ten o'clock to call him in to rest and lunch.

At the same time she cooked for the men, took care of the children, washed and ironed, milked the cows at night, made the butter, and sometimes fed the horses and watered them while her husband kept at the shocking. No slave in the Roman galleys could have toiled so frightfully and lived, for this man thought himself a free man, and that he was working for his wife and babes.

When he sank into his bed with a deep groan of relief, too tired to change his grimy, dripping clothing, he felt that he was getting nearer and nearer to a home of his own, and pushing the wolf of want a little farther from his door.

There is no despair so deep as the despair of a homeless man or woman. To roam the roads of the country or the streets of the city, to feel there is no rood of ground on which the feet can rest, to halt weary and hungry outside lighted windows and hear laughter and song within—these are the hungers and rebellions that drive men to crime and women to shame.

It was the memory of this homelessness, and the fear of its coming again, that spurred Timothy Haskins and Nettie, his wife, to such ferocious labor during that first year.

IV

"'M, yes; 'm, yes; first-rate," said Butler, as his eye took in the neat garden, the pig-pen, and the well-filled barn-yard. "You're gitt'n quite a stock around yeh. Done well, eh?"

Haskins was showing Butler around the place. He had not seen it for a year, having spent the year in Washington and Boston with Ashley, his brother-in-law, who had been elected to Congress.

"Yes, I've laid out a good deal of money durin' the last three years. I've paid out three hundred dollars f'r fencin'."

"Um—h'm! I see, I see," said Butler, while Haskins went on.

"The kitchen there cost two hundred; the barn ain't cost much in money, but I've put a lot o' time on it. I've dug a well, and I——"

"Yes, yes, I see. You've done well. Stock worth a thousand dollars," said Butler, picking his teeth with a straw.

"About that," said Haskins, modestly. "We begin to feel's if we was gitt'n' a home f'r ourselves; but we've worked hard. I tell ye we begin to feel it, Mr. Butler, and we're goin' t' begin to ease up purty soon. We've been kind o' plannin' a trip back t' *her* folks after the fall ploughin's done."

"*Eggs*-actly!" said Butler, who was evidently thinking of something else. "I suppose you've kine o' kalklated on stayin' here three years more?"

"Well, yes. Fact is, I think I c'n buy the farm this fall, if you'll give me a reasonable show."

"Um—m! What do you call a reasonable show?"

"Waal; say a quarter down and three years' time."

Butler looked at the huge stacks of wheat which filled the yard, over which the chickens were fluttering and crawling, catching grasshoppers, and out of which the crickets were singing innumerably. He smiled in a peculiar way as he said, "Oh, I won't be hard on yer. But what did you expect to pay f'r the place?"

"Why, about what you offered it for before, two thousand five hundred, or *possibly* three thousand dollars," he added quickly, as he saw the owner shake his head.

"This farm is worth five thousand and five hundred dollars," said Butler, in a careless and decided voice.

"*What!*" almost shrieked the astounded Haskins. "What's that? Five thousand? Why, that's double what you offered it for three years ago."

"Of course, and it's worth it. It was all run down then; now it's in good shape. You've laid out fifteen hundred dollars in improvements, according to your own story."

"But *you* had nothin' t' do about that. It's my work an' my money."

"You bet it was; but it's my land."

"But what's to pay me for all my——"

"Ain't you had the use of 'em?" replied Butler, smiling calmly into his face.

Haskins was like a man struck on the head with a sandbag; he couldn't think; he stammered as he tried to say: "But—I never'd git the use—You'd rob me! More'n that: you agreed—you promised that I could buy or rent at the end of three years at——"

"That's all right. But I didn't say I'd let you carry off the improvements, nor that I'd go on renting the farm at two-fifty. The land is doubled in value, it don't matter how; it don't enter into the question; an' now you can pay me five hundred dollars a year rent, or take it on your own terms at fifty-five hundred, or—git out."

He was turning away when Haskins, the sweat pouring from his face, fronted him, saying again:

"But *you've* done nothing to make it so. You hain't added a cent. I put it all there myself, expectin' to buy. I worked an' sweat to improve it. I was workin' for myself an' babes——"

"Well, why didn't you buy when I offered to sell? What y' kickin' about?"

"I'm kickin' about payin' you twice f'r my own things,—my own fences, my own kitchen, my own garden."

Butler laughed. "You're too green t' eat, young feller. *Your* improvements! The law will sing another tune."

"But I trusted your word."

"Never trust anybody, my friend. Besides, I didn't promise not to do this thing. Why, man, don't look at me like that. Don't take me for a thief. It's the law. The reg'lar thing. Everybody does it."

"I don't care if they do. It's stealin' jest the same. You take three thousand dollars of my money. The work o' my hands and my wife's." He broke down at this point. He was not a strong man mentally. He could face hardship, ceaseless toil, but he could not face the cold and sneering face of Butler.

"But I don't take it," said Butler coolly. "All you've got to do is to go on jest as you've been a-doin', or give me a thousand dollars down and a mortgage at ten per cent on the rest."

Haskins sat down blindly on a bundle of oats near by, and with staring eyes and drooping head went over the situation. He was under the lion's paw. He felt a horrible numbness in his heart and limbs. He was hid in a mist, and there was no path out.

Butler walked about, looking at the huge stacks of grain, and pulling now and again a few handfuls out, shelling the heads in his hands and blowing the chaff away. He hummed a little tune as he did so. He had an accommodating air of waiting.

Haskins was in the midst of the terrible toil of the last year. He was walking again in the rain and the mud behind his plough; he felt the dust and dirt of the threshing. The ferocious husking-time, with its cutting wind and biting, clinging snows, lay hard upon him. Then he thought of his wife, how she had cheerfully cooked and baked without holiday and without rest.

"Well, what do you think of it?" inquired the cool, mocking, insinuating voice of Butler.

"I think you're a thief and a liar!" shouted Haskins, leaping up. "A black-hearted houn'!" Butler's smile maddened him; with a sudden leap he caught a fork in his hands, and whirled it in the air. "You'll never rob another man, damn ye!" he grated through his teeth, a look of pitiless ferocity in his accusing eyes.

Butler shrank and quivered, expecting the blow; stood, held hypnotized by the eyes of the man he had a moment before despised—a man transformed into an avenging demon. But in the deadly hush between the lift of the weapon and its fall there came a gush of faint, childish laughter and then across the range of his vision, far away and dim, he saw the sun-bright head of his baby girl, as, with the pretty, tottering run of a two-year-old, she moved across the grass of the dooryard. His hands relaxed; the fork fell to the ground; his head lowered.

"Make out y'r deed an' morgige, an' git off'n my land, an' don't ye never cross my line again; if y' do, I'll kill ye."

Butler backed away from the man in wild haste, and climbing into his buggy with trembling limbs, drove off down the road, leaving Haskins seated dumbly on the sunny pile of sheaves, his head sunk into his hands.

OLIVER WENDELL HOLMES, JR.

(1841–1935)

Holmes was born in Boston, the son of the famous physician and poet, Oliver Wendell Holmes. Holmes, Sr., in turn, was the son of Abiel Holmes, a Calvinist minister, who was grieved when his son rejected the Calvinist doctrines of predestination and damnation. This revolt against paternal discipline foreshadowed Oliver Wendell Holmes, Jr.'s refusal to accept the benevolent deity who was the god of his father's universe. In Holmes, Jr.'s view, such a deity was worse than no deity at all, and he opted for the latter alternative.

After graduating from Harvard (A.B., 1861), Holmes received an army commission—the Civil War having just begun—and was soon under fire. In three years of fighting, he rose to the rank of captain and was thrice wounded. For Holmes, the Civil War was the great experience of his life.

After the war, Holmes studied and taught law at Harvard. In 1881 he published The Common Law, *which interpreted its subject not as a rigid, immutable code, but as an accumulation, painfully built up over many centuries. "The life of the law," Holmes wrote, "has not been logic; it has been experience . . . , and it cannot be dealt with as if it contained only the axioms and corollaries of a book of mathematics." From 1883 to 1903, Holmes served first as Justice, then as Chief Justice of the Massachusetts Supreme Court, and from 1903 to 1932 as Justice of the United States Supreme Court.*

Holmes believed that the universe was anarchic and materialistic. Remembering his war experience, however, he believed that there was nevertheless room for faith in such a world—a faith that sprang out of the dauntlessness of the human spirit.

The Soldier's Faith

ANY DAY in Washington Street, when the throng is greatest and busiest, you may see a blind man playing a flute. I suppose that some one hears him. Perhaps also my pipe may reach the heart of some passer in the crowd.

I once heard a man say, "Where Vanderbilt sits, there is the head of the table. I teach my son to be rich." He said what many think. For although the generation born about 1840, and now governing the world, has fought two at least of the greatest wars in history, and has witnessed others, war is out of fashion, and the man who commands the attention of his fellows is the man of wealth. Commerce is the great power. The aspirations of the world are those of commerce. Moralists and philosophers, following its lead, declare that war is wicked, foolish, and soon to disappear.

The society for which many philanthropists, labor reformers, and men of fashion unite in longing is one in which they may be comfortable and may shine without much trouble or any danger. The unfortunately growing hatred of the poor for the rich seems to me to rest on the belief that money is the main thing (a belief in which the poor have been encouraged by the rich), more than on any grievance. Most of my hearers would rather that their daughters or their sisters should marry a son of one of the great rich families than a regular army officer, were he as beautiful, brave, and gifted as Sir William Napier. I have heard the question asked whether our war was worth fighting, after all. There are many, poor and rich, who think that love of country is an old wife's tale, to be replaced by interest in a labor union, or, under the name of cosmopolitanism, by a rootless self-seeking search for a place where the most enjoyment may be had at the least cost.

Meantime we have learned the doctrine that evil means pain, and the revolt against pain in all its forms has grown more and more marked. From societies for the prevention of cruelty to animals up to socialism, we express in numberless ways the notion that suffering is a

From Oliver Wendell Holmes, Jr., *Speeches*, 1896.

wrong which can be and ought to be prevented, and a whole literature of sympathy has sprung into being which points out in story and in verse how hard it is to be wounded in the battle of life, how terrible, how unjust it is that any one should fail.

Even science has had its part in the tendencies which we observe. It has shaken established religion in the minds of very many. It has pursued analysis until at last this thrilling world of colors and sounds and passions has seemed fatally to resolve itself into one vast network of vibrations endlessly weaving an aimless web, and the rainbow flush of cathedral windows, which once to enraptured eyes appeared the very smile of God, fades slowly out into the pale irony of the void.

And yet from vast orchestras still comes the music of mighty symphonies. Our painters even now are spreading along the walls of our Library glowing symbols of mysteries still real, and the hardly silenced cannon of the East proclaim once more that combat and pain still are the portion of man. For my own part, I believe that the struggle for life is the order of the world, at which it is vain to repine. I can imagine the burden changed in the way in which it is to be borne, but I cannot imagine that it ever will be lifted from men's backs. I can imagine a future in which science shall have passed from the combative to the dogmatic stage, and shall have gained such catholic acceptance that it shall take control of life, and condemn at once with instant execution what now is left for nature to destroy. But we are far from such a future, and we cannot stop to amuse or to terrify ourselves with dreams. Now, at least, and perhaps as long as man dwells upon the globe, his destiny is battle, and he has to take the chances of war. If it is our business to fight, the book for the army is a war-song, not a hospital-sketch. It is not well for soldiers to think much about wounds. Sooner or later we shall fall; but meantime it is for us to fix our eyes upon the point to be stormed, and to get there if we can.

Behind every scheme to make the world over, lies the question, What kind of a world do you want? The ideals of the past for men have been drawn from war, as those for women have been drawn from motherhood. For all our prophecies, I doubt if we are ready to give up our inheritance. Who is there who would not like to be thought a gentleman? Yet what has that name been built on but the soldier's choice of honor rather than life? To be a soldier or de-scended from soldiers, in time of peace to be ready to give one's life rather than to suffer disgrace, that is what the word has meant; and if we try to claim it at less cost than a splendid carelessness for life, we are trying to steal the good will without the responsibilities of the place. We will not dispute about tastes. The man of the future may want something different. But who of us could endure a world, al-though cut up into five-acre lots and having no man upon it who was not well fed and well housed, without the divine folly of honor, with-out the senseless passion for knowledge out-reaching the flaming bounds of the possible, without ideals the essence of which is that they never can be achieved? I do not know what is true. I do not know the meaning of the universe. But in the midst of doubt, in the collapse of creeds, there is one thing I do not doubt, that no man who lives in the same world with most of us can doubt, and that is that the faith is true and adorable which leads a soldier to throw away his life in obedience to a blindly accepted duty, in a cause which he little understands, in a plan of campaign of which he has no notion, under tactics of which he does not see the use.

HENRY ADAMS (1838–1918)

The son of Charles Francis Adams (the American Minister to England during the Civil War), the grandson of President John Quincy Adams, and the great-grandson of President John Adams, Henry Adams inevitably felt that the traditions of his family imposed upon him a moral obligation to participate in the leadership of the American democracy.

Endowed with a brilliant mind and an almost too great sensitivity, Adams received a rich and varied education, although he himself later disparaged it, at Harvard (A. B., 1858), on the Continent, and in England, where he served as his father's private secretary.

In 1868, Adams returned to Washington, D. C., but his revulsion at the corruption of the Reconstruction era caused him to decide against an active political career. Instead, Adams became a journalist, a position which allowed him to be observer and judge at the same time. In 1870, Adams returned to Harvard as assistant professor of history. During his years as a professor, Adams was also editor of the influential North American Review. *Resigning his position in 1877, Adams and his wife, whom he had married in 1872, moved back to Washington, where they became the leaders of the intellectual life of the nation's capital.*

If Adams could not be an active participant in politics, he could recall for a generation which seemed to have lost its moral bearings the ideals which had motivated the men who founded the republic. His monumental History of the United States *covering the Administrations of Jefferson and Madison is one of the great achievements of American historiography. Adams also wrote two novels,* Democracy (1880), *which caused an uproar because of its satire of the Gilded Age, and* Esther (1884), *the heroine of which was modeled after*

Adams' wife, a brilliant and beautiful woman, whose suicide in 1885 left Adams a restless wanderer for the rest of his life.

Despite his personal tragedy, Adams continued to write, and he began to formulate a theory of history which he hoped would make history as scientifically predictable as the laws of physics. During the summer of 1895, Adams visited the cathedral of Chartres, which subsequently inspired his book Mont-Saint-Michel and Chartres *(1904), subtitled "A Study of Thirteenth-Century Unity." The medieval worship of the Virgin, which found expression in magnificent cathedrals, was for Adams the driving historical force of an age "when man held the highest idea of himself as a unit in a unified universe."*

As a contrast to the Chartres, *Adams wrote* The Education of Henry Adams *(1907), subtitled "A Study of Twentieth-Century Multiplicity," in which Adams attempted to show his own unfitness for the modern age and expressed his belief that just as the Virgin represented the unity of the Middle Ages, so the dynamo symbolized the acceleratingly anarchic forces at work in the universe and in modern society.*

If we cannot accept Adams' equation of history and physics, his writings—especially the Education—*nevertheless illuminate a most significant historical phenomenon: the alienation of the post-Civil War American intellectual from his traditional role as a leader of American society. As his essay on "American Ideals" makes clear, Adams was an ardent patriot—a fact which only deepened the pain of his alienation and his sense of loss.*

American Ideals

O F ALL POETS, living or dead, Wordsworth felt most keenly what he called the still, sad music of humanity; yet the highest conception he could create of America was not more poetical than that of any Cumberland beggar he might have met in his morning walk:—

From Henry Adams, *History of the United States of America During the Adminstrations of Thomas Jefferson and James Madison,* 1889-91.

"Long-wished-for sight, the Western World appeared;
And when the ship was moored, I leaped ashore
Indignantly,—resolved to be a man,
Who, having o'er the past no power, would live
No longer in subjection to the past,
With abject mind—from a tyrannic lord
Inviting penance, fruitlessly endured.
So, like a fugitive whose feet have cleared
Some boundary which his followers may not cross
In prosecution of their deadly chase,
Respiring, I looked round. How bright the sun,
The breeze how soft! Can anything produced
In the Old World compare, thought I, for power
And majesty, with this tremendous stream
Sprung from the desert? And behold a city
Fresh, youthful, and aspiring! . . .
                                        Sooth to say,
On nearer view, a motley spectacle
Appeared, of high pretensions—unreproved
But by the obstreperous voice of higher still;
Big passions strutting on a petty stage,
Which a detached spectator may regard
Not unamused. But ridicule demands
Quick change of objects; and to laugh alone,
. . . in the very centre of the crowd
To keep the secret of a poignant scorn,
                                . . . is least fit
For the gross spirit of mankind."

Thus Wordsworth, although then at his prime, indulging in what sounded like a boast that he alone had felt the sense sublime of something interfused, whose dwelling is the light of setting suns, and the round ocean, and the living air, and the blue sky, and in the mind of man,—even he, whose moods the heavy and the weary weight of all this unintelligible world was lightened by his deeper sympathies with nature and the soul, could do no better, when he stood in the face of American democracy, than "keep the secret of a poignant scorn."

Possibly the view of Wordsworth and Moore, of Weld, Dennie, and Dickens was right. The American democrat possessed little art of expression, and did not watch his own emotions with a view of uttering them either in prose or verse; he never told more of himself than the world might have assumed without listening to him. Only with diffidence could history attribute to such a class of men a wider range of thought or feeling than they themselves cared to proclaim. Yet the difficulty of denying or even ignoring the wider range was still greater, for no one questioned the force or the scope of an emotion which caused the poorest peasant in Europe to see what was invisible to poet and philosopher,—the dim outline of a mountain-summit across the ocean, rising high above the mist and mud of American democracy. As though to call attention to some such difficulty, European and American critics, while affirming that Americans were a race without illusions or enlarged ideas, declared in the same breath that Jefferson was a visionary whose theories would cause the heavens to fall upon them. Year after year, with endless iteration, in every accent of contempt, rage, and despair, they repeated this charge against Jefferson. Every foreigner and Federalist agreed that he was a man of illusions, dangerous to society and unbounded in power of evil; but if this view of his character was right, the same visionary qualities seemed also to be a national trait, for every one admitted that Jefferson's opinions, in one form or another, were shared by a majority of the American people.

Illustrations might be carried much further, and might be drawn from every social class and from every period in national history. Of all presidents, Abraham Lincoln has been considered the most typical representative of American society, chiefly because his mind, with all its practical qualities, also inclined, in certain directions, to idealism. Lincoln was born in 1809, the moment when American character stood in lowest esteem. Ralph Waldo Emerson, a more distinct idealist, was born in 1803. William Ellery Channing, another idealist, was born in 1780. Men like John Fitch, Oliver Evans, Robert Fulton, Joel Barlow, John Stevens, and Eli Whitney were all classed among visionaries. The whole society of Quakers belonged in the same category. The records of the popular religious sects abounded in examples of idealism and illusion to such an extent that the masses seemed hardly to find comfort or hope in any authority, however old or well established. In religion as in politics, Americans seemed to require a system which gave play to their imagination and their hopes.

Some misunderstanding must always take place when the observer is at cross-purposes with the society he describes. Wordsworth might have convinced himself by a moment's thought that no country could act on the imagination as America acted upon the instincts of the ignorant and poor, without some quality that deserved better treatment than poignant scorn; but perhaps this was only one among innumerable cases in which the unconscious poet breathed in atmosphere which the self-conscious poet could not penetrate. With equal reason he might have taken the opposite view,—that the hard, practical, money-getting American democrat, who had neither generosity nor honor nor imagination, and who inhabited cold shades where fancy sickened and where genius died, was in truth living in a world of dream, and acting a drama more instinct with poetry than all the avatars of the East, walking in gardens of emerald and rubies, in ambition already ruling the world and guiding Nature with a kinder and wiser hand than had ever yet been felt in human history. From this point his critics never approached him,—they stopped at a stone's throw; and at the moment when they declared that the man's mind had no illusions, they added that he was a knave or a lunatic. Even on his practical and sordid side, the American might easily have been represented as a victim to illusion. If the Englishman had lived as the American speculator did,—in the future,—the hyperbole of enthusiasm would have seemed less monstrous. "Look at my wealth!" cried the American to his foreign visitor. "See these solid mountains of salt and iron, of lead, copper, silver, and gold! See these magnificent cities scattered broadcast to the Pacific! See my cornfields rustling and waving in the summer breeze from ocean to ocean, so far that the sun itself is not high enough to mark where the distant mountains bound my golden seas! Look at this continent of mine, fairest of created worlds, as she lies turning up to the sun's never-failing caress her broad and exuberant breasts, overflowing with milk for her hundred million children! See how she glows with youth, health, and love!" Perhaps it was not altogether unnatural that the foreigner, on being asked to see what needed centuries to produce, should have looked about him with bewilderment and indignation. "Gold! cities! cornfields! continents! Nothing of the sort! I see nothing but tremendous wastes, where sickly men and women are dying of homesickness or are scalped by savages! mountain-ranges a thousand miles long, with no means of getting to them, and nothing in them when you get there! swamps and forests choked with their own rotten ruins! nor hope of better for a thousand years! Your story is a fraud, and you are a liar and swindler!"

Met in this spirit, the American, half perplexed and half defiant, retaliated by calling his antagonist a fool, and by mimicking his heavy tricks of manner. For himself he cared little, but his dream was his whole existence. The men who denounced him admitted that they left him in his forest-swamp quaking with fever, but clinging in the delirium of death to the illusions of his dazzled brain. No class of men could be required to support their convictions with a steadier faith, or pay more devotedly with their persons for the mistakes of their judgment. Whether imagination or greed led them to describe more than actually existed, they still saw no more than any inventor or discoverer must have seen in order to give him the energy of success. They said to the rich as to the poor, "Come and share our limitless riches! Come and help us bring to light these unimaginable stores of wealth and power!" The poor came, and from them were seldom heard complaints of deception or delusion. Within a moment, by the mere contact of a moral atmosphere, they saw the gold and jewels, the summer cornfields and the growing continent. The rich for a long time stood aloof,—they were timid and narrow-minded; but this was not all,—between them and the American democrat was a gulf.

The charge that Americans were too fond of money to win the confidence of Europeans was a curious inconsistency; yet this was a common belief. If the American deluded himself and led others to their death by baseless speculations; if he buried those he loved in a gloomy forest where they quaked and died while he persisted in seeing there a splendid, healthy, and well-built city,—no one could deny that he sacrificed wife and child to his greed for gain, that the dollar was his god, and a sordid avarice his demon. Yet had this been the whole truth, no European capitalist would have hesitated to make money out of his grave; for, avarice against avarice, no more sordid or meaner type existed in America than could be shown on every 'Change in Europe. With much more reason Americans might have suspected that in America Englishmen found everywhere a silent influence, which they found nowhere in Europe, and which had nothing to do with avarice or with the dollar, but, on the contrary, seemed likely at any moment to sacrifice the dollar in a cause and for an object so illusory that most Englishmen could not endure to hear it discussed. European travellers who passed through America noticed that everywhere, in the White House at Washington and in log-cabins beyond the Alleghanies, except for a few Federalists, every American, from Jefferson and Gallatin down to the poorest squatter, seemed to nourish an idea that he was doing what he could to over-throw the tyranny which the past had fastened on the human mind. Nothing was easier than to laugh at the ludicrous expressions of this simple-minded conviction, or to cry out against its coarseness, or grow angry with its prejudices; to see its nobler side, to feel the beatings of a heart underneath the sordid surface of a gross humanity, was not so easy. Europeans seemed seldom or never conscious that the sentiment could possess a noble side, but found only matter for complaint in the remark that every American democrat believed himself to be working for the overthrow of tyranny, aristocracy, hereditary privilege, and priesthood, wherever they existed. Even where the American did not openly proclaim this conviction in words, he carried so dense an at-mosphere of the sentiment with him in his daily life as to give re-spectable Europeans an uneasy sense of remoteness. . . .

In the early days of colonization, every new settlement represented an idea and proclaimed a mission. Virginia was founded by a great, liberal movement aiming at the spread of English liberty and empire. The Pilgrims of Plymouth, the Puritans of Boston, the Quakers of Pennsylvania, all avowed a moral purpose, and began by making in-stitutions that consciously reflected a moral idea. No such character belonged to the colonization of 1800. From Lake Erie to Florida, in long, unbroken line, pioneers were at work, cutting into the forests with the energy of so many beavers, and with no more express moral purpose than the beavers they drove away. The civilization they car-ried with them was rarely illumined by an idea; they sought room for no new truth, and aimed neither at creating, like the Puritans, a government of saints, nor, like the Quakers, one of love and peace; they left such experiments behind them, and wrestled only with the hardest problems of frontier life. No wonder that foreign observers, and even the educated, well-to-do Americans of the sea-coast, could seldom see anything to admire in the ignorance and brutality of fron-tiersmen, and should declare that virtue and wisdom no longer guided the United States! What they saw was not encouraging. To a new society, ignorant and semi-barbarous, a mass of demagogues in-sisted on applying every stimulant that could inflame its worst appe-tites, while at the same instant taking away every influence that had hitherto helped to restrain its passions. Greed for wealth, lust for power, yearning for the blank void of savage freedom such as Indians and wolves delighted in,—these were the fires that flamed under the caldron of American society, in which, as conservatives believed, the old, well-proven, conservative crust of religion, government, family, and even common respect for age, education, and experience was rapidly melting away, and was indeed already broken into fragments, swept about by the seething mass of scum ever rising in greater quan-tities to the surface. . . .

Yet even then one part of the American social system was proving itself to be rich in results. The average American was more intelligent than the average European, and was becoming every year still more active-minded as the new movement of society caught him up and swept him through a life of more varied experiences. On all sides the national mind responded to its stimulants. Deficient as the American was in the machinery of higher instruction; remote, poor; unable by any exertion to acquire the training, the capital, or even the elemen-tary textbooks he needed for a fair development of his natural pow-ers,—his native energy and ambition already responded to the spur applied to them. Some of his triumphs were famous throughout the world; for Benjamin Franklin had raised high the reputation of American printers, and the actual President of the United States, who signed with Franklin the treaty of peace with Great Britain, was the son of a small farmer, and had himself kept a school in his youth. In both these cases social recognition followed success; but the later tri-umphs of the American mind were becoming more and more popular. John Fitch was not only one of the poorest, but one of the least-educated Yankees who ever made a name; he could never spell with tolerable correctness, and his life ended as it began,—in the lowest social obscurity. Eli Whitney was better educated than Fitch, but had neither wealth, social influence, nor patron to back his ingenuity. In the year 1800 Eli Terry, another Connecticut Yankee of the same class, took into his employ two young men to help him make wooden clocks, and this was the capital on which the greatest clock-manufactory in the world began its operations. In 1797 Asa Whittemore, a Massachusetts Yankee, invented a machine to make cards for carding wool, which "operated as if it had a soul," and became the foundation for a hundred subsequent patents. In 1790 Jacob Perkins, of Newburyport, invented a machine capable of cutting and turning out two hundred thousand nails a day; and then invented a process for transferring engraving from a very small steel cylinder to copper, which revolutionized cotton-printing. The British traveller Weld, passing through Wilmington, stopped, as Liancourt had done before him, to see the great flour-mills on the Brandywine. "The improvements," he said, "which have been made in the machinery of the flour-mills in America are very great. The chief of these consist in a new application of the screw, and the introduction of what are called elevators, the idea of which was evidently borrowed from the chain-pump." This was the invention of Oliver Evans, a native of Delaware, whose parents were in very humble life, but who was himself, in spite of every disadvantage, an inventive genius of the first order. Robert Fulton, who in 1800 was in Paris with Joel Barlow, sprang from the same source in Pennsylvania. John Stevens, a native of New York, belonged to a more favored class, but followed the same impulses. All these men were the outcome of typical American society, and all their inventions transmuted the democratic instinct into a practical and tangible shape. Who would undertake to say that there was a limit to the fecundity of this teeming source? Who that saw only the narrow, practical, money-getting nature of these devices could venture to assert that as they wrought their end and raised the standard of millions, they would not also raise the creative power of those millions to a higher plane? If the priests and barons who set their names to Magna Charta had been told that in a few centuries every swine-herd and cobbler's apprentice would write and read with an ease such as few kings could then command, and reason with better logic than any university could then practise, the priest and baron would have been more incredulous than any man who was told in 1800 that within another five centuries the ploughboy would go a-field whistling a sonata of Beethoven, and figure out in quaternions the relation of his furrows. The American democrat knew so little of art that among his popular illusions he could not then nourish artistic ambition; but leaders like Jefferson, Gallatin, and Barlow might without extravagance count upon a coming time when diffused ease and education should bring the masses into familiar contact with higher forms of human achievement, and their vast creative power, turned toward a nobler culture, might rise to the level of that democratic genius which found expression in the Parthenon; might revel in the delights of a new Buonarotti and a richer Titian; might create for five hundred million people the America of thought and art which alone could satisfy their omnivorous ambition.

Whether the illusions, so often affirmed and so often denied to the American people, took such forms or not, there were in effect the problems that lay before American society: Could it transmute its social power into the higher forms of thought? Could it provide for the moral and intellectual needs of mankind? Could it take permanent political shape? Could it give new life to religion and art? Could it create and maintain in the mass of mankind those habits of mind which had hitherto belonged to men of science alone? Could it physically develop the convolutions of the human brain? Could it produce, or was it compatible with, the differentiation of a higher variety of the human race? Nothing less than this was necessary for its complete success.

WILLIAM JAMES (1842–1910)

William James and his equally famous brother, Henry, the nove-list, received a rich and cosmopolitan education in the United States, England, Switzerland, France, and Germany. Their father, Henry James, Sr., was also a vital source of ideas.

In his young manhood, William James embarked on a variety of careers. For a time, he thought of becoming a painter. He spent some time as a student at the Lawrence Scientific School at Harvard. In 1869, he took a degree at the Harvard Medical School. During these years, James suffered periods of physical semi-invalidism and pro-found psychological depression. He was plagued by the conflict be-tween science and theology, centering around the question of whether man was merely a biological organism whose life was determined by circumstance, or whether he was a free moral agent. In 1870, James read Charles Renouvier's Rational Psychology *which convinced him that man does indeed possess a moral freedom, a conviction that helped James immensely in his battle to regain his health.*

Beginning in 1872, James taught psychology at Harvard. In 1890, he published his Principles of Psychology, *in which he asserted that the mind is a determiner of events in the sense that one's response to external events can help to shape future events. "The knower," James wrote, "is an actor and coefficient of the truth on one side, whilst on the other he registers the truth which he helps to create."*

From this concept of human psychology sprang James's pragmatic philosophy, which he expounded in The Will to Believe and Other Essays *(1897),* The Varieties of Religious Experience *(1902), and* Pragmatism: A New Name for Some Old Ways of Thinking *(1907). James's pragmatism centers around the theory that the ideas which the mind in its totality conceives cannot be abstracted from the inter-action of intellect and environment. Thus only by being practically*

*tested can ideas prove their emotional validity for the individual.
James asserted that there were no universal dogmas which sum up
truth, for what is true for one man may not be for another. Similarly,
he maintained that supernatural beliefs, which cannot be proved
scientifically, are justifiable in that religious faith can give an impetus
to action and are therefore "real."*

What Pragmatism Means

S OME YEARS ago, being with a camping party in the mountains, I
returned from a solitary ramble to find every one engaged in a ferocious metaphysical dispute. The *corpus* of the dispute was a squirrel
—a live squirrel supposed to be clinging to one side of a tree-trunk;
while over against the tree's opposite side a human being was imagined to stand. This human witness tries to get sight of the squirrel
by moving rapidly round the tree, but no matter how fast he goes,
the squirrel moves as fast in the opposite direction, and always keeps
the tree between himself and the man, so that never a glimpse of him
is caught. The resultant metaphysical problem now is this: *Does the
man go round the squirrel or not?* He goes round the tree, sure
enough, and the squirrel is on the tree; but does he go round the
squirrel? In the unlimited leisure of the wilderness discussion had
been worn threadbare. Every one had taken sides and was obstinate;
and the numbers on both sides were even. Each side, when I appeared, therefore appealed to me to make it a majority. Mindful of
the scolastic adage that whenever you meet a contradiction you must
make a distinction, I immediately sought and found one, as follows;
"Which party is right," I said, "depends on what you *practically
mean* by 'going round' the squirrel. If you mean passing from the
north of him to the east, then to the south, then to the west, and then
to the north of him again, obviously the man does go round him, for
he occupies these successive positions. But if on the contrary you mean
being first in front of him, then on the right of him, then behind him,

From William James, *Pragmatism* (New York; Longmans, Green; 1907), pp. 43-55.

then on his left, and finally in front again, it is quite obvious that the man fails to go round him, for by compensating movements the squirrel makes, he keeps his belly turned towards the man all the time, and his back turned away. Make the distinction, and there is no occasion for any further dispute. You are both right and both wrong, according as you conceive the verb 'to go round' in one practical fashion or the other."

Although one or two of the hotter disputants called my speech a shuffling evasion, saying they wanted no quibbling or scholastic hair-splitting, but meant just plain honest English "round," the majority seemed to think that the distinction had assuaged the dispute.

I tell this trivial anecdote because it is a peculiarly simple example of what I wish now to speak of as *the pragmatic method*. The pragmatic method is primarily a method of settling metaphysical disputes that otherwise might be interminable. Is the world one or many?—fated or free?—material or spiritual?—here are notions either of which may or may not hold good of the world; and disputes over such notions are unending. The pragmatic method in such cases is to try to interpret each notion by tracing its respective practical consequences. What difference would it practically make to any one if this notion rather than that notion were true? If no practical difference whatever can be traced, then the alternatives mean practically the same thing, and all dispute is idle. Whenever a dispute is serious, we ought to be able to show some practical difference that must follow from one side or the other's being right.

A glance at the history of the idea will show you still better what pragmatism means. The term is derived from the same Greek word πράγμα, meaning action, from which our words "practice" and "practical" come. It was first introduced into philosophy by Mr. Charles Peirce in 1878. In an article entitled "How to Make Our Ideas Clear," in the *Popular Science Monthly* for January of 1879, Mr. Peirce, after pointing out that our beliefs are really rules for action, said that, to develop a thought's meaning, we need only determine what conduct it is fitted to produce: that conduct is for us its sole significance. And the tangible fact at the root of all our thought-distinctions, however subtle, is that there is no one of them so fine as to consist in anything but a possible difference of practice. To attain perfect clearness in our thoughts of an object, then, we need only consider what conceivable effects of a practical kind the object may involve—what sensations we are to expect from it, and what reactions we must prepare. Our conception of these effects, whether immediate or remote, is then for us the whole of our conception of the object, so far as that conception has positive significance at all.

This is the principle of Peirce, the principle of pragmatism. It lay entirely unnoticed by any one for twenty years, until I, in an address before Professor Howison's philosophical union at the university of California, brought it forward again and made a special application of it to religion. By that date (1898) the times seemed ripe for its reception. The word "pragmatism" spread, and at present it fairly spots the pages of the philosophic journals. On all hands we find the "pragmatic movement" spoken of, sometimes with respect, sometimes with contumely, seldom with clear understanding. It is evident that the term applies itself conveniently to a number of tendencies that hitherto have lacked a collective name, and that it has "come to stay."

To take in the importance of Peirce's principle, one must get accustomed to applying it to concrete cases. I found a few years ago that Ostwald, the illustrious Leipzig chemist, had been making perfectly distinct use of the principle of pragmatism in his lectures on the philosophy of science, though he had not called it by that name.

"All realities influence our practice," he wrote me, "and that influence is their meaning for us. I am accustomed to put questions to my classes in this way: In what respects would the world be different if this alternative or that were true? If I can find nothing that would become different, then the alternative has no sense."

That is, the rival views mean practically the same thing, and meaning, other than practical, there is for us none. Ostwald in a published lecture gives this example of what he means. Chemists have long wrangled over the inner constitution of certain bodies called "tautomerous." Their properties seemed equally consistent with the notion that an instable hydrogen atom oscillates inside of them, or that they are instable mixtures of two bodies. Controversy raged, but never was decided. "It would never have begun," says Ostwald, "if the combatants had asked themselves what particular experimental

fact could have been made different by one or the other view being
correct. For it would then have appeared that no difference of fact
could possibly ensue; and the quarrel was as unreal as if, theorising
in primitive times about the raising of dough by yeast, one party
should have invoked a 'brownie,' while another insisted on an 'elf' as
the true cause of the phenomenon."

It is astonishing to see how many philosophical disputes collapse
into insignificance the moment you subject them to this simple test of
tracing a concrete consequence. There can *be* no difference anywhere
that doesn't *make* a difference elsewhere—no difference in abstract
truth that doesn't express itself in a difference in concrete fact and
in conduct consequent upon that fact, imposed on somebody, somehow, somewhere, and somewhen. The whole function of philosophy
ought to be to find out what definite difference it will make to you
and me, at definite instants of our life, if this world-formula or that
world-formula be the true one.

There is absolutely nothing new in the pragmatic method. Socrates
was an adept at it. Aristotle used it methodically. Locke, Berkeley,
and Hume made momentous contributions to truth by its means.
Shadworth Hodgson keeps insisting that realities are only what they
are "known as." But these forerunners of pragmatism used it in
fragments: they were a prelude only. Not until in our time has it
generalized itself, become conscious of a universal mission, pretended
to a conquering destiny. I believe in that destiny, and I hope I may
end by inspiring you with my belief.

Pragmatism represents a perfectly familiar attitude in philosophy,
the empiricist attitude, but it represents it, as it seems to me, both in
a more radical and in a less objectionable form than it has ever yet
assumed. A pragmatist turns his back resolutely and once for all upon
a lot of inveterate habits dear to professional philosophers. He turns
away from abstraction and insufficiency, from verbal solutions, from
bad *a priori* reasons, from fixed principles, closed systems, and pretended absolutes and origins. He turns towards concreteness and
adequacy, towards facts, towards action and towards power. That
means the empiricist temper regnant and the rationalist temper sincerely given up. It means the open air and possibilities of nature, as
against dogma, artificiality, and the pretence of finality in truth.

At the same time it does not stand for any special results. It is a method only. But the general triumph of that method would mean an enormous change in what I called in my last lecture the "temperament" of philosophy. Teachers of the ultra-rationalistic type would be frozen out, much as the courtier type is frozen out in republics, as the ultra-montane type of priest is frozen out in protestant lands. Science and metaphysics would come much nearer together, would in fact work absolutely hand in hand.

Metaphysics has usually followed a very primitive kind of quest. You know how men have always hankered after unlawful magic, and you know what a great part in magic *words* have always played. If you have his name, or the formula of incantation that binds him, you can control the spirit, genie, afrite, or whatever the power may be. Solomon knew the names of all the spirits, and having their names, he held them subject to his will. So the universe has always appeared to the natural mind as a kind of enigma, of which the key must be sought in the shape of some illuminating or power-bringing word or name. That word names the universe's *principle*, and to possess it is after a fashion to possess the universe itself. "God," "Matter," "Reason," "the Absolute," "Energy," are so many solving names. You can rest when you have them. You are at the end of your metaphysical quest.

But if you follow the pragmatic method you cannot look on any such word as closing your quest. You must bring out of each word its practical cash-value, set it at work within the stream of your experience. It appears less as a solution, then, than as a programme for more work, and more particularly as an indication of the ways in which existing realities may be *changed*.

Theories thus become instruments, not answers to enigmas, in which we can rest. We don't lie back upon them, we move forward, and, on occasion, make nature over again by their aid. Pragmatism unstiffens all our theories, limbers them up and sets each one at work. Being nothing essentially new, it harmonizes with many ancient philosophic tendencies. It agrees with nominalism, for instance, in always appealing to particulars; with utilitarianism in emphasizing practical aspects; with positivism in its disdain for verbal solutions, useless questions, and metaphysical abstractions.

All these, you see, are *anti-intellectualist* tendencies. Against rationalism as a pretension and a method pragmatism is fully armed and militant. But, at the outset, at least, it stands for no particular results. It has no dogmas, and no doctrines save its method. As the young Italian pragmatist Papini has well said, it lies in the midst of our theories like a corridor in a hotel. Innumerable chambers open out of it. In one you may find a man writing an atheistic volume; in the next some one on his knees praying for faith and strength; in a third a chemist investigating a body's properties; in a fourth a system of idealistic metaphysics is being excogitated; in a fifth the impossibility of metaphysics is being shown. But they all own the corridor, and all must pass through it if they want a practicable way of getting into or out of their respective rooms.

No particular results then, so far, but only an attitude of orientation, is what the pragmatic method means. *The attitude of looking away from first things, principles, "categories," supposed necessities; and of looking towards last things, fruits, consequences, facts.*

JANE ADDAMS (1860–1935)

The rapid expansion of American industry in the post-Civil War years caused a phenomenal urban growth. Thus Chicago had 150 inhabitants in 1833, but by 1890 had a population of more than a million, mostly industrial workers crowded into extensive slums. The difficulty of this situation was aggravated by the fact that nearly three fourths of the workers were first-generation immigrants from eastern and southern Europe who spoke little or no English and were regarded as innately inferior by many Americans of Protestant, Anglo-Saxon stock.

Yet there were also Americans of the older breed who, imbued with a sense of social responsibility and thoroughly optimistic about their capacity to influence history, felt an obligation to improve the living conditions of the urban immigrant.

One of the most famous and successful experiments in social improvement was Jane Addams's Hull-House, founded in Chicago in 1889. The daughter of a miller in Cedarville, Illinois, Jane Addams went to Rockford College (A.B., 1882), then entered the Women's Medical College of Philadelphia. On a trip to England, however, she visited Toynbee Hall, an East End settlement house, and was inspired to found Hull-House. The activities at Hull-House eventually included an art gallery, kindergartens, classes in arts and crafts, concerts, women's cooperatives, counseling for juvenile delinquents, as well as a soup kitchen for the needy. Jane Addams was also a champion of women's rights and a pacifist, serving as president for many years of the Women's International League for Peace and Freedom. Her vision of the increasingly important role to be played by women in modern society illuminates an important aspect of twentieth-century American culture.

The following selection is from Twenty Years at Hull-House *(1910), which gives a classic description of Chicago slum life.*

Public Activities and Investigations

O N E of the striking features of our neighborhood twenty years ago, and one to which we never became reconciled, was the presence of huge wooden garbage boxes fastened to the street pavements in which the undisturbed refuse accumulated day by day. The system of garbage collecting was inadequate throughout the city but it became the greatest menace in a ward such as ours, where the normal amount of waste was much increased by the decayed fruit and vegetables discarded by the Italian and Greek fruit peddlers, and by the residuum left over from the piles of filthy rags which were fished out of the city dumps and brought to the homes of the rag pickers for further sorting and washing.

The children of our neighborhood twenty years ago played their games in and around these huge garbage boxes. They were the first objects that the toddling child learned to climb; their bulk afforded a barricade and their contents provided missiles in all the battles of the older boys; and finally they became the seats upon which absorbed lovers held enchanted converse. We are obliged to remember that all children eat everything which they find and that odors have a curious and intimate power of entwining themselves into our tenderest memories, before even the residents of Hull-House can understand their own early enthusiasm for the removal of these boxes and the establishment of a better system of refuse collection.

It is easy for even the most conscientious citizen of Chicago to forget the foul smells of the stockyards and the garbage dumps, when he is living so far from them that he is only occasionally made conscious of their existence but the residents of a Settlement are perforce constantly surrounded by them. During our first three years on Halsted Street, we had established a small incinerator at Hull-House

From Jane Addams, *Twenty Years at Hull House* (New York, Macmillan, 1910, 1938), pp. 281-291.

and we had many times reported the untoward conditions of the ward to the city hall. We had also arranged many talks for the immigrants, pointing out that although a woman may sweep her own doorway in her native village and allow the refuse to innocently decay in the open air and sunshine, in a crowded city quarter, if the garbage is not properly collected and destroyed, a tenement-house mother may see her children sicken and die, and that the immigrants must therefore, not only keep their own houses clean, but must also help the authorities to keep the city clean.

Possibly our efforts slightly modified the worst conditions but they still remained intolerable, and the fourth summer the situation became for me absolutely desperate when I realized in a moment of panic that my delicate little nephew for whom I was guardian, could not be with me at Hull-House at all unless the sickening odors were reduced. I may well be ashamed that other delicate children who were torn from their families, not into boarding school but into eternity, had not long before driven me to effective action. Under the direction of the first man who came as a resident to Hull-House we began a systematic investigation of the city system of garbage collection, both as to its efficiency in other wards and its possible connection with the death rate in the various wards of the city.

The Hull-House Woman's Club had been organized the year before by the resident kindergartner who had first inaugurated a mothers' meeting. The members came together, however, in quite a new way that summer when we discussed with them the high death rate so persistent in our ward. After several club meetings devoted to the subject, despite the fact that the death rate rose highest in the congested foreign colonies and not in the streets in which most of the Irish American club women lived, twelve of their number undertook in connection with the residents, to carefully investigate the condition of the alleys. During August and September the substantiated reports of violations of the law sent in from Hull-House to the health department were one thousand and thirty-seven. For the club woman who had finished a long day's work of washing or ironing followed by the cooking of a hot supper, it would have been much easier to sit on her doorstep during a summer evening than to go up and down ill-kept alleys and get into trouble with her neighbors over the condition of their garbage boxes. It required both civic enterprise and moral conviction to be willing to do this three evenings a week during the hottest and most uncomfortable months of the year. Nevertheless, a certain number of women persisted, as did the residents and three city inspectors in succession were transferred from the ward because of unsatisfactory services. Still the death rate remained high and the condition seemed little improved throughout the next winter. In sheer desperation, the following spring when the city contracts were awarded for the removal of garbage, with the backing of two well-known business men, I put in a bid for the garbage removal of the nineteenth ward. My paper was thrown out on a technicality but the incident induced the mayor to appoint me the garbage inspector of the ward.

The salary was a thousand dollars a year, and the loss of that political "plum" made a great stir among the politicians. The position was no sinecure whether regarded from the point of view of getting up at six in the morning to see that the men were early at work; or of following the loaded wagons, uneasily dropping their contents at intervals, to their dreary destination at the dump; or of insisting that the contractor must increase the number of his wagons from nine to thirteen and from thirteen to seventeen, although he assured me that he lost money on every one and that the former inspector had let him off with seven; or of taking careless landlords into court because they would not provide the proper garbage receptacles; or of arresting the tenant who tried to make the garbage wagons carry away the contents of his stable.

With the two or three residents who nobly stood by, we set up six of those doleful incinerators which are supposed to burn garbage with the fuel collected in the alley itself. The one factory in town which could utilize old tin cans was a window weight factory, and we deluged that with ten times as many tin cans as it could use—much less would pay for. We made desperate attempts to have the dead animals removed by the contractor who was paid most liberally by the city for that purpose but who, we slowly discovered, always made the police ambulances do the work, delivering the carcasses upon freight cars for shipment to a soap factory in Indiana where they were sold for a good price although the contractor himself was the largest stockholder in the concern. Perhaps our greatest achievement was the discovery of a pavement eighteen inches under the surface in a narrow street; although after it was found we triumphantly discovered a record of its existence in the city archives. The Italians living on the street were much interested but displayed little astonishment, perhaps because they were accustomed to see buried cities exhumed. This pavement became the *casus belli* between myself and the street commissioner when I insisted that its restoration belonged to him, after I had removed the first eight inches of garbage. The matter was finally settled by the mayor himself, who permitted me to drive him to the entrance of the street in what the children called my "garbage phaëton" and who took my side of the controversy.

A graduate of the University of Wisconsin, who had done some excellent volunteer inspection in both Chicago and Pittsburg, became my deputy and performed the work in a most thoroughgoing manner for three years. During the last two she was under the régime of civil service for in 1895, to the great joy of many citizens, the Illinois legislature made that possible.

Many of the foreign-born women of the ward were much shocked by this abrupt departure into the ways of men, and it took a great deal of explanation to convey the idea even remotely that if it were a womanly task to go about in tenement houses in order to nurse the sick, it might be quite as womanly to go through the same district in order to prevent the breeding of so-called "filth diseases." While some of the women enthusiastically approved the slowly changing conditions and saw that their housewifely duties logically extended to the adjacent alleys and streets, they yet were quite certain that "it was not a lady's job." A revelation of this attitude was made one day in a conversation which the inspector heard vigorously carried on in a laundry. One of the employees was leaving and was expressing her mind concerning the place in no measured terms, summing up her contempt for it as follows: "I would rather be the girl who goes about in the alleys than to stay here any longer!"

And yet the spectacle of eight hours' work for eight hours' pay, the even-handed justice to all citizens irrespective of "pull," the dividing of responsibility between landlord and tenant, and the readiness to enforce obedience to law from both, was, perhaps, one of the most valuable demonstrations which could have been made. Such daily living on the part of the office holder is of infinitely more value than many talks on civics for, after all, we credit most easily that which we see. The careful inspection combined with other causes, brought about a great improvement in the cleanliness and comfort of the neighborhood and one happy day, when the death rate of our ward was found to have dropped from third to seventh in the list of city wards and was so reported to our Woman's Club, the applause which followed recorded the genuine sense of participation in the result, and a public spirit which had "made good." But the cleanliness of the ward was becoming much too popular to suit our all-powerful alderman and, although we felt fatuously secure under the régime of civil service, he found a way to circumvent us by eliminating the position altogether. He introduced an ordinance into the city council which combined the collection of refuse with the cleaning and repairing of the streets, the whole to be placed under a ward superintendent. The office of course was to be filled under civil service regulations but only men were eligible to the examination. Although this latter regulation was afterwards modified in favor of one woman, it was retained long enough to put the nineteenth ward inspector out of office.

Of course our experience in inspecting only made us more conscious of the wretched housing conditions over which we had been distressed from the first. It was during the World's Fair summer that one of the Hull-House residents in a public address upon housing reform used as an example of indifferent landlordism a large block in the neighborhood occupied by small tenements and stables unconnected with a street sewer, as was much similar property in the vicinity. In the lecture the resident spared neither a description of the property nor the name of the owner. The young man who owned the property was justly indignant at this public method of attack and promptly came to investigate the condition of the property. Together we made a careful tour of the houses and stables and in the face of the conditions that we found there, I could not but agree with him that supplying South Italian peasants with sanitary appliances seemed a difficult undertaking. Nevertheless he was unwilling that the block should remain in its deplorable state, and he finally cut through the dilemma with the rash proposition that he would give a free lease of the entire tract to Hull-House, accompanying the offer, however, with the warning remark, that if we should choose to use the income from the rents in sanitary improvements we should be throwing our money away.

Even when we decided that the houses were so bad that we could not undertake the task of improving them, he was game and stuck to his proposition that we should have a free lease. We finally submitted a plan that the houses should be torn down and the entire tract turned into a playground, although cautious advisers intimated that it would be very inconsistent to ask for subscriptions for the support of Hull-House when we were known to have thrown away an income of two thousand dollars a year. We, however, felt that a spectacle of inconsistency was better than one of bad landlordism and so the worst of the houses were demolished, the best three were sold and moved across the street under careful provision that they might never be used for junk shops or saloons, and a public playground was finally established. Hull-House became responsible for its management for ten years, at the end of which time it was turned over to the City Playground Commission although from the first the city detailed a policeman who was responsible for its general order and who became a valued adjunct of the House.

During fifteen years this public-spirited owner of the property paid all the taxes, and when the block was finally sold he made possible the playground equipment of a near-by school yard. On the other hand, the dispossessed tenants, a group of whom had to be evicted by legal process before their houses could be torn down, have never ceased to mourn their former estates. Only the other day I met upon the street an old Italian harness maker, who said that he had never succeeded so well anywhere else nor found a place that "seemed so much like Italy."

V. Faith and Doubt

ROBERT FROST (1874–1963)

The most New England of poets, Frost was actually born in San Francisco, California, the son of a man who had sympathized with the Southern side during the Civil War.

After his father's death, however, Frost returned to his ancestral New England. A year's study at Dartmouth was followed by work in a New Hampshire mill and country-school teaching. In 1895, Frost married Elinor White. Two years later, he entered Harvard as a special student. After two years of study, he left Harvard for a farm in West Derry, New Hampshire. His settling on a farm in a period when countless rural New Englanders were moving to industrial cities and towns symbolizes an idea that would become recurrent in his poetry: life must be based on the continual rediscovery of nature's lessons, albeit man is as much at odds with nature as he is intimately tied to it.

It was not until Frost moved to England in 1912 that he was finally able to find adequate appreciation of his poetry. A Boy's Will *(1913) and* North of Boston *(1914), both published in London, were received very favorably by English critics; when Frost returned to the United States in 1915 he was at last honored in his own country. Later collections of his poetry include* Mountain Interval *(1916),* New Hampshire *(1923), and* West-Running Brook *(1928).*

The Gift Outright

The land was ours before we were the land's.
She was our land more than a hundred years

From Robert Frost, *A Witness Tree* (New York, Henry Holt, 1942), p. 41.

Before we were her people. She was ours
In Massachusetts, in Virginia,
But we were England's, still colonials,
Possessing what we still were unpossessed by,
Possessed by what we now no more possessed.
Something we were withholding made us weak
Until we found out that it was ourselves
We were withholding from our land of living,
And forthwith found salvation in surrender.
Such as we were we gave ourselves outright
(The deed of gift was many deeds of war)
To the land vaguely realizing westward,
But still unstoried, artless, unenhanced,
Such as she was, such as she would become.

T. S. ELIOT (1888——)

Eliot was born in St. Louis, Missouri, of an old New England family which had moved to the Middle West in the 1830's. After graduating from Harvard College in 1910, Eliot spent a year in Paris, then returned to Harvard in order to study Oriental philosophy and Sanskrit. In 1914, Eliot left America and settled permanently in England.

Eliot's first two collections of poems, Prufrock and Other Observations *(1917) and* The Waste Land *(1922) caught the disillusionment and despair of the World War I generation. However, unlike many spokesmen of the postwar years, Eliot was not content simply to record the destruction of all traditional values and faiths; rather, he was concerned that they prevail. His conversion to Anglo-Catholicism toward the end of the twenties and the religious themes of his poetry since 1930 demonstrate this concern.*

In his critical tenets as in his theology, Eliot is a traditionalist. The Sacred Wood *(1920),* Homage to John Dryden *(1924), and* The Use of Poetry *(1933) are examples of his "classical" criticism.*

The Boston Evening Transcript

The readers of the *Boston Evening Transcript*
Sway in the wind like a field of ripe corn.

When evening quickens faintly in the street,
Wakening the appetites of life in some
And to others bringing the *Boston Evening Transcript,*

From *Collected Poems of T. S. Eliot* (New York; Harcourt, Brace; 1936), p. 32.

I mount the steps and ring the bell, turning
Wearily, as one would turn to nod good-bye to Rochefoucauld,
If the street were time and he at the end of the street,
And I say, "Cousin Harriet, here is the *Boston Evening Tran-
script.*"

JOHN DOS PASSOS (1896——)

Dos Passos' grandfather was a Portuguese immigrant whose son made a fortune as a New York lawyer and married into a Tidewater Virginia family. The future novelist consequently spent his childhood in New York, Mexico, Virginia, and Europe; attended a fashionable New England prep school; and was admitted to Harvard. As a Harvard undergraduate Dos Passos was one of a group of young aesthetes who, following the lead of the French symbolists, regarded the growing importance of science and technology as a threat to humanity and hailed art as man's only salvation.

After his graduation from college in 1916, Dos Passos had planned to study architecture in Spain, but World War I changed his mind and he joined a French ambulance unit instead. His subsequent disillusionment with war, and with the future prospects of Western civilization, are evident in his first two novels, One Man's Initiation *(1920) and* Three Soldiers *(1921).* Manhattan Transfer *(1925), which made Dos Passos' national reputation, asserts that beneath the surface confusion and variety of American life there are economic and social forces which brutally restrict individual freedom.*

In U.S.A., *a trilogy of novels comprising* The 42nd Parallel *(1930),* Nineteen Nineteen *(1932), and* The Big Money *(1936), Dos Passos depicted modern American society as a mechanical triumph and a human waste land. For Dos Passos, the horrors of war, which—as the following passage shows—he could describe as graphically as Hemingway, were simply dramatic illustrations of the continuing tragedy of industrial civilization.*

The Body of an American

Whereasthe Congressoftheunitedstates byaconcurrentresolutionadopted-
on the4thdayofmarch lastauthorizedthe Secretaryofwar to cause to be
brought to theunitedstatesthe body of an Americanwhowasamemberofthe-
americanexpeditionaryforcesineurope wholosthislifeduringtheworldwarand-
whoseidentityhasnotbeenestablished for burial inthememorialamphitheatre-
ofthe nationalcemeteryatarlingtonvirginia

In the tarpaper morgue at Chalons-sur-Marne in the reek of
chloride of lime and the dead, they picked out the pine box that held
all that was left of
enie menie minie moe plenty other pine boxes stacked up there
containing what they'd scraped up of Richard Roe
and other person or persons unknown. Only one can go. How did
they pick John Doe?
Make sure he aint a dinge, boys,
make sure he aint a guinea or a kike,
how can you tell a guy's a hunredpercent when all you've got's a
gunnysack full of bones, bronze buttons stamped with the screaming
eagle and a pair of roll puttees?
. . . and the gagging chloride and the puky dirt-stench of the year-
old dead . . .

The day withal was too meaningful and tragic for applause. Silence, tears,
songs and prayer, muffled drums and soft music were the instrumentalities
today of national approbation.

John Doe was born (thudding din of blood in love into the shud-
dering soar of a man and a woman alone indeed together lurching
into
and ninemonths sick drowse waking into scared agony and the pain
and blood and mess of birth). John Doe was born
and raised in Brooklyn, in Memphis, near the lakefront in Cleveland, Ohio, in the stench of the stockyards in Chi, on Beacon Hill, in
an old brick house in Alexandria Virginia, on Telegraph Hill, in a
half-timbered Tudor cottage in Portland the city of roses,

From John Dos Passos, *Nineteen Nineteen* (Boston, Houghton Mifflin Co., 1946) pp. 539-
545.

in the Lying-In Hospital old Morgan endowed on Stuyvesant Square,

across the railroad tracks, out near the country club, in a shack cabin tenement apartmenthouse exclusive residential suburb;

scion of one of the best families in the social register, won first prize in the baby parade at Coronado Beach, was marbles champion of the Little Rock grammarschools, crack basketballplayer at the Booneville High, quarterback at the State Reformatory, having saved the sheriff's kid from drowning in the Little Missouri River was invited to Washington to be photographed shaking hands with the President on the White House steps;—

though this was a time of mourning, such an assemblage necessarily has about it a touch of color. In the boxes are seen the court uniforms of foreign diplomats, the gold braid of our own and foreign fleets and armies, the black of the conventional morning dress of American statesmen, the varicolored furs and outdoor wrapping garments of mothers and sisters come to mourn, the drab and blue of soldiers and sailors, the glitter of musical instruments and the white and black of a vested choir

—busboy harveststiff hogcaller boyscout champeen cornshucker of Western Kansas bellhop at the United States Hotel at Saratoga Springs office boy callboy fruiter telephone lineman longshoreman lumberjack plumber's helper,

worked for an exterminating company in Union City, filled pipes in an opium joint in Trenton, N.J.

Y.M.C.A. secretary, express agent, truckdriver, fordmechanic, sold books in Denver Colorado: Madam would you be willing to help a young man work his way through college?

President Harding, with a reverence seemingly more significant because of his high temporal station, concluded his speech:

We are met today to pay the impersonal tribute;
the name of him whose body lies before us took flight with his imperishable soul . . .
as a typical soldier of this representative democracy he fought and died believing in the indisputable justice of his country's cause . . .

by raising his right hand and asking the thousands within the sound of his voice to join in the prayer:

Our Father which art in heaven hallowed be thy name . . .

Naked he went into the army;
they weighed you, measured you, looked for flat feet, squeezed your penis to see if you had clap, looked up your anus to see if you had piles, counted your teeth, made you cough, listened to your heart and lungs, made you read the letters on the card, charted your urine and your intelligence,
gave you a service record for a future (imperishable soul)
and an identification tag stamped with your serial number to hang around your neck, issued OD regulation equipment, a condiment can and a copy of the articles of war.
Atten'SHUN suck in your gut you c——r wipe that smile off your face eyes right wattja tink dis is a choirch-social? For-war-D'ARCH.
John Doe
and Richard Roe and other person or persons unknown
drilled hiked, manual of arms, ate slum, learned to salute, to soldier, to loaf in the latrines, forbidden to smoke on deck, overseas guard duty, forty men and eight horses, shortarm inspection and the ping of shrapnel and the shrill bullets combing the air and the sorehead woodpeckers the machineguns mud cooties gas-masks and the itch.
Say feller tell me how I can get back to my outfit.

John Doe had a head
for twentyodd years intensely the nerves of the eyes the ears the palate the tongue the fingers the toes the armpits, the nerves warmfeeling under the skin charged the coiled brain with hurt sweet warm cold mine must dont sayings print headlines:
Thou shalt not the multiplication table long division, Now is the time for all good men knocks but once at a young man's door, It's a great life if Ish gebibbel, The first five years'll be the Safety First, Suppose a hun tried to rape your my country right or wrong, Catch 'em young, What he dont know wont treat 'em rough, Tell 'em nothin, He got what was coming to him he got his, This is a white

man's country, Kick the bucket, Gone west, If you dont like it you
can croaked him

Say buddy cant you tell me how I can get back to my outfit?

Cant help jumpin when them things go off, give me the trots
them things do. I lost my identification tag swimming in the Marne,
roughhousin with a guy while he was waitin to be deloused, in bed
with a girl named Jeanne (Love moving picture wet French postcard
dream began with saltpeter in the coffee and ended at the propho
station);—

*Say soldier for chrissake cant you tell me how I can get back to
my outfit?*

John Doe's
heart pumped blood:
alive thudding silence of blood in your ears
down in the clearing in the Oregon forest where the punkins were
punkincolor pouring into the blood through the eyes and the fall-
colored trees and the bronze hoopers were hopping through the dry
grass, where tiny striped snails hung on the underside of the blades
and the flies hummed, wasps droned, bumblebees buzzed, and the
woods smelt of wine and mushrooms and apples, homey smell of fall
pouring into the blood,
and I dropped the tin hat and the sweaty pack and lay flat with the
dogday sun licking my throat and adamsapple and the tight skin
over the breastbone.

The shell had his number on it.

The blood ran into the ground.

The service record dropped out of the filing cabinet when the
quartermaster sergeant got blotto that time they had to pack up and
leave the billets in a hurry.
The identification tag was in the bottom of the Marne.

The blood ran into the ground, the brains oozed out of the cracked

skull and were licked up by the trenchrats, the belly swelled and
raised a generation of bluebottle flies,
    and the incorruptible skeleton,
    and the scraps of dried viscera and skin bundled in khaki

    they took to Chalons-sur-Marne
    and laid it out neat in a pine coffin
    and took it home to God's Country on a battleship
    and buried it in a sarcophagus in the Memorial Amphitheatre in
the Arlington National Cemetery
    and draped the Old Glory over it
    and the bugler played taps
    and Mr. Harding prayed to God and the diplomats and the gen-
erals and the admirals and the brasshats and the politicians and the
handsomely dressed ladies out of the society column of the *Washington Post* stood up solemn
    and thought how beautiful sad Old Glory God's Country it was
to have the bugler play taps and the three volleys made their ears
ring.

    Where his chest ought to have been they pinned
    the Congressional Medal, the D.S.C., the Medaille Militaire, the
Belgian Croix de Guerre, the Italian gold medal, the Vitutea Mili-
tara sent by Queen Marie of Rumania, the Czechoslovak war cross,
the Virtuti Militari of the Poles, a wreath sent by Hamilton Fish, Jr.,
of New York, and a little wampum presented by a deputation of Ari-
zona redskins in warpaint and feathers. All the Washingtonians
brought flowers.

    Woodrow Wilson brought a bouquet of poppies.

H. L. MENCKEN (1880–1956)

After graduating from Polytechnic Institute in his native Balti-more, Mencken went to work in his father's business. Three years later, in 1899, he began his lifelong career as a newspaperman when he was taken on by the Baltimore Herald. *In 1908, he became the drama critic for the* Smart Set *magazine, which he and George Jean Nathan later edited. In 1923, Mencken and Nathan started the* American Mercury.

Mencken's attacks on the genteel tradition and his cynical debunk-ing of all the ideals which Americans of the older generation thought sacred and inviolable, delighted the young rebels of the jazz age. It was his purpose, Mencken said, to write in a "spirit of boisterous scepticism" about "the gaudy, gorgeous American scene," and few aspects of American culture escaped his satire. Many of Mencken's contemporaries considered him a dangerous radical, but later criti-cism has found Mencken to be essentially a conservative, whose aim was not revolution but reform.

In addition to denouncing politicians, Prohibitionists and profes-sors, Mencken encouraged many of the new writers of his time, in-cluding Sherwood Anderson, Theodore Dreiser, Carl Sandburg, Eu-gene O'Neill, and Sinclair Lewis. His book, The American Lan-guage *(1919), many times revised and republished, is a pioneer study of American English.*

On Being an American

$\mathcal{A}$ pparently there are those who begin to find it disagreeable
—nay, impossible. Their anguish fills the Liberal weeklies, and every
ship that puts out from New York carries a groaning cargo of them,
bound for Paris, London, Munich, Rome and way points—anywhere
to escape the great curses and atrocities that make life intolerable for
them at home. Let me say at once that I find little to cavil at in their
basic complaints. In more than one direction, indeed, I probably go
a great deal further than even the Young Intellectuals. It is, for
example, one of my firmest and most sacred beliefs, reached after an
inquiry extending over a score of years and supported by incessant
prayer and meditation, that the government of the United States, in
both its legislative arm and its executive arm, is ignorant, incompe-
tent, corrupt, and disgusting—and from this judgment I except no
more than twenty living lawmakers and no more than twenty execu-
tioners of their laws. It is a belief no less piously cherished that the
administration of justice in the Republic is stupid, dishonest, and
against all reason and equity—and from this judgment I except no
more than thirty judges, including two upon the bench of the Supreme Court of the United States. It is another that the foreign policy
of the United States—its habitual manner of dealing with other nations, whether friend or foe—is hypocritical, disingenuous, knavish,
and dishonorable—and from this judgment I consent to no exceptions whatever, either recent or long past. And it is my fourth (and,
to avoid too depressing a bill, final) conviction that the American
people taking one with another, constitute the most timorous, sniveling, poltroonish, ignominious mob of serfs and goose-steppers ever
gathered under one flag in Christendom since the end of the Middle
Ages, and that they grow more timorous, more sniveling, more poltroonish, more ignominious every day.

So far I go with the fugitive Young Intellectuals—and into the
Bad Lands beyond. Such, in brief, are the cardinal articles of my
political faith, held passionately since my admission to citizenship and
now growing stronger and stronger as I gradually disintegrate into

From H. L. Mencken, *Prejudices, Third Series* (New York, Alfred A. Knopf, 1922,
1949), pp. 9-14.

my component carbon, oxygen, hydrogen, phosphorus, calcium, sodium, nitrogen and iron. This is what I believe and preach, *in nomine Domini,* Amen. Yet I remain on the dock, wrapped in the flag, when the Young Intellectuals set sail. Yet here I stand, unshaken and undespairing, a loyal and devoted Americano, even a chauvinist, paying taxes without complaint, obeying all laws that are physiologically obeyable, accepting all the searching duties and responsibilities of citizenship unprotestingly, investing the sparse usufructs of my miserable toil in the obligations of the nation, avoiding all commerce with men sworn to overthrow the government, contributing my mite toward the glory of the national arts and sciences, enriching and embellishing the native language, spurning all lures (and even all invitations) to get out and stay out—here am I, a bachelor of easy means, forty-two years old, unhampered by debts or issue, able to go wherever I please and to stay as long as I please—here am I, contentedly and even smugly basking beneath the Stars and Stripes, a better citizen, I daresay, and certainly a less murmurous and exigent one, than thousands who put the Hon. Warren Gamaliel Harding beside Friedrich Barbarossa and Charlemagne, and hold the Supreme Court to be directly inspired by the Holy Spirit, and belong ardently to every Rotary Club, Ku Klux Klan, and Anti-Saloon League, and choke with emotion when the band plays "The Star-Spangled Banner," and believe with the faith of little children that one of Our Boys, taken at random, could dispose in a fair fight of ten Englishmen, twenty Germans, thirty Frogs, forty Wops, fifty Japs, or a hundred Bolsheviki.

Well, then, why am I still here? Why am I so complacent (perhaps even to the point of offensiveness), so free from bile, so little fretting and indignant, so curiously happy? Why did I answer only with a few academic "Hear, Hears" when Henry James, Ezra Pound, Harold Stearns and the *emigrés* of Greenwich Village issued their successive calls to the corn-fed *intelligentsia* to flee the shambles, escape to fairer lands, throw off the curse forever? The answer, of course, is to be sought in the nature of happiness, which tempts to metaphysics. But let me keep upon the ground. To me, at least (and I can only follow my own nose), happiness presents itself in an aspect that is tripartite. To be happy (reducing the thing to its elementals) I must be:

a. Well-fed, unhounded by sordid cares, at ease in Zion.
b. Full of a comfortable feeling of superiority to the masses of my fellow-men.
c. Delicately and unceasingly amused according to my taste.

It is my contention that, if this definition be accepted, there is no country on the face of the earth wherein a man roughly constituted as I am—a man of my general weaknesses, vanities, appetites, prejudices, and aversions—can be so happy, or even one-half so happy, as he can be in these free and independent states. Going further, I lay down the proposition that it is a sheer physical impossibility for such a man to live in These States and *not* be happy—that it is as impossible to him as it would be to a schoolboy to weep over the burning down of his school-house. If he says that he isn't happy here, then he either lies or is insane. Here the business of getting a living, particularly since the war brought the loot of all Europe to the national strong-box, is enormously easier than it is in any other Christian land —so easy, in fact, that an educated and forehanded man who fails at it must actually make deliberate efforts to that end. Here the general average of intelligence, of knowledge, of competence, of integrity, of self-respect, of honor is so low that any man who knows his trade, does not fear ghosts, has read fifty good books, and practices the common decencies stands out as brilliantly as a wart on a bald head, and is thrown willy-nilly into a meager and exclusive aristocracy. And here, more than anywhere else that I know of or have heard of, the daily panorama of human existence, of private and communal folly— the unending procession of governmental extortions and chicaneries, of commercial brigandages and throat-slittings, of theological buffooneries, of aesthetic ribaldries, of legal swindles and harlotries, of miscellaneous rogueries, villainies, imbecilities, grotesqueries, and extravagances—is so inordinately gross and preposterous, so perfectly brought up to the highest conceivable amperage, so steadily enriched with an almost fabulous daring and originality, that only the man who was born with a petrified diaphragm can fail to laugh himself to sleep every night, and to awake every morning with all the eager, unflagging expectation of a Sunday-school superintendent touring the Paris peep-shows.

F. SCOTT FITZGERALD (1896–1940)

Fitzgerald was born and grew up in St. Paul, Minnesota, where his parents never had quite enough money or social status to be fully accepted by St. Paul society.

The refusal to accord Fitzgerald what he considered his natural place in society helps to account for his complicated attitude toward the very rich. On the one hand, he imitated them, sometimes surpassing his richest friends in gaudy displays of conspicuous consumption; on the other hand, his sense of not belonging enabled him to stand apart and observe his friends with an objective and yet compassionate eye.

Admitted to Princeton in 1913, Fitzgerald left before getting his degree in order to join the American Army. However, instead of fighting heroically in France, as he had hoped, he spent the war being shifted from one training camp to another in the United States. After the Armistice, Fitzgerald worked as an advertising copy writer in New York. In 1920, he published This Side of Paradise, *which became an overnight sensation. His subsequent novels and short stories,* Flappers and Philosophers *(1920),* The Beautiful and Damned *(1922), and* Tales of the Jazz Age *(1922) established him as a spokesman of the jazz-age generation and enabled him and his beautiful wife, Zelda, to live in the style Fitzgerald had always aspired to.*

In 1925, while living on the French Riviera, Fitzgerald finished The Great Gatsby, *which—with the possible exception of* Tender Is the Night *(1934)—stands as his finest achievement. Both novels display a deep understanding of the American character. In extraordinarily moving detail, Fitzgerald shows that the American striving after money springs from a strangely innocent desire to live fully and passionately. At the same time, this striving is tragic and doomed, because the attainment of their material ambitions leads to the corrup-*

tion of his characters' moral and spiritual values, and thus to the betrayal of themselves and others.

After the stock market crash of 1929, American writers turned to novels of social criticism and Fitzgerald was relegated to the past as the irresponsible pied piper of an adolescent generation. Tender Is the Night *was regarded as irrelevant to the needs of the 1930's by both the critics and the reading public. In order to make a living, Fitzgerald went to Hollywood and wrote scripts for the movies. Almost forgotten, he died in 1940, before he could complete* The Last Tycoon, *a novel about Hollywood.*

The following selection from The Great Gatsby *shows the great excitement, and the loneliness, which a young man from the Middle West can experience in New York.*

Young Man in New York

R̲ EADING OVER what I have written so far, I see I have given the impression that the events of three nights several weeks apart were all that absorbed me. On the contrary, they were merely casual events in a crowded summer, and, until much later, they absorbed me infinitely less than my personal affairs.

Most of the time I worked. In the early morning the sun threw my shadow westward as I hurried down the white chasms of lower New York to the Probity Trust. I knew the other clerks and young bond-salesmen by their first names, and lunched with them in dark, crowded restaurants on little pig sausages and mashed potatoes and coffee. I even had a short affair with a girl who lived in Jersey City and worked in the accounting department, but her brother began throwing mean looks in my direction, so when she went on her vacation in July I let it blow quietly away.

I took dinner usually at the Yale Club—for some reason it was the gloomiest event of my day—and then I went upstairs to the library and studied investments and securities for a conscientious hour. There

From F. Scott Fitzgerald, *The Great Gatsby* (New York, Charles Scribner's Sons, 1925, 1953), pp. 68-70.

were generally a few rioters around, but they never came into the library, so it was a good place to work. After that, if the night was mellow, I strolled down Madison Avenue past the old Murray Hill Hotel, and over 33rd Street to the Pennsylvania Station.

I began to like New York, the racy, adventurous feel of it at night, and the satisfaction that the constant flicker of men and women and machines gives to the restless eye. I liked to walk up Fifth Avenue and pick out romantic women from the crowd and imagine that in a few minutes I was going to enter into their lives, and no one would ever know or disapprove. Sometimes, in my mind, I followed them to their apartments on the corners of hidden streets, and they turned and smiled back at me before they faded through a door into warm darkness. At the enchanted metropolitan twilight I felt a haunting loneliness sometimes, and felt it in others—poor young clerks who loitered in front of windows waiting until it was time for a solitary restaurant dinner—young clerks in the dusk, wasting the most poignant moments of night and life.

Again at eight o'clock, when the dark lanes of the Forties were lined five deep with throbbing taxicabs, bound for the theater district, I felt a sinking in my heart. Forms leaned together in the taxis as they waited, and voices sang, and there was laughter from unheard jokes, and lighted cigarettes made unintelligible circles inside. Imagining that I, too, was hurrying toward gayety and sharing their intimate excitement, I wished them well.

THEODORE DREISER (1871-1945)

Dreiser's father was a German Catholic immigrant who had settled in the small Indiana town of Sullivan. A harshly religious man, the father became more and more fanatically strict with his family as he found himself unable to make a decent living in America. Dreiser's mother, by contrast, was a warm and kind woman to whom Theodore was deeply attached.

Revolting against his father, the family's poverty, and small-town boredom, Dreiser left high school when he was sixteen and went to Chicago. After working at a number of jobs, he left the city in 1889 and enrolled at the University of Indiana, only to return to Chicago after one year. In 1892, he landed a reporter's job on the Chicago Globe. Later he worked on newspapers in St. Louis, Pittsburgh, and Cleveland, and edited several popular magazines in New York.

When he began writing fiction, Dreiser sought to convey to his readers a vision of the universe as a sequence of amoral forces. Human beings, to Dreiser, were merely biological organisms, the products of blind accident, whose lives were totally dominated by their sexual and materialistic appetites. Sister Carrie, the heroine of Dreiser's first novel (published in 1900), is not to be blamed for her love affairs, for she cannot help herself. Yet there was also in Dreiser a religious mysticism (his mother was a Mennonite) which expressed itself in his belief that man might eventually create a society based on love and not on the brutal fight for existence.

The disparity between his vision of a future America and the reality he saw around him provides the basic tension in Dreiser's masterpiece, An American Tragedy (1925). The central character, Clyde Griffiths, is a weakling who dreams of getting rich quick and living happily ever after. His dreams, however, lead him to plot the murder of a factory girl whom he has seduced, so that she will not inter-

*fere with his plans to marry the richest girl in town. Although the
factory girl drowns by accident, Clyde is convicted of having killed
her. In the following selection, we see the agony of Clyde's mother
at the fate of her son. Drawing on all the tensions of his own early
life and his love for his own mother, Dreiser illuminates more brilliantly than any other writer has done the pathos of the American
Mom.*

Among Dreiser's other important books are Jennie Gerhardt
(1911), The Financier *(1912), and* The Titan *(1914).*

Clyde Griffiths' Mother

*T*HE DREARY AFTERMATH of a great contest and a great failure,
with the general public from coast to coast—in view of this stern local
interpretation of the tragedy—firmly convinced that Clyde was guilty
and, as heralded by the newspapers everywhere, that he had been
properly convicted. The pathos of that poor little murdered country
girl! Her sad letters! How she must have suffered! That weak
defense! Even the Griffiths of Denver were so shaken by the evidence
as the trial had progressed that they scarcely dared read the papers
openly—one to the other—but, for the most part, read of it sepa-
rately and alone, whispering together afterwards of the damning,
awful deluge of circumstantial evidence. Yet, after reading Belknap's
speech and Clyde's own testimony, this little family group that had
struggled along together for so long coming to believe in their own
son and brother in spite of all they had previously read against him.
And because of this—during the trial as well as afterwards—writing
him cheerful and hopeful letters, based frequently on letters from
him in which he insisted over and over again that he was not guilty.
Yet once convicted, and out of the depths of his despair wiring his
mother as he did—and the papers confirming it—absolute consternation in the Griffiths family. For was not this proof? Or, was it? All
the papers seemed to think so. And they rushed reporters to Mrs.

From Theodore Dreiser, *An American Tragedy* (New York, The World Publishing Co.,
Cleveland and New York, 1948), pp. 797-804.

Griffiths, who, together with her little brood, had sought refuge from the unbearable publicity in a remote part of Denver entirely removed from the mission world. A venal moving-van company had revealed her address.

And now this American witness to the rule of God upon earth, sitting in a chair in her shabby, nondescript apartment, hard-pressed for the very means to sustain herself—degraded by the milling forces of life and the fell and brutal blows of chance—yet serene in her trust—and declaring: "I cannot think this morning. I seem numb and things look strange to me. My boy found guilty of murder! But I am his mother and I am not convinced of his guilt by any means! He has written me that he is not guilty and I believe him. And to whom should he turn with the truth and for trust if not to me? But there is He who sees all things and who knows."

At the same time there was so much in the long stream of evidence, as well as Clyde's first folly in Kansas City, that had caused her to wonder—and fear. Why was he unable to explain that folder? Why couldn't he have gone to the girl's aid when he could swim so well? And why did he proceed so swiftly to the mysterious Miss X—whoever she was? Oh, surely, surely, surely, she was not going to be compelled, in spite of all her faith, to believe that her eldest—the most ambitious and hopeful, if restless, of all of her children, was guilty of such a crime! No! She could not doubt him—even now. Under the merciful direction of a living God, was it not evil in a mother to believe evil of a child, however dread his erring ways might seem? In the silence of the different rooms of the mission, before she had been compelled to remove from there because of curious and troublesome visitors, had she not stood many times in the center of one of those miserable rooms while sweeping and dusting, free from the eye of any observer—her head thrown back, her eyes closed, her strong, brown face molded in homely and yet convinced and earnest lines—a figure out of the early Biblical days of her six thousand-year-old world—and earnestly directing her thoughts to that imaginary throne which she saw as occupied by the living, giant mind and body of the living God—her Creator. And praying by the quarter and the half hour that she be given strength and understanding and guidance to know of her son's innocence or guilt—and if innocent that this searing burden of suffering be lifted from him and her and all those dear to him and her—or if guilty, she be shown how to do—how to endure the while he be shown how to wash from his immortal soul forever the horror of the thing he had done—make himself once more, if possible, white before the Lord.

"Thou art mighty, O God, and there is none beside Thee. Behold, to Thee all things are possible. In Thy favor is Life. Have mercy, O God. Though his sins be as scarlet, make him white as snow. Though they be red like crimson, make them as wool."

Yet in her then—and as she prayed—was the wisdom of Eve in regard to the daughters of Eve. That girl whom Clyde was alleged to have slain—what about her? Had she not sinned too? And was she not older than Clyde? The papers said so. Examining the letters, line by line, she was moved by their pathos and was intensely and pathetically grieved for the misery that had befallen the Aldens. Nevertheless, as a mother and woman full of wisdom of ancient Eve, she saw how Roberta herself must have consented—how the lure of her must have aided in the weakening and the betrayal of her son. A strong, good girl would not have consented—could not have. How many confessions about this same thing had she not heard in the mission and at street meetings? And might it not be said in Clyde's favor— as in the very beginning of life in the Garden of Eden—"the woman tempted me?"

Truly—and because of that—

"His mercy endureth forever," she quoted. And if His mercy endureth—must that of Clyde's mother be less?

"If ye have faith, so much as the grain of a mustard seed," she quoted to herself—and now, in the face of these importuning reporters added: "Did my son kill her? That is the question. Nothing else matters in the eyes of our Maker," and she looked at the sophisticated, callous youths with the look of one who was sure that her God would make them understand. And even so they were impressed by her profound sincerity and faith. "Whether or not the jury has found him guilty or innocent is neither here nor there in the eyes of Him who holds the stars in the hollow of His hand. The jury's finding is of men. It is of the earth's earthy. I have read his lawyer's plea. My son himself has told me in his letters that he is not guilty. I believe my son. I am convinced that he is innocent."

And Asa in another corner of the room, saying little. Because of his lack of comprehension of the actualities as well as his lack of experience of the stern and motivating forces of passion, he was unable to grasp even a tithe of the meaning of this. He had never understood Clyde or his lacks or his feverish imaginings, so he said, and preferred not to discuss him.

"But," continued Mrs. Griffiths, "at no time have I shielded Clyde in his sin against Roberta Alden. He did wrong, but she did wrong too in not resisting him. There can be no compromising with sin in any one. And though my heart goes out in sympathy and love to the bleeding heart of her dear mother and father who have suffered so, still we must not fail to see that this sin was mutual and that the world should know and judge accordingly. Not that I want to shield him," she repeated. "He should have remembered the teachings of his youth." And here her lips compressed in a sad and somewhat critical misery. "But I have read her letters too. And I feel that but for them, the prosecuting attorney would have had no real case against my son. He used them to work on the emotions of the jury." She got up, tried as by fire, and exclaimed, tensely and beautifully: "But he is my son! He has just been convicted. I must think as a mother how to help him, however I feel as to his sin." She gripped her hands together, and even the reporters were touched by her misery. "I must go to him! I should have gone before. I see it now." She paused, discovering herself to be addressing her innocent agony, need, fear, to these public ears and voices, which might in no wise understand or care.

"Some people wonder," now interrupted one of these same—a most practical and emotionally calloused youth of Clyde's own age—"why you weren't there during the trial. Didn't you have the money to go?"

"I had no money," she replied simply. "Not enough, anyhow. And besides, they advised me not to come—that they did not need me. But now—now I must go—in some way—I must find out how." She went to a small shabby desk, which was a part of the sparse and colorless equipment of the room. "You boys are going downtown," she said. "Would one of you send a telegram for me if I give you the money."

"Sure!" exclaimed the one who had asked her the rudest question.

"Give it to me. You don't need any money. I'll have the paper send it." Also, as he thought, he would write it up, or in, as a part of his story.

She seated herself at the yellow and scratched desk and after finding a small pad and pen, she wrote: "Clyde—Trust in God. All things are possible to Him. Appeal at once. Read Psalm 51. Another trial will prove your innocence. We will come to you soon. Father and Mother."

"Perhaps I had just better give you the money," she added, nervously, wondering whether it would be well to permit a newspaper to pay for this and wondering at the same time if Clyde's uncle would be willing to pay for an appeal. It might cost a great deal. Then she added: "It's rather long."

"Oh, don't bother about that!" exclaimed another of the trio, who was anxious to read the telegram. "Write all you want. We'll see that it goes."

"I want a copy of that," added the third, in a sharp and uncompromising tone, seeing that the first reporter was proceeding to take and pocket the message. "This isn't private. I get it from you or her —now!"

And at this, number one, in order to avoid a scene, which Mrs. Griffiths, in her slow way, was beginning to sense, extracted the slip from his pocket and turned it over to the others, who there and then proceeded to copy it.

At the same time that this was going on, the Griffiths of Lycurgus, having been consulted as to the wisdom and cost of a new trial, disclosed themselves as by no means interested, let alone convinced, that an appeal—at least at their expense—was justified. The torture and socially—if not commercially—destroying force of all this—every hour of it a Golgotha! Bella and her social future, to say nothing of Gilbert and his—completely overcast and charred by this awful public picture of the plot and crime that one of their immediate blood had conceived and executed! Samuel Griffiths himself, as well as his wife, fairly macerated by this blasting flash from his well-intentioned, though seemingly impractical and nonsensical good deed. Had not a long, practical struggle with life taught him that sentiment in business was folly? Up to the hour he had met Clyde he had never allowed it to influence him in any way. But his mistaken notion that his youngest brother had been unfairly dealt with by their father! And now this! This! His wife and daughter compelled to remove from the scene of their happiest years and comforts and live as exiles— perhaps forever—in one of the suburbs of Boston, or elsewhere—or forever endure the eyes and sympathy of their friends! And himself and Gilbert almost steadily conferring ever since as to the wisdom of uniting the business in stock form with some of the others of Lycurgus or elsewhere—or, if not that, of transferring, not by de- grees but speedily, to either Rochester or Buffalo or Boston or Brook- lyn, where a main plant might be erected. The disgrace of this could only be overcome by absenting themselves from Lycurgus and all that it represented to them. They must begin life all over again— socially at least. That did not mean so much to himself or his wife— their day was about over anyhow. But Bella and Gilbert and Myra— how to rehabilitate them in some way, somewhere?

And so, even before the trial was finished, a decision on the part of Samuel and Gilbert Griffiths to remove the business to South Boston, where they might decently submerge themselves until the misery and shame of this had in part at least been forgotten.

And because of this further aid to Clyde absolutely refused. And Belknap and Jephson then sitting down together to consider. For obviously, their time being as valuable as it was—devoted hitherto to the most successful practice in Bridgeburg—and with many mat- ters waiting on account of the pressure of this particular case— they were by no means persuaded that either their practical self- interest or their charity permitted or demanded their assisting Clyde without further recompense. In fact, the expense of appealing this case was going to be considerable as they saw it. The record was enormous. The briefs would be large and expensive, and the State's allowance for them was pitifully small. At the same time, as Jephson pointed out, it was folly to assume that the western Griffiths might not be able to do anything at all. Had they not been identified with religious and charitable work this long while? And was it not possible, the tragedy of Clyde's present predicament pointed out to them, that they might through appeals of various kinds raise at least sufficient money to defray the actual costs of such an appeal? Of course, they had not aided Clyde up to the present time but that was because his mother had been notified that she was not needed. It was different now.

"Better wire her to come on," suggested Jephson, practically. "We can get Oberwaltzer to set the sentence over until the tenth if we say that she is trying to come on here. Besides, just tell her to do it and if she says she can't we'll see about the money then. But she'll be likely to get it and maybe some towards the appeal too."

And forthwith a telegram and a letter to Mrs. Griffiths, saying that as yet no word had been said to Clyde but none-the-less his Lycurgus relatives had declined to assist him further in any way. Besides, he was to be sentenced not later than the tenth, and for his own future welfare it was necessary that some one—preferably herself—appear. Also that funds to cover the cost of an appeal be raised, or at least the same guaranteed.

And then Mrs. Griffiths, on her knees praying to her God to help her. Here, *now*, he must show his Almighty hand—his never-failing mercy. Enlightenment and help must come from somewhere—otherwise how was she to get the fare, let alone raise money for Clyde's appeal?

Yet as she prayed—on her knees—a thought. The newspapers had been hounding her for interviews. They had followed her here and there. Why had she not gone to her son's aid? What did she think of this? What of that? And now she said to herself, why should she not go to the editor of one of the great papers so anxious to question her always and tell him how great was her need? Also, that if he would help her to reach her son in time to be with him on his day of sentence that she, his mother, would report the same for him. These papers were sending their reporters here, there—even to the trial, as she had read. Why not her—his mother? Could she not speak and write too? How many, many tracts had she not composed?

And so now to her feet—only to sink once more on her knees: "Thou hast answered me, oh, my God!" she exclaimed. Then rising, she got out her ancient brown coat, the commonplace brown bonnet with strings—based on some mood in regard to religious livery— and at once proceeded to the largest and most important newspaper. And because of the notoriety of her son's trial she was shown directly to the managing editor, who was as much interested as he was impressed and who listened to her with respect and sympathy. He understood her situation and was under the impression that the paper would be interested in this. He disappeared for a few moments—then returned. She would be employed as a correspondent for a period of three weeks, and after that until further notice. Her expenses to and fro would be covered. An assistant, into whose hands he would now deliver her would instruct her as to the method of preparing and filing her communications. He would also provide her with some ready cash. She might even leave to-night if she chose—the sooner, the better. The paper would like a photograph or two before she left. But as he talked, and as he noticed, her eyes were closed—her head back. She was offering thanks to the God who had thus directly answered her plea.

SINCLAIR LEWIS (1885-1951)

The son of a doctor, Lewis grew up in the small town of Sauk Centre, Minnesota. Awkward and self-conscious, Lewis cut a curious, if erratically brilliant, figure as an undergraduate at Yale, where he was graduated in 1908.

After a trip to Panama, Lewis became a contributor to popular magazines, worked as a publisher's reader in New York, married, and published his first novel, Our Mr. Wrenn *(1914). In 1920, Lewis achieved fame overnight with* Main Street. *Like so many books of the twenties,* Main Street *rebelled against the genteel standards of morality and culture which had dominated the American scene since the Civil War. The novel is set in Gopher Prairie in the Middle West, but as the title suggests, it could be any one of a thousand communities located anywhere in the United States. The people of Gopher Prairie are not the stalwart and idealistic pioneers of the popular imagination, but bigoted, gossipy, and narrow-minded, and when Carol Kennicott, the novel's heroine, attempts to bring enlightenment to Gopher Prairie, she is crushed.*

Among the best of Lewis' later novels are Babbitt *(1922),* Arrowsmith *(1925),* Elmer Gantry *(1927), and* Dodsworth *(1929).*

The following selection is the preface to Main Street. *It conveys Lewis' passionate belief that America is the heir of all the ages, as well as his terrified conviction that the American dream has somehow been cheapened and is in danger of being destroyed.*

Gopher Prairie, Minnesota

*T*HIS IS AMERICA—a town of a few thousand, in a region of wheat and corn and dairies and little groves.

The town is, in our tale, called "Gopher Prairie, Minnesota." But its Main Street is the continuation of Main Streets everywhere. The story would be the same in Ohio or Montana, in Kansas or Kentucky or Illinois, and not very differently would it be told Up York State or in the Carolina hills.

Main Street is the climax of civilization. That this Ford car might stand in front of the Bon Ton Store, Hannibal invaded Rome and Erasmus wrote in Oxford cloisters. What Ole Jenson the grocer says to Ezra Stowbody the banker is the new law for London, Prague, and the unprofitable isles of the sea; whatsoever Ezra does not know and sanction, that thing is heresy, worthless for knowing and wicked to consider.

Our railway station is the final aspiration of architecture. Sam Clark's annual hardware turnover is the envy of the four counties which constitute God's Country. In the sensitive art of the Rosebud Movie Palace there is a Message, and humor strictly moral.

Such is our comfortable tradition and sure faith. Would he not betray himself an alien cynic who should otherwise portray Main Street, or distress the citizens by speculating whether there may not be other faiths?

From Sinclair Lewis, *Main Street* (New York; Harcourt, Brace & World, Inc.; 1920, 1948), n.p.

NATHANAEL WEST (1902–1940)

The son of a prosperous New York City contractor, West grew up in solid, middle-class comfort. From the time he entered Brown University, however, he turned his back on his parents' environment. He became a painter; he dabbled in French surrealism and Christian mysticism; he went to Paris. Out of his Paris days came his first novel, The Dream Life of Balso Snell *(1931), which relates the hidden, grotesque, inner life of a young man.*

On his return to New York, West worked as a hotel clerk for several years, but continued to write fiction. His second novel, Miss Lonelyhearts *(1933), is the story of a columnist for the lovelorn who gradually becomes convinced that only Christian love can save the world. When he attempts to express his love, however, he is shot by a cripple who thinks he is being attacked. The violence and absurdity which West saw at the center of American society are even more evident in his next two novels,* A Cool Million *(1934), a Horatio Alger story in which the hero is shot to death, and* The Day of the Locust *(1939), West's last novel and his finest.*

The Day of the Locust deals with the little people—the failures, the pretenders, and the merely hopeful—who live on the fringes of Hollywood. Drawing on his own experiences as a Hollywood scriptwriter, West portrayed a young artist who has sold out to the movies and expends his talent on building cardboard castles and other scenic illusions; a cheap blonde and her father, who is a forgotten music-hall star; a dwarf; and a clerk who has been told to come to California (the "last Garden of Eden in America") to regain his health. As West conceived it, Hollywood was the perfect symbol of all the meretriciousness, the materialism and the nightmare-violence of American culture.

The following selection is from The Day of the Locust. *Tod Hackett is the young painter.*

The Last Garden of Eden

*F*AYE moved out of the San Berdoo the day after the funeral.
Tod didn't know where she had gone and was getting up the courage
to call Mrs. Jenning when he saw her from the window of his office.
She was dressed in the costume of a Napoleonic vivandière. By the
time he got the window open, she had almost turned the corner of the
building. He shouted for her to wait. She waved, but when he got
downstairs she was gone.

From her dress, he was sure that she was working in the picture
called "Waterloo." He asked a studio policeman where the company
was shooting and was told on the back lot. He started toward it at
once. A platoon of cuirassiers, big men mounted on gigantic horses,
went by. He knew that they must be headed for the same set and followed them. They broke into a gallop and he was soon outdistanced.

The sun was very hot. His eyes and throat were choked with the
dust thrown up by the horses' hooves and his head throbbed. The
only bit of shade he could find was under an ocean liner made of
painted canvas with real life boats hanging from its davits. He stood
in its narrow shadow for a while, then went on toward a great forty-
foot papier mâché sphinx that loomed up in the distance. He had to
cross a desert to reach it, a desert that was continually made larger by
a fleet of trucks dumping white sand. He had gone only a few feet
when a man with a megaphone ordered him off.

He skirted the desert, making a wide turn to the right, and came
to a Western street with a plank sidewalk. On the porch of the "Last
Chance Saloon" was a rocking chair. He sat down on it and lit a
cigarette.

From there he could see a jungle compound with a water buffalo
tethered to the side of a conical grass hut. Every few seconds the
animal groaned musically. Suddenly an Arab charged by on a white
stallion. He shouted at the man, but got no answer. A little while
later he saw a truck with a load of snow and several malamute dogs.

From Nathanael West, *The Day of the Locust* (New York, New Directions, 1939),
pp. 94-100.

He shouted again. The driver shouted something back, but didn't stop.

Throwing away his cigarette, he went through the swinging doors of the saloon. There was no back to the building and he found himself in a Paris street. He followed it to its end, coming out in a Romanesque courtyard. He heard voices a short distance away and went toward them. On a lawn of fiber, a group of men and women in riding costume were picnicking. They were eating cardboard food in front of a cellophane waterfall. He started toward them to ask his way, but was stopped by a man who scowled and held up a sign—"Quiet, Please, We're Shooting." When Tod took another step forward, the man shook his fist threateningly.

Next he came to a small pond with large celluloid swans floating on it. Across one end was a bridge with a sign that read, "To Kamp Komfit." He crossed the bridge and followed a little path that ended at a Greek temple dedicated to Eros. The god himself lay face downward in a pile of old newspapers and bottles.

From the steps of the temple, he could see in the distance a road lined with Lombardy poplars. It was the one on which he had lost the cuirassiers. He pushed his way through a tangle of briars, old flats and iron junk, skirting the skeleton of a Zeppelin, a bamboo stockade, an adobe fort, the wooden horse of Troy, a flight of baroque palace stairs that started in a bed of weeds and ended against the branches of an oak, part of the Fourteenth Street elevated station, a Dutch windmill, the bones of a dinosaur, the upper half of the Merrimac, a corner of a Mayan temple, until he finally reached the road.

He was out of breath. He sat down under one of the poplars on a rock made of brown plaster and took off his jacket. There was a cool breeze blowing and he soon felt more comfortable.

He had lately begun to think not only of Goya and Daumier but also of certain Italian artists of the seventeenth and eighteenth centuries, of Salvator Rosa, Francesco Guardi and Monsu Desiderio, the painters of Decay and Mystery. Looking down hill now, he could see compositions that might have actually been arranged from the Calabrian work of Rosa. There were partially demolished buildings and broken monuments, half hidden by great, tortured trees, whose exposed roots writhed dramatically in the arid ground, and by shrubs that carried, not flowers, but armories of spikes, hooks and swords.

For Guardi and Desiderio there were bridges which bridged nothing, sculpture in trees, palaces that seemed of marble until a whole stone portico began to flap in the light breeze. And there were figures as well. A hundred yards from where Tod was sitting a man in a derby hat leaned drowsily against the gilded poop of a Venetian barque and peeled an apple. Still farther on, a charwoman on a step-ladder was scrubbing with soap and water the face of a Buddha thirty feet high.

He left the road and climbed across the spine of the hill to look down on the other side. From there he could see a ten-acre field of cockleburs spotted with clumps of sunflowers and wild gum. In the center of the field was a gigantic pile of sets, flats and props. While he watched, a ten-ton truck added another load to it. This was the final dumping ground. He thought of Janvier's "Sargasso Sea." Just as that imaginary body of water was a history of civilization in the form of a marine junkyard, the studio lot was one in the form of a dream dump. A Sargasso of the imagination! And the dump grew continually, for there wasn't a dream afloat somewhere which wouldn't sooner or later turn up on it, having first been made photographic by plaster, canvas, lath and paint. Many boats sink and never reach the Sargasso, but no dream ever entirely disappears. Somewhere it troubles some unfortunate person and some day, when that person has been sufficiently troubled, it will be reproduced on the lot.

When he saw a red glare in the sky and heard the rumble of cannon, he knew it must be Waterloo. From around a bend in the road trotted several cavalry regiments. They wore casques and chest armor of black cardboard and carried long horse pistols in their saddle holsters. They were Victor Hugo's soldiers. He had worked on some of the drawings for their uniforms himself, following carefully the descriptions in "Les Miserables."

He went in the direction they took. Before long he was passed by the men of Lefebvre-Desnouttes, followed by a regiment of gendarmes d'élite, several companies of chasseurs of the guard and a flying detachment of Rimbaud's lancers.

They must be moving up for the disastrous attack on La Haite

Santée. He hadn't read the scenario and wondered if it had rained yesterday. Would Grouchy or Blucher arrive? Grotenstein, the producer, might have changed it.

The sound of cannon was becoming louder all the time and the red fan in the sky more intense. He could smell the sweet, pungent odor of blank powder. It might be over before he could get there. He started to run. When he topped a rise after a sharp bend in the road, he found a great plain below him covered with early nineteenth-century troops, wearing all the gay and elaborate uniforms that used to please him so much when he was a child and spent long hours looking at the soldiers in an old dictionary. At the far end of the field, he could see an enormous hump around which the English and their allies were gathered. It was Mont St. Jean and they were getting ready to defend it gallantly. It wasn't quite finished, however, and swarmed with grips, property men, set dressers, carpenters and painters.

Tod stood near a eucalyptus tree to watch, concealing himself behind a sign that read, " 'Waterloo'—A Charles H. Grotenstein Production." Nearby a youth in a carefully torn horse guard's uniform was being rehearsed in his lines by one of the assistant directors.

"Vive l'Empereur!" the young man shouted, then clutched his breast and fell forward dead. The assistant director was a hard man to please and made him do it over and over again.

In the center of the plain, the battle was going ahead briskly. Things looked tough for the British and their allies. The Prince of Orange commanding the center, Hill the right and Picton the left wing, were being pressed hard by the veteran French. The desperate and intrepid Prince was in an especially bad spot. Tod heard him cry hoarsely above the din of battle, shouting to the Hollande-Belgians, "Nassau! Brunswick! Never retreat!" Nevertheless, the retreat began. Hill, too, fell back. The French killed General Picton with a ball through the head and he returned to his dressing room. Alten was put to the sword and also retired. The colors of the Lunenberg battalion, borne by a prince of the family of Deux-Ponts, were captured by a famous child star in the uniform of a Parisian drummer boy. The Scotch Greys were destroyed and went to change into another uniform. Ponsonby's heavy dragoons were also cut to ribbons.

Mr. Grotenstein would have a large bill to pay at the Western Costume Company.

Neither Napoleon nor Wellington was to be seen. In Wellington's absence, one of the assistant directors, a Mr. Crane, was in command of the allies. He reinforced his center with one of Chasse's brigades and one of Wincke's. He supported these with infantry from Brunswick, Welsh foot, Devon yeomanry and Hanoverian light horse with oblong leather caps and flowing plumes of horsehair.

For the French, a man in a checked cap ordered Milhaud's cuirassiers to carry Mont St. Jean. With their sabers in their teeth and their pistols in their hands, they charged. It was a fearful sight.

The man in the checked cap was making a fatal error. Mont St. Jean was unfinished. The paint was not yet dry and all the struts were not in place. Because of the thickness of the cannon smoke, he had failed to see that the hill was still being worked on by property men, grips and carpenters.

It was the classic mistake, Tod realized, the same one Napoleon had made. Then it had been wrong for a different reason. The Emperor had ordered the cuirassiers to charge Mont St. Jean not knowing that a deep ditch was hidden at its foot to trap his heavy cavalry. The result had been disaster for the French; the beginning of the end.

This time the same mistake had a different outcome. Waterloo, instead of being the end of the Grand Army, resulted in a draw. Neither side won, and it would have to be fought over again the next day. Big losses, however, were sustained by the insurance company in workmen's compensation. The man in the checked cap was sent to the dog house by Mr. Grotenstein just as Napoleon was sent to St. Helena.

When the front rank of Milhaud's heavy division started up the slope of Mont St. Jean, the hill collapsed. The noise was terrific. Nails screamed with agony as they pulled out of joists. The sound of ripping canvas was like that of little children whimpering. Lath and scantling snapped as though they were brittle bones. The whole hill folded like an enormous umbrella and covered Napoleon's army with painted cloth.

It turned into a rout. The victors of Berezina, Leipsic, Austerlitz, fled like schoolboys who had broken a pane of glass. "Sauve qui peut!" they cried, or, rather, "Scram!"

The armies of England and her allies were too deep in scenery to flee. They had to wait for the carpenters and ambulances to come up. The men of the gallant Seventy-Fifth Highlanders were lifted out of the wreck with block and tackle. They were carted off by the stretcher-bearers, still clinging bravely to their claymores.

VI.   Varieties of Present Experience

DAVID RIESMAN (1909———)

Born in Philadelphia, Riesman was graduated from Harvard Col-
lege in 1931 and the Harvard Law School in 1934. In 1935–36 he
worked as a law clerk to Supreme Court Justice Louis Brandeis.
After some years of teaching law and working as a district attorney in
New York, Riesman became professor of social science at the Univer-
sity of Chicago and, since 1958, at Harvard.

In 1950, Riesman, in collaboration with Reuel Denney and Nathan
Glazer, published The Lonely Crowd: A Study of the Changing
American Character. *In this influential book Riesman distinguishes*
between two types of individuals, the inner-directed, for whom "the
source of direction . . . is 'inner' in the sense that it is implanted early
in life by the elders and directed toward generalized but nonetheless
inescapably destined goals," and the other-directed, whose source of
direction comes from his "contemporaries . . . either those known to
him or those with whom he is indirectly acquainted, through friends
and through the mass media." Riesman finds that earlier generations
of Americans were, on the whole, inner-directed, but that modern
Americans have become other-directed, conforming to the standards
of their peer-groups.

The adherence to the group has not, however, relieved the other-
directed individual of the loneliness which he is trying to escape, a
loneliness which the inner-directed man tended to feel less intensely,
because his ideas and standards of behavior were ingrained in him
from early childhood and were not the result of the influence of a
variety of rapidly changing external factors.

"The Talk of the Town": The Socialization of
Consumption Preferences

*I*N THE SOCIETIES depending on inner-direction that developed in
the west, all values were translatable, at least in principle, into the
impersonal standard of money. This was the possession that gave
value to all other possessions. True, money itself fluctuated in value,
depending not only on directly technological factors but also on socio-
psychological ones. Nevertheless, money felt substantial to parents,
was made to feel so to children, and served in countless subtle ways
as the goal and norm of both society and socialization.

"Money talks," people said, meaning that it also smiles on those
who have it and frowns on those who do not. Money, little as we like
to recognize the fact today in our ascetic or self-righteous attitudes
about it, permitted the cash customer to pursue his private purposes—
good or bad—with no other justification than his pocketbook. Today
the currency into which all values tend to be translated is no longer
money but appraisal by the peer-group. And this value, much more
patently than money, is subject to booms and busts on manifest socio-
psychological grounds; it does not feel substantial either to parents
or to children. The appraisal of the peer-group is always stated, in
the final analysis, in terms of a consumption preference. Whereas the
simple cost of a commodity was the most important fact about it in
the days of inner-direction, today in other-directed circles, though
money still makes a difference, it is the peer-group that does most of
the "talking." Price influences the group's verdict—but only up to a
point. Children and adolescents, far more sophisticated than the old
people, form a consumers' union; indeed each child in the middle
class is automatically a consumer trainee before he can walk; and his
practice in consumer's research begins long before he can count
change. To a degree he will be judged on his ability as a trainee as,
in earlier eras, he might have been sized up as a potential recruit for
the army or for the production economy.

From David Riesman, *The Lonely Crowd* (New Haven, Yale University Press, 1950),
pp. 78-82.

Such changes constitute our most dramatic evidence that, in the phase of incipient population decline, there is a great advance in the standard of living and in the position of children. Children are not subjected to a period of deprivation and hardship which leads to compensatory dreams of a life of ease and pleasure. Girls are not, as they were in some earlier societies, drudges at home until, at puberty, they were suddenly given the only "capital" they were ever likely to find—that of their bodies—to live on as income, or exhaust as principal. Even boys from comfortable homes were expected until recently to hit the sunrise trail with paper routes or other economically profitable and "character-building" chores. Other-directed children who have not faced such deprivations and dreamed compensatory dreams of wild purchasing power find it easier than these dream-driven children to become sophisticated consumers, more preoccupied with their sophistication—the verdict on consumption—than with consumption itself.

While the other-directed person's tremendous outpouring of energy is channeled into the ever expanding frontiers of consumption, the inner-directed person's energy was channeled relentlessly into production—production that underwent fantastic expansion in the phase of transitional growth of population. Inner-directed patterns often discouraged consumption for adults as well as children. But at other times, and especially in the higher social strata less affected by Puritan asceticism, the inner-directed person consumed—with time out, so to speak, for saving and for good behavior—as relentlessly as he (or his progenitors) produced. Most clearly in the case of upper-class conspicuous consumption he lusted for possessions and display, once the old tradition-directed restraints had worn away. He pursued clear acquisition and consumption goals with a fierce individualism. To be sure, his goals were socially determined, but less by a contemporary union of consumers than by inherited patterns of desire, hardly less stable than the desire for money itself. Goals such as fine houses, fine horses, fine women, fine objets d'art—these could be investments because their value scarcely changed in the scale of consumption preference.

These relatively stable and individualistic pursuits are today being replaced by the fluctuating tastes which the other-directed person accepts from his peer-group. (Women, as we shall see in Chapter VII, are still desired objects of consumption, but judgments as to what is desirable in a woman change with the same rapidity as women's styles in dress—indeed, these styles symbolize the degrees and kinds of fashionableness and femininity that men will want or accept.) Moreover, many of the desires that drove men to work and to madness in societies depending on inner-direction are now satisfied relatively easily; they are incorporated into the standard of living taken for granted by millions. But the craving remains. It is a craving for the satisfactions others seem to have, an *objectless craving*. The consumer today has most of his potential individuality trained out of him by his membership in the consumers' union. He is kept within his consumption limits not by goal-directed but by other-directed guidance, kept from splurging too much by fear of others' envy, and from consuming too little by fear of his own envy of the others.

These observations would amount to a digression from the child's world into the adult's were it not for the fact that today there is no fast line that separates the consumption patterns of the adult world from those of the child, except the consumption objects themselves. The child may consume comics or toys while the adult consumes editorials and cars; more and more both consume in the same way. Some of the reasons for the increasing over-all conformity of consumption are analyzed in later chapters which deal specifically with the adult world of consumption. It is sufficient to remark here that we can think of the child as one among the many kinds of consumer trainees we find in our economy.

In the consumers' union of the peer-group the child's discipline as a consumer begins today very early in life—and lasts late. It is true that in the era of inner-direction it was difficult enough for children to understand the work roles of their parents. It was perhaps as difficult then, especially for boys, as it is today. But this did not mean that the inner-directed child displaced his energies for judging work into judging consumption; he was supposed to be "job-minded" even if the job itself was not clear in his mind. Today the future occupation of all moppets is to be skilled consumers.

This is visible early in children's play-at-consumption. In this area there is a noticeable increase in the range of children's toys. Added to boys' toys, for example production-imitating equipment like trucks and steam shovels or toy soldiers and miniature war material, is a whole new range of objects modeled after the service trades: laundry trucks, toy telephones, service stations, and so forth. Added to girls' toys, the doll and her wardrobe, are juvenile make-up outfits and voice recorders.

These props of the child's playtime hours, however, are not so striking as the increasing rationalization of children's preferences in everything they consume. In the period of inner-direction children accepted trade-marked cereals largely because that was what was set for them at table. Today they eat Wheaties, or other cereal, influenced by some specific reason that all can talk about: "Wheaties makes champions." And comics, children will say if pressed, "relax champions." In this way the other-directed child rapidly learns that there always is and always must be a reason for consuming anything. One "reason" is that the commodity he is consuming is the "best" in its line. As the child develops as a consumer trainee, advertising no longer is given all the credit for answering the question of what is the best in its line. The product approved by most of the others, or by a suitable testimonial from a peer consumer, becomes the "best." The most popular products, by this formula, are the products that happen to be used by the most popular peer or group of peers. And to be sure, these pace setters themselves have a "reason," often enough picked out from the mass media, if not from the advertising pages; thus the hunt for the reason goes on in an endless regress.

These patterns place extra burdens on girls, partly because women are the accepted consumption leaders in our society, partly because women, much more than men, feel pressure to play any role they are accepted in by the men. At every social level boys are permitted a greater amount of aggression than girls; they are also permitted a wider range of preferences and can get by with a good deal of aggressive resistance to the taste-exchanging process. The media may exaggerate, but do not greatly exaggerate, the role of young girls in the pattern which requires that what is learned in the peer-group must be marketed at home, rather than vice versa.

Finally, the child consumer trainee becomes a consumer tutor in the home circle, "bringing up" mother as well as father. *Life* magazine recently ran a leading article on "Teen-age Fun," showing the etiquettes and pastimes prevailing in certain American cities; these pastimes were news even to some recent high-school graduates. Teenagers must initiate adults rather than vice versa; typical is the case, also cited in *Life*, where teachers at a Denver high school imitated the idiomatic greeting style of the "most popular" boy.

WILLIAM H. WHYTE, JR. (1917——)

Born in West Chester, Pennsylvania, Whyte was graduated from Princeton in 1939 and went to work for the Vick Chemical Company. After service in World War II, he became a writer and editor for Fortune. *His interest in the business personality culminated in* The Organization Man *(1956), from which the following excerpt is taken. In this book Whyte contends that the individualistic ethic of American business has been replaced by a social ethic, the aim of which is "togetherness" and conformity.*

Human Relations

THE MOST noteworthy feature of the General Electric approach is the emphasis on the "professional" manager. As in all training programs, the bulk of the instruction is on specifics. Unlike most, however, there is considerable study in subjects that cut across every kind of job. Trainees study personnel philosophy, labor relations, law, and, most important, the managerial viewpoint. . . .

Not surprisingly, the part of the curriculum for which they have the greatest affinity is the human-relations instruction. They are particularly enthusiastic about the "Effective Presentation" course worked up by the sales-training department. They can hardly be blamed. "YOU CAN ALWAYS GET ANYBODY TO DO WHAT YOU WISH," the textbook proclaims. To this end the students spend four months eagerly studying a battery of communication techniques and psychological principles which General Electric tells them will help them

From William H. Whyte, Jr., *The Organization Man* (New York, Simon & Schuster, 1956), pp. 121-124.

to be good managers. (Sample principle: "Never say anything controversial.")

There is nothing novel about teaching people how to manipulate other people, and GE's scientific psychological techniques bear a strong resemblance to the how-to-be-a-success precepts standard in the U.S. for decades. What is different about them is their justification. They are not presented on the grounds that they will help make people do what you want them to do so that you can make more money. GE trainees see it in much more eleemosynary terms. They do like the part about selling yourself to others so you can get ahead, for they think a lot about this. But they don't abide the thought of enemies on the other side of the counter; they see the manipulative skills as something that in the long run will make other people *happy*. When in years to come the trainees are charged with the destiny of subordinates—a possibility most take remarkably much for granted—they will be able to achieve a stable, well-adjusted work group. They won't drive subordinates, they explain. They will motivate them.

Trainees are also predisposed to emphasis on co-operation rather than competition, and this they get too. The emphasis is built into the structure of the school. For one thing, the student is given a high measure of security from the beginning, and while there may be promotion of the fittest there can be survival for all. There are exceptions, but one must be a very odd ball to be one. For the first two years the trainee is part of a system in which his salary raises will be automatic, and while later on he will be more on his own there will be no planned elimination as there was at Vick, nor an up-or-out policy such as the Navy's.

To get ahead, of course, one must compete—but not too much, and certainly not too obviously. While overt ambition is a bad posture for the ambitious anywhere, the GE system has especial sanctions for the rate-buster. The trainee is, first of all, a member of a group, and the group is entrusted to a surprising degree with the resolution of his future. How well, the company wants to know, does he fit in? His fellow trainees provide the answer, and in the "case study" group discussions the eager beaver or the deviant is quickly exposed. And brought to heel. Trainees speak frequently of the way close fraternity life atmosphere is valuable in ironing out some trainees' aberrant tendencies. It may be tough on him, they concede, but better now than later. In a few years the trainee will be released from this close association and the social character that he has perfected will be a fundamental necessity; he will be moving from one company branch to another, and he must be able to fit into the same kind of integrated social system.

The company officially recognizes the disciplining of the group. In its periodic rating of the man, the company frequently calls on his comrades to participate in the rating. If a man is liked especially well not only by his superiors but by his peers, he may be given the job of guiding about eight or ten of his fellow trainees. He is now a "sign-up," and if he keeps on maturing he may become a "head-of-tests," the seven "sign-ups" reporting to him. Since the opinions of one's peers are so integral to advancement, this system virtually insures that the overzealous or the " knocker" type of man will not get ahead—or, at the very least, that he will successfully remold himself to the managerial image.

The fact that the trainee must spend so much time thinking of what other people think of him does not oppress him. Quite the opposite, the constant surveillance is one of the things the average trainee talks about most enthusiastically. The rating system is highly standardized, he explains; it is the product of *many* people rather than one, and this denominator of judgments frees him from the harshness or caprice that might result from the traditional boss-employee relationship. He is also freed from being ignored; the system insures that other people must be thinking about him quite as much as he is thinking about them, and for this reason he won't get pigeonholed. At General Electric, as one trainee remarked, not only can't you get lost, you can't even hide.

Needless to say, ambition still pulses, and I am not trying to suggest that the General Electric man is any less set on the main chance than my Vick comrades. It is quite obvious, nevertheless, that he must pursue the main chance in a much more delicate fashion. To get ahead, he must co-operate with the others—but co-operate *better* than they do.

JAMES BALDWIN (1924——)

With the possible exception of Ralph Ellison, James Baldwin is the most important contemporary Negro writer in the United States. Born and raised in New York City, Baldwin was the son of a clergyman and the eldest of nine children. His first novel, Go Tell It on the Mountain *(1953) is the story of the religious salvation of an adolescent Negro boy. His latest novel is* Another Country *(1962). Notes of a Native Son *(1955), from which the following selection is taken, is a collection of essays dealing with Baldwin's life in America and his sojourn in Europe.*

Autobiographical Notes

I WAS BORN in Harlem thirty-one years ago. I began plotting novels at about the time I learned to read. The story of my childhood is the usual bleak fantasy, and we can dismiss it with the restrained observation that I certainly would not consider living it again. In those days my mother was given to the exasperating and mysterious habit of having babies. As they were born, I took them over with one hand and held a book with the other. The children probably suffered, though they have since been kind enough to deny it, and in this way I read *Uncle Tom's Cabin* and *A Tale of Two Cities* over and over and over again; in this way, in fact, I read just about everything I could get my hands on—except the Bible, probably because it was the only book I was encouraged to read. I must also confess that I wrote—a great deal—and my first professional triumph, in

From James Baldwin, *Notes of a Native Son* (Boston, Beacon Press, 1955), pp. 3-9.

any case, the first effort of mine to be seen in print, occurred at the age of twelve or thereabouts, when a short story I had written about the Spanish revolution won some sort of prize in an extremely short-lived church newspaper. I remember the story was censored by the lady editor, though I don't remember why, and I was outraged.

Also wrote plays, and songs, for one of which I received a letter of congratulations from Mayor La Guardia, and poetry, about which the less said, the better. My mother was delighted by all these go-ings-on, but my father wasn't; he wanted me to be a preacher. When I was fourteen I became a preacher, and when I was seventeen I stopped. Very shortly thereafter I left home. For God knows how long I struggled with the world of commerce and industry—I guess they would say they struggled with *me*—and when I was about twenty-one I had enough done of a novel to get a Saxton Fellowship. When I was twenty-two the fellowship was over, the novel turned out to be unsalable, and I started waiting on tables in a Village res-taurant and writing book reviews—mostly, as it turned out, about the Negro problem, concerning which the color of my skin made me automatically an expert. Did another book, in company with photog-rapher Theodore Pelatowski, about the store-front churches in Har-lem. This book met exactly the same fate as my first—fellowship, but no sale. (It was a Rosenwald Fellowship.) By the time I was twenty-four I had decided to stop reviewing books about the Negro problem—which, by this time, was only slightly less horrible in print than it was in life—and I packed my bags and went to France, where I finished, God knows how, *Go Tell It on the Mountain*.

Any writer, I suppose, feels that the world into which he was born is nothing less than a conspiracy against the cultivation of his talent—which attitude certainly has a great deal to support it. On the other hand, it is only because the world looks on his talent with such a frightening indifference that the artist is compelled to make his talent important. So that any writer, looking back over even so short a span of time as I am here forced to assess, finds that the things which hurt him and the things which helped him cannot be divorced from each other; he could be helped in a certain way only because he was hurt in a certain way; and his help is simply to be enabled to move from one conundrum to the next—one is tempted to say that he moves from one disaster to the next. When one begins looking for influences one finds them by the score. I haven't thought much about my own, not enough anyway; I hazard that the King James Bible, the rhetoric of the store-front church, something ironic and violent and perpetually understated in Negro speech—and something of Dickens' love for bravura—have something to do with me today; but I wouldn't stake my life on it. Likewise, innumerable people have helped me in many ways; but finally, I suppose, the most difficult (and most rewarding) thing in my life has been the fact that I was born a Negro and was forced, therefore, to effect some kind of truce with this reality. (Truce, by the way, is the best one can hope for.)

One of the difficulties about being a Negro writer (and this is not special pleading, since I don't mean to suggest that he has it worse than anybody else) is that the Negro problem is written about so widely. The bookshelves groan under the weight of information, and everyone therefore considers himself informed. And this information, furthermore, operates usually (generally, popularly) to reinforce traditional attitudes. Of traditional attitudes there are only two—For or Against—and I, personally, find it difficult to say which attitude has caused me the most pain. I am speaking as a writer; from a social point of view I am perfectly aware that the change from ill-will to good-will, however motivated, however imperfect, however expressed, is better than no change at all.

But it is part of the business of the writer—as I see it—to examine attitudes, to go beneath the surface, to tap the source. From this point of view the Negro problem is nearly inaccessible. It is not only written about so widely; it is written about so badly. It is quite possible to say that the price a Negro pays for becoming articulate is to find himself, at length, with nothing to be articulate about. ("You taught me language," says Caliban to Prospero, "and my profit on't is I know how to curse.") Consider: the tremendous social activity that this problem generates imposes on whites and Negroes alike the necessity of looking forward, of working to bring about a better day. This is fine, it keeps the waters troubled; it is all, indeed, that has made possible the Negro's progress. Nevertheless, social affairs are not generally speaking the writer's prime concern, whether they ought to be or not; it is absolutely necessary that he establish between himself and these affairs a distance which will allow, at least, for clarity, so that before he can look forward in any meaningful sense, he must first be allowed to take a long look back. In the context of the Negro problem neither whites nor blacks, for excellent reasons of their own, have the faintest desire to look back; but I think that the past is all that makes the present coherent, and further, that the past will remain horrible for exactly as long as we refuse to assess it honestly.

I know, in any case, that the most crucial time in my own development came when I was forced to recognize that I was a kind of bastard of the West; when I followed the line of my past I did not find myself in Europe but in Africa. And this meant that in some subtle way, in a really profound way, I brought to Shakespeare, Bach, Rembrandt, to the stones of Paris, to the cathedral at Chartres, and to the Empire State Building, a special attitude. These were not really my creations, they did not contain my history; I might search in them in vain forever for any reflection of myself. I was an interloper; this was not my heritage. At the same time I had no other heritage which I could possibly hope to use—I had certainly been unfitted for the jungle or the tribe. I would have to appropriate these white centuries, I would have to make them mine—I would have to accept my special attitude, my special place in this scheme—otherwise I would have no place in *any* scheme. What was the most difficult was the fact that I was forced to admit something I had always hidden from myself, which the American Negro has had to hide from himself as the price of his public progress; that I hated and feared white people. This did not mean that I loved black people; on the contrary, I despised them, possibly because they failed to produce Rembrandt. In effect, I hated and feared the world. And this meant, not only that I thus gave the world an altogether murderous power over me, but also that in such a self-destroying limbo I could never hope to write.

One writes out of one thing only—one's own experience. Everything depends on how relentlessly one forces from this experience the last drop, sweet or bitter, it can possibly give. This is the only real concern of the artist, to recreate out of the disorder of life that order which is art. The difficulty then, for me, of being a Negro writer was the fact that I was, in effect, prohibited from examining my own experience too closely by the tremendous demands and the very real dangers of my social situation.

I don't think the dilemma outlined above is uncommon. I do think, since writers work in the disastrously explicit medium of language, that it goes a little way towards explaining why, out of the enormous resources of Negro speech and life, and despite the example of Negro music, prose written by Negroes has been generally speaking so pallid and so harsh. I have not written about being a Negro at such length because I expect that to be my only subject, but only because it was the gate I had to unlock before I could hope to write about anything else. I don't think that the Negro problem in America can be even discussed coherently without bearing in mind its context; its context being the history, traditions, customs, the moral assumptions and preoccupations of the country; in short, the general social fabric. Appearances to the contrary, no one in America escapes its effects and everyone in America bears some responsibility for it. I believe this the more firmly because it is the overwhelming tendency to speak of this problem as though it were a thing apart. But in the work of Faulkner, in the general attitude and certain specific passages in Robert Penn Warren, and, most significantly, in the advent of Ralph Ellison, one sees the beginnings—at least—of a more genuinely penetrating search. Mr. Ellison, by the way, is the first Negro novelist I have ever read to utilize in language, and brilliantly, some of the ambiguity and irony of Negro life.

About my interests: I don't know if I have any, unless the morbid desire to own a sixteen-millimeter camera and make experimental movies can be so classified. Otherwise, I love to eat and drink—it's my melancholy conviction that I've scarcely ever had enough to eat (this is because it's *impossible* to eat enough if you're worried about the next meal)—and I love to argue with people who do not disagree with me too profoundly, and I love to laugh. I do *not* like bohemia, or bohemians, I do not like people whose principal aim is pleasure, and I do not like people who are *earnest* about anything. I don't like people who like me because I'm a Negro; neither do I like people who find in the same accident grounds for contempt. I love America more than any other country in the world, and, exactly for this reason, I insist on the right to criticize her perpetually. I think all theories are suspect, that the finest principles may have to be modified, or may even be pulverized by the demands of life, and that one must find, therefore, one's own moral center and move through the world hoping that this center will guide one aright. I consider that I have many responsibilities, but none greater than this: to last, as Hemingway says, and get my work done.

I want to be an honest man and a good writer.